THE AMERICAN JEWISH
PHILANTHROPIC COMPLEX

The American Jewish Philanthropic Complex

THE HISTORY OF A MULTIBILLION-DOLLAR INSTITUTION

LILA CORWIN BERMAN

PRINCETON UNIVERSITY PRESS

PRINCETON & OXFORD

Copyright © 2020 by Princeton University Press

Requests for permission to reproduce material from this work should be sent to permissions@press.princeton.edu

Published by Princeton University Press
41 William Street, Princeton, New Jersey 08540
6 Oxford Street, Woodstock, Oxfordshire OX20 1TR

press.princeton.edu

Library of Congress Cataloging-in-Publication Data

Names: Berman, Lila Corwin, 1976– author.
Title: The American Jewish philanthropic complex : the history of
    a multibillion-dollar institution / Lila Corwin Berman.
Description: Princeton : Princeton University Press, [2021] |
    Includes bibliographical references and index.
Identifiers: LCCN 2020018930 (print) | LCCN 2020018931 (ebook) |
    ISBN 9780691170732 (hardback) | ISBN 9780691209791 (ebook)
Subjects: LCSH: Jews—United States—Charities—History. |
    Charity organization—United States—History.
Classification: LCC HV3191 .B374 2021 (print) | LCC HV3191 (ebook) |
    DDC 361.7089/924073—dc23
LC record available at https://lccn.loc.gov/2020018930
LC ebook record available at https://lccn.loc.gov/2020018931

British Library Cataloging-in-Publication Data is available

Editorial: Fred Appel and Jenny Tan
Production Editorial: Leslie Grundfest
Jacket Design: Leslie Flis
Production: Erin Suydam
Publicity: Kate Hensley and Kathryn Stevens
Copyeditor: Karen Verde

Jacket Credit: Shutterstock

This book has been composed in Arno

Printed on acid-free paper. ∞

Printed in the United States of America

10 9 8 7 6 5 4 3 2 1

CONTENTS

THE AMERICAN JEWISH
PHILANTHROPIC COMPLEX

The State of Philanthropy

A PORTION of my salary as a professor is paid out of an endowment, donated three decades ago by a small group of funders to my public university. My children attend a public magnet school with a rooftop garden, computers, and books contributed by corporations, businesses, and individuals. The local newspaper I read every morning is owned by a charitable foundation, the public radio station I tune in to reminds me on the hour that private family foundations support it, and my city's art museum is filled with galleries named after its supporters. Not a single day in my life passes untouched by philanthropy. The same is true for most Americans, whether they recognize it or not.

When I try to account for the scope of philanthropy in my life, I also have to acknowledge the particular contribution of Jewish philanthropy. Add to the above ledger my graduate education, multiple trips to Israel, my children's first summer at Jewish overnight camp, hundreds of books I have read to them, and much more, all supported in entirety or large part through grants from Jewish private family foundations, community foundations, and public charities. The ubiquity of Jewish philanthropy in my life is also not unique. Almost any person who affiliates with an American Jewish community could make a similar accounting of the benefits they have reaped from Jewish philanthropy.

If I were to tally philanthropy's contributions to my own life, I would confront a startlingly large figure. And if I were to try to calculate what proportion of that total figure could be classified as Jewish philanthropy, the sum would still be substantial, but the process of categorization would be riddled with unanswerable questions. When a Jewish family donates to an art museum, or endows a professorship—such as the one I hold—for the study of Jewish history at an American public university, is it engaging in Jewish philanthropy? Or when a non-Jewish family donates to a cause in Israel, is that Jewish philanthropy?

No wonder, then, that over the last decade, reports of the total value of American Jewish philanthropy have varied from $24 billion to $46.3 billion, depending on the criteria researchers use to define it. Even qualitative measures of American Jewish philanthropy run into similar problems, as researchers try to decide what makes an individual donate to a "Jewish" cause as opposed to an "American" one. Similarly, when investigative journalists probe the recesses of American Jewish philanthropy, they, too, confront these same definitional problems.[1]

A historian of American Jewish philanthropy might feel pressed to define exactly what it is, a task that several other researchers have attempted. I wrote this book, however, because I think there is a better way to approach the topic. The more I have learned about American Jewish philanthropy, the more I have come to see that its significance has been grossly underestimated in blinkered attempts to account for it as distinct from American philanthropy or the American state.

When I began to explore the history of American Jewish philanthropy, I realized that it was leading me to examine the historical formation of the core ideologies of American democracy and capitalism. Never far below the surface of the institutions and practices of American Jewish philanthropy was a persistent puzzle of American statecraft: how to balance the interests of democracy with those of capitalism. Thus, to understand American Jewish philanthropy, I had to study the laws and policies that facilitated private means to act as a proxy for the public good. Over time, the institutions of the American state enriched private resources with public support. In squaring its obligations to a democratically empowered public and to capitalist growth, the state increasingly resolved that the good of the whole could be met best by not only freeing but, indeed, subsidizing private interests and markets. In this way, American democracy invested in capitalism. More than the sum of dollars and their donors and more than any rigid distinction between Jewish philanthropy and American philanthropy, what I have come to characterize as the American Jewish philanthropic complex emerged at the intersection of the American state—the laws, policies, agencies, officials, and practices that regulated the public good and protected private freedoms—and Jewish communal aspirations in the United States.

A complex generally refers to something that brings together several parts into one formation, sometimes so successfully that we lose sight of its constituent pieces or its process of construction. This is exactly what I mean by the American Jewish philanthropic complex. With its beginnings in the nineteenth and early twentieth centuries and its full maturation over the second half of the twentieth century, it brought together the shifting terrain of American political economy and statecraft with the technical and psychological task of provisioning for American Jewish life. The parts—policies, political and economic ideologies, and cataclysmic events that reshaped global Jewish life—resolved into a complex, made to appear timeless and whole as much by the efforts of its institutions, leaders, and supporters as by its validation of late-twentieth-century American statecraft.

In 1961, during his last days in office, President Dwight Eisenhower delivered his now famous military-industrial-complex speech. In it he observed the ascendance of private interests (specifically, those of military producers) within government circles and public policies. He admonished that democratic principles would suffer should the trend continue. In this same period, a similar dynamic could be observed in the historical development of American philanthropy. Even with new regulatory measures enacted in the following decades, philanthropic institutions were nourished by and fostered an array of policies that empowered private entities to exercise governance over the American public. On one level, then, the American Jewish philanthropic complex was just one manifestation of an American philanthropic complex, which was simply a manifestation of the private control over public life about which Eisenhower had warned.[2]

A complex is, also, complicated, and the American Jewish philanthropic complex was as well. With their countless acronyms, name changes, mergers, and ties to global Jewish philanthropic efforts, American Jewish philanthropic institutions were organizationally and historically intricate. More than just an indication of their internal complexity, however, the nature of these institutions also reflected the regulatory complexity of American laws and policies in the twentieth century. Similar to other philanthropic institutions, Jewish ones crafted technologies and employed new classes of professionals to help them adhere to regulatory standards, simultaneously abiding by and interpreting them.

Finally, the word complex brings to mind a set of psychological patterns. This, too, must be accounted for in order to understand the American Jewish philanthropic complex. As it developed, the complex served as a channel for the shifting anxieties, vulnerabilities, and uncertainties that many American Jewish leaders experienced. While they struggled to raise funds to sustain their institutions, they also worried about the deleterious perceptions their efforts might fuel. Few Jewish philanthropic leaders could ignore the ongoing threat posed by long-standing antisemitic suspicions that equated Jewish financial activity with Jews' alleged exploitative and conspiratorial inclinations. Visible Jewish wealth, while a boon to communal endeavors, could also stoke antisemitic ideas and behaviors.

The history of the American Jewish philanthropic complex is both a broad chronicle of the complicated and ever-shifting arrangements of the American state and a very specific story about how these shifts repositioned Jewish communal institutions into state actors. It draws attention to how the leaders of those institutions interpreted American laws and policies to address their changing needs, desires, and fears. When we account for American Jewish philanthropy as a governing instrument—reflecting the state and, also, transforming it—we can more precisely apprehend its significance to American life.

———

The majority of Jews arrived in the United States during a period of incredible expansion over the nineteenth and early twentieth centuries. Territory, population, and industrial production all grew massively in this period, as did the conception of an American national identity that included a greater diversity of citizens than ever before. The largest wave of Jewish immigration coincided with the migration of millions of other newcomers to the United States and, also, followed on the heels of the passage of the Thirteenth, Fourteenth, and Fifteenth Amendments, which abolished slavery and extended, in law though not necessarily its application, citizenship to "all persons born or naturalized in the United States."[3]

In the late nineteenth and early twentieth centuries, American Jews established philanthropic institutions to channel private Jewish dollars to serve global Jewish populations and, also, to meet domestic communal needs. Similar to other Americans, Jews organized the means to distribute private capital within the parameters of evolving rules and regulations issued by state and federal governments. The experience of building philanthropic organizations exposed them to national debates over the extents of capitalism, its ability to serve broad public needs, and the limits of democracy in the face of a rapidly diversifying American population. The spectacular growth of philanthropic institutions over these years could be interpreted as proving the felicitous co-existence of capitalism with democracy, as an ever-wider array of Americans divested themselves of their private earnings for the public good. However, that same growth could threaten a democratic process, as private entities took hold of their capital power to serve the public as they saw fit.

The American Jewish philanthropic complex developed in the context of the American state's expansion and its attendant and varied efforts to reconcile democratic protections with capitalist growth over the course of the twentieth century. For historians of American Jews, my invocation of the American state as central to Jewish life may feel counterintuitive. The work of American Jewish history has rested on a foundational claim that Jews as individuals gained full and unmitigated citizenship rights in the United States, unlike under other ruling regimes that approached Jewish emancipation as a process, with fits and starts and myriad regulatory experiments. Accordingly, American Jewish historians tend to maintain that Jews as a collective have not experienced state-based regulation to any significant degree in the United States, a conclusion that continues to fuel an exceptionalist approach to the field. In such a framework, the American state only matters insofar as it was so exceptionally different from other state apparatuses. Under the sway of this approach, American Jewish historians have based their research questions on a presumption about the American state—namely, its radical difference from other states—but not on a critical examination of the effects it had on Jewish life.[1]

For a long time, American Jewish historians were not alone in eschewing the American state as a relevant category of analysis. In his now classic 2008 article entitled "The Myth of the 'Weak' American State," William Novak called fellow American historians to task for uncritically reproducing an ideological fashioning of the US government as small and limited, giving its citizens rights and then setting them free. He argued that this portrayal, core to Cold War politics, was contrary to the twentieth-century history of American state growth, tracked through the expansion of agencies and bureaucracies and the rise of interventionist social and economic policies. Following Novak's lead, historians over the last decade have produced a bounty of new scholarship about sexuality, immigration, military service, and urban and suburban space that all shows how state policies delimited individual possibilities and, also, conscripted individuals into state-produced categories for the purposes of social and legal control.[5]

To understand the history of American Jewish philanthropy, I contend, we must ask similar questions about the role the state played in classifying and regulating American Jews. When they created state-recognized associations, whether religious organizations or other kinds of corporate bodies with property holdings and legal standing, American Jews as a collective became visible to and governable by state laws, bureaucracies, and agencies. Indeed, as political scientist Theda Skocpol notes, the basic tension between state control over resources and its apportionment of those resources to citizens and collective groups acting in the interest of the public has long been "literally at the heart of American public policy."[6]

The few scholars who have studied the history of American Jewish philanthropy, however, have depicted it as removed from state policies or affairs. Instead, they have portrayed its development as illustrative of the broad freedom Jews had to flourish in the United States, with the full tolerance of, but little interference from, the American government. Daniel Elazar, a political scientist who in 1976 published one of the only broad studies of American Jewish philanthropy, asserted, "The American tradition is one of *public* rather than *state* institutions, with all that the semantic distinction implies." He went on to portray American Jewish philanthropy as a product of one of the many publics fostered by "the American tradition" and, thus, as "*sui generis*" within Jewish history and "quite compatible with the evolving American culture." Likewise, Jonathan Woocher, a sociologist and author of the most recent—though now more than three-decades-old—interpretive study of American Jewish philanthropy, explained that American Jews drew upon their philanthropic traditions "to express the meaning of Jewishness" in a way that "was thoroughly compatible with American values." He characterized philanthropy as the core of "the American Jewish civil religion," and argued that its practice placed Jews "firmly within the embrace of American pluralism," while "link[ing] American Jews to the totality of the Jewish people at a level beyond ideological diversity."[7]

The dual impulse to connect American Jewish philanthropy to the broad sweep of Jewish history and to claim it as evidence of a peerless, exceptional synthesis between Jews and the United States has guided the ahistorical assumptions embedded in many studies of it, even those written by historians (which Woocher and Elazar were not). Popular historical accounts tend to weave together episodes drawn from many centuries of Jewish life throughout the globe to create the impression that American Jewish philanthropy was just one expression of timeless Jewish values, often rendered through Hebrew words such as *tsedakah* (the word commonly used for charity, from the root for righteousness) and *tikkun olam* (literally "repair of the world"), now allowed to thrive freely in the United States.[8]

The story of American Jewish philanthropy as the survival and efflorescence of Jewish traditions on American soil obscures the massive transformations that reordered Jewish philanthropy in the United States and implanted it firmly in the political economy of the American state. Even when it moved across national lines and flowed through global channels, American Jewish philanthropy bore the deep imprint of the American state. The American Jewish philanthropic complex was a by-product of American statecraft, making Jewish philanthropy far more than a Jewish endeavor, but rather an instrument, alongside other philanthropic bodies and putatively nonstate actors, of the state.[9]

As Novak and other historians tell us, the concept of the American state is a slippery one, dispersed across layers of agencies, bureaucracies, and courts at the federal, individual state, and local levels; and yet this protean profile must not deter us from studying it. By telling the history of American Jewish philanthropy as the historical formation of a complex, I reveal an often-neglected dimension of American Jewish history: its ever-shifting entanglement with the state.

Over the course of the middle to late twentieth century, a wide array of individuals, collective institutions, and state bodies became reliant on the American Jewish philanthropic complex, both for its material benefits and also for its authorization of a model of American governance that empowered private interests to define and serve the public good. Far from simply adhering to state efforts to regulate collective bodies and their property, American Jewish philanthropic entities entered into a dialogue with state institutions about the nature of regulation, protection, and freedom; that is, they participated in state-level negotiations over how best to balance the interests of capitalism with those of democracy. They worked alongside other philanthropic associations to interpret and craft American policy. Furthermore, they used their proximity to state agencies in order to advocate expanding the way that private entities could act, with state encouragement, in the name of the public good. In all of these ways, American Jewish philanthropy transformed into a complex arrangement of knowledge, institutions, and capital thoroughly embedded in the American state.

Readers will find here neither an exhaustive review of every American Jewish philanthropic organization that has existed nor a deep discussion of how American Jewish philanthropy shaped the lives of everyday American Jews. I have tried to provide references for those interested in these topics and others that I similarly treat only superficially. Indeed, I am hopeful that my work will contribute to and inspire new research that explores questions that exceed my own analysis. For example, this book only touches on the gender and sexual politics ingrained in philanthropy, but its focus on systems of authority may suggest to others a fruitful starting point for examining those dynamics. Likewise, although this is not a comparative study, I offer a framework for thinking about the role of the American state in limning Jews' collective experiments that may enable other scholars to draw new comparisons among American Jews and other American groups and, also, among Jews in the United States and Jewish communities elsewhere. In these ways and others, I hope to contribute to a scholarly shift to reconsider the role of the American state in American Jewish history, thereby dismantling the exceptionalist foundations upon which the field has rested.[10]

————

Chapter by chapter, I trace the development of the American Jewish philanthropic complex's core concepts—association, regulation, property, taxation, politics, finance and identity, and the market—beginning in the nineteenth century, with particular focus on the decades after World War II, and concluding in the early twenty-first century. The chapters illuminate how each of these concepts built upon the prior and supported the next. The book's structure is intended to illustrate the process of historical formation, contingency, and relationality that shaped Jewish philanthropy into a complex that, to many people's eyes, came to appear a natural feature of American Jewish life, beyond the history that created it.

The first chapter considers state-based experiments to govern a diversity of American groups or "associations" starting in the nineteenth century. Not able to adjudicate how every single group acted, individual states and then the federal government instead legislated uniform practices to tether collective associations to American law without demanding uniform beliefs. The legal framework of the association acted as a lever of power for governmental entities, allowing them to control and extract resources from groups in different ways than they acted upon individuals. In theory, so long as American Jews' collective enterprises adhered to these practices, they would be treated similarly to any other collective group. By forming associations, Jews made themselves legible to governing bodies and formed a relationship with the American state, as it emerged locally and nationally through agencies, courts, and elected officials.

The second chapter examines how increasingly centralized governing bodies enacted regulations on collective associations. In their infancy, these regulations provided only the skeletal outlines of an evolving relationship between the American state and those associations classified as acting in the interest of the public. Often, associations filled the gaps through their own bylaws and inter-pretations of what different state bodies could expect from and offer to them. For American Jews, the federation system, a city-by-city effort that emerged in the early twentieth century to coordinate fund-raising for Jewish agencies, played a critical role in defining the relationship between American Jewish col-lective life and state-based regulatory claims. Most important, federations disci-plined themselves by requiring that dollars raised through annual fund-raising campaigns be allocated fully and expeditiously to service-providing agencies.

The third chapter focuses on the changing meaning and nature of Jewish communal property, from dollars to investments to real estate. In the years of the Great Depression and its wake, federal state power grew ever more central-ized, most evident through the expansion of social welfare programs and the creation of agencies and bureaucracies charged with regulating economic growth. In this environment, some Jewish leaders began to challenge the valu-ation of Jewish communal property through only the immediate needs it could fulfill. The Depression had depleted the shallow wells of financial reserves that Jewish organizations held, and now, with a government newly committed to providing for its citizens' social welfare, some Jewish leaders considered whether Jewish philanthropy could invest more substantially in the future by holding back immediate expenditures. Endowments—savings accounts that invest their corpus for growth and, generally, spend below their investment returns as a strategy for perpetual growth—would change the valuation and purpose of Jewish communal property.

Whether circulated immediately or reserved for the future in savings or endowment accounts, Jewish communal property reflected the American tax structure, the sustained focus of the fourth chapter. American tax policies markedly changed in the decades after World War II. In these same years, American Jewish institutions turned unprecedented time and resources to the task of understanding the policies governing philanthropic transactions. They retained tax lawyers, often members of their community, to help them inter-pret and apply tax codes. As they grew reliant on these tax experts, Jewish philanthropic institutions also began to define a set of tax-related interests around which to lobby agencies, bureaucrats, and elected officials. More than ever, they understood their existence as intertwined with how the American state decided to underwrite various forms of philanthropic practice.

The fifth chapter explores the political position that American Jewish phil-anthropic institutions and their leaders occupied as they became enmeshed in state processes and amassed capital in new ways. I describe these institutions and their leaders as participating in "depoliticized" politics. Through tax policy, American policymakers had advanced a precise and enforceable definition of the types of political behavior that would disqualify a philanthropic organization from receiving state enrichment through a tax exemption. Narrowing political behavior to electoral campaigning and "substantial" legislative lobbying, state regulations allowed philanthropic bodies to maintain a posture of remove from political matters while acting in profoundly political ways; in other words, these regulations gave birth to depoliticized politics. Jewish philanthropic institutions and leaders used their communal standing and the capital they held to access American state leaders. In multiple ways, they worked to sway policy discussions, yet all the while operating in the name of Jewish consensus and with the cover of a tax status that categorized them as not political. Hardly unique to American Jews, the mode of depoliticized politics was open to myriad philanthropic organizations that likewise saw great benefit in seemingly standing at a distance from politically fractious ideologies while claiming to represent a consensus or set of shared interests by virtue of their standing.

Parallel to the political consolidation that tax policy enabled Jewish philanthropic institutions and leaders to achieve was a similar consolidation of finance and so-called Jewish identity, the twinned subjects of chapter 6. In the late 1960s and 1970s, Jewish philanthropic organizations gained new tools to build financial strength through endowment vehicles and, simultaneously, to render Jewish identity through the prism of financial perpetuity. Until that time, endowment-building had existed only at the margins of Jewish philanthropy, pursued quietly if at all by Jewish federations and some private Jewish foundations. Yet American Jews' rising wealth alongside the passage of new tax legislation in 1969 helped strengthen the case for Jewish philanthropic institutions to choose capital accumulation, through endowment vehicles, over its rapid distribution. A growing communal fixation on Jewish identity and its looming crisis—precipitated in part by American Jews' rising socioeconomic status—reinforced future-oriented financial practices, where today's dollars could invest in and secure the next generation's identity.

Chapter 7 explores how Jewish philanthropic institutions braided together the strands of finance, politics, and identity by the early 1980s to align with the pro-market ideals espoused during the Reagan years. Regardless of whether Jewish philanthropic leaders personally supported the new administration, they participated in a structure that endorsed its central terms of a small state with a large private market, unfettered by regulation yet nurtured by incredibly significant and favorable tax policies. Furthermore, more than simple observers of the political scene, Jewish philanthropic leaders believed their position provided them with a platform to influence state policy, especially related to Israel. In the name of asserting and preserving a consensus-based Jewish identity, they leveraged the financial and political consolidation they had achieved and entered the American political scene as Jewish spokespeople more visibly than ever before.

Herein, the American Jewish philanthropic complex emerged in full force. Chapter 8 draws attention to how the complex affirmed and enacted the structure of late-twentieth-century American political economy, in its inequality and its support of private forms of power over public goods and processes. Before any philanthropic dollars were even distributed to serve public interests, philanthropic funds grew and accumulated as if they were any other capital investment. But, unlike most other forms of private capital, one of their biggest investors was the American state. Treating a portion of its tax revenue as public venture capital, the American government invested public dollars in these private entities, on the promissory note that they would expend their gains for the good of the public. At least in the short term, this practice had the consequence of hardening the lines of inequality that a more redistributive logic of philanthropy had once gestured toward remedying. The American Jewish philanthropic complex, like American philanthropy more generally and like the American state, had entrusted democracy to capitalism, a far cry from efforts to balance the two.

On the eve of the new millennium, the American Jewish philanthropic complex mirrored the structure of America itself, in its wildly uneven distribution of capital and its dependence on a very few and empowered private entities. The only way the isomorphism between American Jewish philanthropy and American political economy would be surprising was if one disregarded the structuring power of the American state across well over a century's formation of American Jewish philanthropy. By the same token, the only way one could conclude that this arrangement of American Jewish philanthropy was timeless, inevitable, or uniquely Jewish was by neglecting the massive historical transformations, chronicled in this book, that made way for the formation of the American Jewish philanthropic complex.

———

Just as some of the individuals in this book were anxious about putting Jewish wealth on display or making Jewish communal finances too visible, I have also worried about the consequences of writing a book that traces the growth of American Jewish philanthropy and its alignment with American capitalism. For almost a century, a long shadow cast by nineteenth- and early-twentieth-century antisemitic writing about Jewish economic behavior has warded off precisely the sort of study of Jewish politics and economics I have undertaken. Letting fears about antisemitism guide them away from the topic, many historians may have believed that to write about Jews' economic lives was to play into antisemites' hands. They likely did not think their histories would actually validate antisemitic claims, but they worried about drawing upon a shared vocabulary and, more so, having to concede that certain patterns, tied to antisemitic tropes, were common among Jewish historical actors in specific circumstances.[11]

In recent years, alongside rising interest in the history of capitalism, a growing number of Jewish historians have made a strong case for why the field must nevertheless study Jewish political economy. As historian Derek Penslar argues, "[R]eflection about the economic structure, behavior, and utility of the Jews within the framework of the society in which the Jews lived" has "profoundly affected the course of modern Jewish history." Thus, the topic cannot be ignored or dominated by "apologists, ideologues, and anti-Semites," in the words of intellectual historian Adam Sutcliffe. The defenses that these historians and others have mounted have begun to turn the scholarly tide that for so long pushed against examining Jewish economic behavior; however, their legitimation does not release me from the obligation to explain my approach and evidence as plainly as possible.[12]

I have persistently (and obsessively) asked myself what responsibility I bear when treading the same ground that has provided fodder for antisemitic theories of Jewish power or domination. When I started to study American Jewish philanthropy, I occasionally described my research as focusing on "Jewish power." I no longer find that characterization accurate or interpretively honest. Far from a study of Jewish power, this is a book about how individuals and institutions accessed and exercised power at different moments in time. At points, those actors gained power—through law, property, capital, political sway, expertise, or networks—and, at times, they were in close relationship to sources of power, especially state-based laws and policies. This interpretive lens, focused on relationality and proximity, is quite apart from one that would attempt to name or reify something called Jewish power.

An individual may want to invoke Jewish power as a political or identity claim, but the standards for using the term as a historical framework are different. The historian would have to explain how, precisely, the noun (power) is modified by the adjective (Jewish), when the parts and the whole are constantly changing. I have not pursued that task here because I do not find it instructive for my historical project. To the contrary, I think the term "Jewish power" would compromise my analysis, drawing attention away from the specific relations and contingencies of power to a stable and putatively Jewish mode.[13]

I have attempted to write about power in the most specific and historically informed way possible because I believe doing otherwise is irresponsible and, frankly, dangerous. Decidedly not an institutional or social history, this book is, instead, about the constituent parts that resolved into a complex of American Jewish philanthropy. It calls upon historical sources, from meeting minutes to congressional testimony to tax law and the Internal Revenue Code to personal papers and recollections, in order to illuminate the formation of that complex.

At the end of the day, I have limited control over how others perceive or use my words. My historical subjects could not possibly avert antisemitic perceptions about Jews and finance, and I will not hold out false hope of eradicating antisemitism through reason or history. My aim, however, is to make it impossible—or, at least, an act of willed blindness—to confuse a diffuse category of people with a turgid and fraught abstraction about the totality of their power. The history of American Jewish philanthropy belies the existence of a singular Jewish power, revealing, instead, a complex. Only in teasing apart the tangled webs of interaction among state policies, collective associations, financial transactions, political acts, and ever-shifting sources of norms and authorities within Jewish communities can we begin to understand the broad significance of philanthropy to the history of American Jews and the history of the United States.

1

Associations

IN A 1945 ESSAY, Jewish social worker and researcher Harry Lurie reflected on the historical development of Jewish communal life in the United States: "We have not had 'Jewish unity,' but we have had many free associations of Jewish groups and interests. These have developed naturally in our American democracy associated with free enterprise and voluntary initiative." Compressed into two sentences, Lurie told a quintessential American story about democracy and capitalism, and the fruits of their coupling. As the story went, "free associations" developed as the common American ground upon which a diversity of interests could thrive in harmony. These associations balanced between the public mandate of democracy and the private pull of capitalism. What might have turned into a fatal struggle—between a political ideology of public rule and an economic ideology of private freedom—instead bore American progress.[1]

Well before Lurie's paean to it, the phenomenon of the American association had its biggest booster in the French political theorist Alexis de Tocqueville. Writing about his travels through the United States in the early 1830s, the Frenchman enthused, "In no country in the world has the principle of association been more successfully used, or more unsparingly applied to a multitude of different objects, than in America." Americans, he explained, formed associations for reasons grave and trivial: "to give entertainments, to found establishments for education, to build inns, to construct churches, to diffuse books, to send missionaries to the antipodes; and in this manner they found hospitals, prisons, and schools." In the United States, "the most democratic country on the face of the earth," associations embodied, according to Tocqueville, "the principle of [self-]interest rightly understood."[2]

In his romanticization of the United States, Tocqueville alit upon associations as forming the connective tissue between private interests and public purposes. Reflective of citizens' interests and property holdings, associations could stand guard against the tyranny of the majority and the totalitarianism of a strong state. Although citizens of other countries crafted similar associations, Tocqueville noted that the explicit encouragement of the American government for them, ironically through its hands-off approach, was the hallmark of associationalism. Recognized as an early champion of American exceptionalism, Tocqueville rooted his faith in American democracy in his contention that the American form of government uniquely encouraged its citizens to embody the successful synthesis of democracy and capitalism through their collective, self-governed endeavors.[3]

Lurie, who in 1935 became the first director of the Council of Jewish Federations and Welfare Funds (CJFWF), a national body to coordinate federated Jewish charities across the United States, similarly situated American Jewish life within a sweeping narrative of American progress and exceptionalism. Admirers of associationalism, from Tocqueville to Lurie, and many in between and since, have tended to paint it as a product of the singular American way, combining a strong sense of public-mindedness with an entrepreneurial and self-reliant spirit. Such romantic depictions neglect history in favor of a transcendent vision of an enduring American spirit, always bending toward progress. While powerful, perhaps, as a patriotic ode, this understanding omits the American state's leading role in the historical formation of associationalism. Although American law designated citizenship as an individual status, agents of the American state also operated on collective groups of citizens (and, in some cases, noncitizens) through their legal, political, and economic management over associations. Associational life or what some in more modern parlance may call "civil society," far from a natural outgrowth of democracy and capitalism, cannot be understood apart from the state.[4]

Historians of American Jews have traced the late-nineteenth-century proliferation of Jewish fraternal groups, sisterhoods, mutual benefit societies, denominational bodies, educational institutions, and political and cultural organizations, but they have rarely discerned the connection between these efforts and Jews' collective political and economic status in the eyes of the American state. Quite the opposite: most have shared Tocqueville's admiration for American voluntarism and the entrepreneurial, self-governing verve of associationalism. As a result, they have been more inclined to regard Jewish associations singularly—as if each was fashioned through the unique and spontaneous energies of its founders and supporters and, often, signaled long-standing Jewish traditions—than to situate them within the apparatus of American law and policy.[5]

Jewish associations, similar to other associations, existed within a web of state policies intended to manage their property and interests. To render Jewish collective life in the United States as a series of voluntary activities, indicative of tradition or self-fashioning alone, is to strip it of the governing structures and policies that shaped it and made Jews, through their collective and philanthropic endeavors, visible subjects of the American state.

———

Well before the federal government had much to say about associations, state legislatures built a legal framework around them. Were these young elected bodies to ignore citizens' corporate endeavors, they did so at their own risk. America's founders had worried about how to maintain a centralized form of government that reflected the will of the people in the face of powerful nonstate associations or corporations. The answer emerged in the legal form of the incorporated association. States used incorporation to draw a legal circle around nonstate collective entities. Within its circumscribed limits, incorporation law gave associations remarkable freedom, all the while demanding their adherence to a process controlled by the state. In no realm were the workings of incorporation as a state tool of freedom and regulation more visible than in that of religion.[6]

As late as the 1820s, when Tocqueville toured the United States, several American states maintained official religions. State by state, the gradual and often uneven process of disestablishment offered occasions to construct a legal system that could manage strong collectivist structures through their categorical treatment and not through tests of conscience. Legal historian Sarah Barringer Gordon explains, "Long before businesses were granted the privilege of incorporation, religious societies popularized the corporate form for Americans."[7]

Through incorporation acts, states sought to control the form of religious life. Although many states had initially reserved incorporation rights for entities that explicitly proved their public purpose, they quickly passed general incorporation laws that identified whole categories of groups, such as religious ones, as providing public benefits and, thus, automatically eligible for incorporation. In return for the legal protections of incorporation, which in Barringer's words "extended security of property and state recognition" to religious groups, states required adherence to a uniformity of governance practices, including, in almost every state, an elected lay-led board with terms and limitations on property holdings.[8]

Incorporation law provided states with governing power over collective groups of citizens, not only over individual citizens. Just as individual citizens ceded some of their autonomy to state governments in return for certain protections, likewise collective associations ceded some of their freedoms. Yet the balance between state control and individual or collective control was not an easily settled one. Similar to the large body of case law that developed to determine the extent to which a state could impinge on individual freedoms, legal opinions also grappled with the limits of state power over collective associations.

Although much of the legal framework developed at the state level, federal court rulings, specifically those dealing with potential breaches of contract between states and incorporated associations, slowly transformed the matter into a federal one. A significant Supreme Court decision rendered in 1819 reversed the New Hampshire legislature's efforts to turn Dartmouth College into a public institution. According to the legislature's claim, because Dartmouth College had incorporated in New Hampshire, the state gained the right to control it and mandate, among other things, the elimination of religious requirements for its board, faculty, and students. In the majority opinion, Chief Justice Louis Marshall wrote that an act of incorporation already expressed confidence in a collective entity's public purpose and could not be used as grounds to exercise new power over it: "The character of civil institutions does not grow out of their incorporation, but out of the manner in which they are formed, and the objects for which they are created. The right to change them is not founded on their being incorporated, but on their being the instruments of government, created for its purposes."[9]

In order to gain legal standing, associations had to adhere to a certain level of state scrutiny, but Marshall tried to clarify that even as incorporation made associations visible to the state, it did not require that they act at the will of the state. Incorporation law blurred the lines between public and private and created a new legal space that governed the growth of American associations without resolving their precise standing.[10]

The proliferation of churches and synagogues in the mid-nineteenth century, a period often referred to as the Second Great Awakening, occurred amidst states' efforts to work out the parameters of incorporation law. The explosion of religious institutions in these years was particularly significant for American Jews. Between 1840 and 1870, the number of formally established

Jewish congregations ballooned from eighteen to 277. Patterns of Jewish mobility, both within the United States and transnationally, accounted for the rising number of synagogues. New synagogues appeared in areas of the country where few Jews had lived in prior decades and, also, proliferated as older institutions fractured into multiple congregations, each able to pursue its own interpretation of Jewish ritual and tradition. In some instances, incorporation law paved the way for breakaway religious communities to gain state recognition, even if their co-religionists wished to deny them the recognition. For example, disputes over mixed-gender pews or the introduction of organs into Sabbath services sometimes wound their way into American civil courts, where representatives of different factions hoped judges would rule in their favor. However, in most cases, these doctrinal issues were kicked back to the synagogue and often resulted in the creation of separately incorporated institutions. Furthermore, where xenophobia might have stood in the way of the creation of synagogues or other religious institutions, incorporation law could similarly act as a protector. Most strikingly, black church groups in the nineteenth century mined the protections of incorporation in order to gain civic power that was often denied to African Americans as individuals.[11]

While states' ability to manage associations increased alongside the expansion of incorporation law, states also developed new mechanisms for governing collective bodies through another state-defined legal mode, that of taxation. Much as it did for incorporation law, religious disestablishment served as the testing ground for associational governance by tax policy. Taxation practices allowed the state to monitor the growth of religious institutions by regulating their ability to accumulate property.

Under English common law, which served as precedent for many American legal structures, church property was classified as tax exempt because it was seamlessly connected to the state. Only in certain cases, if a church breached stipulated limits on property use and control or if the state declared an emergency, were churches subject to taxation. Even as they engaged in the process of religious disestablishment, American states tended throughout the nineteenth century to extend the property tax exemption to churches and religious institutions under a similar logic. Critics, however, noted the inconsistency of adopting a legal practice while rejecting the original rationale, here state-run religion, that justified it. If religious property was no longer part of the state, then why should tax law treat it differently from other kinds of property? Most state constitutions, after all, applied an "equal and uniform" standard to their property tax procedures. As critics exposed the logical flaw in states' tax treatment of religious property, defenders helped develop a new rationale.[12]

In the wake of disestablishment, a raft of court opinions, legislative statements, and public writings crafted a new equation: between church property and the public good. Drawing on a different strain of English precedent that treated church property as exempt only when it was used "charitably," this improvised defense of religious property exemptions hinged on the presumed social benefits of religion and became the basis for broader exemptions as American tax law expanded.[13]

By the beginning of the twentieth century, almost every state had constitutional provisions or statutory laws that exempted religious property from taxation. Most demanded proof, often incorporation papers, establishing that a religious association owned property for religious purposes. Once that test was satisfied, and thanks to property tax exemptions, religious institutions could fill their coffers with funds undiminished by taxation, a privilege that enabled them to thrive and diversify in the American landscape. Between 1850 and 1860, the US census of religious bodies recorded that the value of synagogue property doubled, an increase consistent with the general growth of religious property value in the United States.[14]

Hardly a free gift, however, property tax exemption imposed state discipline on religious institutions. A state that could exempt an entity from taxation could also deny an exemption. Practices of taxation provided states with levers to regulate and classify behavior and delineate the boundaries between public interests and private interests more precisely than Chief Justice Marshall had in his Dartmouth College decision. As they developed over the course of the nineteenth century, incorporation law and property tax exemption became the means by which American states, according to Sarah Barringer Gordon, "simultaneously supported and disciplined" religious associations. The process of disestablishment and the explosion of religious diversity set into motion legislative and judicial efforts to refine these strategies and define the precise role a state could play in managing associations.[15]

———

Although states' efforts to disestablish religion were critical in shaping the legal, political, and economic contours of associationalism, states also applied the associational form to rationalize and control collective life beyond religious institutions. In the 1840s, New York State extended the privileges and regulations of general incorporation to all "benevolent, charitable, scientific, and missionary societies," widening the categorical umbrella beyond religious institutions and providing a model for statutory reform in other states. Groups covered under general incorporation did not necessarily gain access to states' property tax exemption, though many did, especially once states started to delineate between "for-profit" corporations and "not-for-profit" ones as a matter of public benefit, beginning in the 1870s. Indeed, by the late nineteenth century, when the federal government first attempted to create a national income tax, the idea that some associations and activities, by their nature, were of public benefit informed the government's view of what was and was not taxable income.[16]

In 1894, the US Congress passed the first peacetime federal income tax. Similar to earlier state property tax policies, the law granted the federal government the powers of taxation and its obverse, exemption. Narrowly understood, the income tax allowed the federal government to generate new sources of revenue, but in a broader and more consequential way, it also empowered the federal government to shape people's lives and to structure their collective interests and properties, much as states' governance of associations did.[17]

Although the Supreme Court quickly struck down the 1894 law, declaring its attempt to levy a direct tax unconstitutional, the legislation's progressive formula for taxation—taxing the wealthiest Americans at the highest rate—and its special treatment of public benefit associations ultimately went on to shape modern American life. Almost two decades would elapse before tax reformers could garner support for the now necessary constitutional amendment enshrining Congress's power to tax income. The battle to pass the Sixteenth Amendment in 1913 required tax reformers to sharpen their case for what one historian has called "the modern American fiscal state." Threading the needle between competing economic philosophies, proponents of the income tax maintained that a direct and progressive tax would hold excessive wealth accumulation in check while still eschewing a socialized state. Their goal, as with so many other progressive reform efforts in the United States, was to establish instruments for safeguarding democracy against the rule of the powerful few without hindering capitalist growth.[18]

In 1913, immediately after the states ratified the Sixteenth Amendment giving Congress the power to tax income, Congress created the Bureau of Internal Revenue, an acknowledgment that its legislation could place unprecedented administrative burdens on the federal government. In its first few years, the new agency's responsibilities were more notional than real, as only 2% of the American labor force earned enough to qualify for taxation—and the top earners among those were assessed a modest 7% marginal tax rate. But with the onset of World War I, the federal government leaned more heavily on income tax for revenue generation, extending the income tax to a greater proportion of Americans and creating a wider graduated scale that progressively increased the rate of taxation as one's income increased.[19]

Along with its progressive approach to taxation, however, the 1913 income tax law reserved for the government the power to exempt certain entities from taxation, a practice that provided the greatest benefit to those who would otherwise be subject to the highest level of taxation—in other words, a regressive measure. Imported in full from the ill-fated 1894 law, the exemption clause wove together English common law, state general incorporation laws, and property tax laws: "[N]othing herein contained shall apply . . . to corporations, companies, or associations organized and conducted solely for charitable, religious, or educational purposes." In 1917, as part of its War Revenue Act, Congress broadened the benefits of exemption to individuals by allowing them to deduct contributions to such organizations from their taxable income. The logic of tax exemptions held that any income already counted on the revenue side of the government's balance sheet should not be subject to taxation; thus, if an expenditure could be classified as contributing to a clear public purpose, for the government to then tax the income used for that expenditure would be akin to double taxation.[20]

In determining what kinds of income—how high, generated by what activities, engaged in what kind of work—already fulfilled a public mission and, thus, deserved a tax exemption, the American state (including the federal legislative branch that passed the law, the agency set up to administer it, and the courts charged with enforcing it) extended its authority over private capital and private lives. Drawing on practices it had developed to manage associations, the state perceived its citizens and their collective activities in categorical terms. Administrative categories, from the composition of boards and property holdings to the classification of religious, educational, or charitable pursuits, served to organize a vast array of activities no matter their particular substance. By conforming to these categories, diverse associations received and were perceived as public benefits.

———

Throughout their history, most American Jews did not belong to synagogues, but the vast majority interacted with Jewish associations, whether mutual aid societies, educational institutions, fraternal organizations, or social welfare agencies. While the purposes and memberships of these associations were diverse, their structures, embedded in the political economy of the American state and subject to its modes of disciplining and provisioning entities that presented themselves as public benefits, were much less so.[21]

If Tocqueville was impressed by the vibrancy of American associations in the early nineteenth century, he would have been astounded by—or, perhaps, claimed to have predicted—the vast array of associations, many of national scope, that had come into existence by the late nineteenth century. Among Jews, mutual aid societies emerged in almost every Jewish settlement in the United States. According to one estimate, by the early twentieth century, one quarter of New York City's Jews held membership in such organizations. Whether assembled by immigrants hailing from the same place in the Old World (called *landsmanshaftn*), organized by trade or profession, or simply created by Jews who settled in the same area, these mutual aid societies tied American Jews to an institutional infrastructure.

The progenitor of mutual aid societies, B'nai B'rith, founded in 1843 in New York City by a small group of men who had emigrated from German states, extended its network of charity, insurance, and sociability to Jewish settlements across the country. B'nai B'rith, similar to most mutual aid societies, sought to provide benefits to its male members' widowed wives and children. It also served as a fraternal organization for Jewish men who generally were excluded from membership in the popular masonic movement and other male social clubs. Echoing the structure and language of masonic organizations, B'nai B'rith was composed of "orders" with local chapters called "lodges" that established and supported libraries, schools, hospitals, old-age homes, and other auxiliary institutions to help Jews implant themselves in the United States. As the foremost historian of Jewish immigration associations has noted, despite their diversity of beliefs and interests (including socialist ones), the broad range of Jewish associations "resembled each other so remarkably. . . . Their membership requirements, leadership structures, benefits, activities, even, in many cases, their names all followed a like pattern."[22]

Throughout the second half of the nineteenth century, American Jews also established a slew of so-called benevolent societies, including a significant number led by women as paid staff members and volunteers. While in some cases women's benevolent or charitable organizations grew as sister organizations to men's associations (including B'nai B'rith), many were either standalone enterprises or linked to synagogues. These organizations served as the backbone of Jewish charitable work. Much like in other communities across the country, charitable activities tended to be recognized as falling within women's domain. Jewish women exercised leadership, managed budgets, learned how to comply with legal codes, and appeared in public life through their involvement in benevolent societies. Just as mutual aid societies resembled each other, even as each had their own character, benevolent organizations also conformed to many of the same patterns, including their gendered nature.[23]

Many Jewish leaders, however, were less likely to see the similarities that existed across their organizational landscape and more likely to perceive a chaotic lack of coordination, resulting in duplication of services, misuse of funds, and needs gone unmet. Setting their sights specifically on the vast array of benevolent societies, predominantly male Jewish leaders began to propose the creation of coordinating structures for the sake of efficiency. The "federation" movement was the most durable product to emerge from their efforts, though it took many decades for the model to succeed. As historian Beth Wenger has shown, in the early decades of the twentieth century, the Jewish federation model gradually "squeezed out" women from leadership roles, as male leaders reconfigured benevolent organizations into federation agencies, generally consolidating several organizations into one and appointing male experts to coordinate new agencies. In the cases that women resisted the process of consolidation, their organizations tended to become sidelined from Jewish communal priorities and funding. Even the agencies recognized by and funded through a Jewish federation often bristled at its control and worried about their loss of autonomy, but women and their organizations suffered the steepest losses from the growth of this new centralized funding structure of American Jewish associational life.[24]

Jewish charitable federations promised a new method for raising and disbursing funds to the growing array of Jewish associations—addressing everything from social uplift, immigrant settlement, education, and occupational training—by centralizing the collection and allocation of capital within any given community. Boosters of the model envisioned a federated structure to reduce the nuisance of competitive fund-raising, while maintaining a commitment to decentralized service providers for American Jews—a strikingly similar vision to the one that many Progressive-movement thinkers had for the federal government. Political scientists who have examined American associations from the early republic through the late nineteenth century trace the striking rise of nationally coordinated associations, explaining that their development "closely mirrored the representative and federal arrangements of U.S. government and proliferated in close relationship to key episodes of nation-state formation." Thus, as much as associations may have appeared separate from governmental bodies, they reflected the shifting patterns of American statecraft and, specifically, bore the mark of growingly robust state-based infrastructures to coordinate and regulate broader dimensions of American life.[25]

The Jewish federation system embraced the Progressive movement's ideological hybridity—its commitment to democratic institutions and its investment in capitalism—as well as the technological advances of the era. To be certain, some American Jews, especially immigrants and their children, endorsed a far more revolutionary call for socialism as the only pathway toward true social improvement. Most, however, joined with other Americans in favoring a reformist program that fell far short of capitalist overthrow and, instead, in the words of a historian of the Progressive movement, advanced an American "creed" of reform that relied on "associations and the state to end class conflict and the other problems of industrial capitalism."[26]

Pressure to coordinate and improve Jewish social services came most forcefully from cities absorbing swelling numbers of new immigrants. In New York City in the 1870s, economic recession spurred the *Jewish Messenger*, one of the leading Jewish weeklies at the time, to strengthen its call for a united infrastructure to meet changing needs. Drawing on the model of New York Protestant groups, the editor of the newspaper helped organize the United Hebrew Charities in 1874, with the participation of five major Jewish charities. As a model for coordination, the United Hebrew Charities was noteworthy, but its achievements were short-lived, as new organizations in the city formed at breathtaking speed over the coming decades and defied its unifying impulse.[27]

Two decades later, in Boston, the same impulse to centralize and coordinate fund-raising efforts led to the creation of the Federation of Jewish Charities. Pursuing an almost identical course to that of the United Hebrew Charities, the Federation of Jewish Charities began by coordinating the city's core Jewish charitable institutions, including an orphanage, an employment bureau, and a burial association. Yet similar to New York's, Boston's first attempt to unify Jewish charitable life fell prey to rapid population expansion and the proliferation of Jewish organizations to meet new needs, and in the early twentieth century, a second attempt, Federated Jewish Charities, sought to cast a much wider net and coordinate the funding for a larger set of Jewish agencies.

Indeed, in almost every decade until the 1950s, the federation system in Boston renamed itself and announced its intentions to serve an even broader swathe of the city's Jewish population.[28]

In like fashion, Jewish federations sprung up across the United States, often reforming and renaming themselves multiple times throughout the early twentieth century. In 1904, Cleveland's Jewish community established a federation—with one name and then another only a few years later—that would emerge as the federation system's most significant financial innovator after World War II. Returning to their federated experiments, New York Jews in 1917 created the Federation for the Support of Jewish Philanthropic Societies, renamed in the coming decades to reflect mergers with other Jewish organizations. By World War I, twenty-three cities in the United States had formed Jewish federations. At no time were these federations inclusive of the vast universe of Jewish associations—for example, they almost never included synagogues within their structure—but they organized a larger portion of American Jewish collective life than any other institution, and just as notably they served as a model for other communities.[29]

Exhibiting similar patterns, a broad array of federated charitable structures, both religiously based ones, such as the National Conference of Catholic Charities, and putatively nonsectarian ones, such as the community chest movement that preceded the founding of the United Way, established chapters in communities across the United States in the early twentieth century. Furthermore, the field of social work—and the term itself—emerged directly from the trend of developing more coordinated and systematic approaches to reform. Focusing on families, communities, and entire cities, social workers hoped to help individuals while also reforming the structures that hindered their well-being. What once had been the work of primarily small-scale ethnic and religious organizations was transformed into a professional field with training institutions, textbooks, and conferences. Connected to this transformation was the consolidation of funding for social welfare work and the emergence of nonsectarian funding agencies.[30]

Even as American laws and policies impressed themselves upon these emerging philanthropic conglomerates, especially through incorporation regulations and tax codes, many of the same philanthropic associations developed mechanisms both to extend the reaches and to skirt the limits of American national sovereignty. From missionary networks embedded in American religious organizations to the international connections that immigrant populations brought with them to the United States, the earliest incarnations of internationally oriented associations already began to develop in the late nineteenth century, anticipating the rise of international nongovernmental organizations in the era of the First World War.[31]

Individual American Jews channeled resources to Jews outside of the United States throughout the nineteenth century to care for family members living across the Atlantic, to help rebuild villages decimated by pogroms and acts of state violence under the Russian Empire, to support Jewish settlements in Palestine, to assist high-profile Jewish legal battles, and more. In Europe, Jewish organizations, such as the Alliance Israélite Universelle established in France in 1860, were wholly dedicated to safeguarding the rights of global Jewish communities through advocacy and funding. Gradually, American Jewish leaders developed a communal infrastructure to coordinate international philanthropic efforts. Initially, they worked through their existing associations, such as B'nai B'rith and other mutual aid societies, but by the early twentieth century, they began to consolidate these efforts through the creation of new associations, much as they did through domestically oriented federations. In 1914, just as World War I began, Jewish leaders established the American Jewish Joint Distribution Committee (JDC). First formed to send assistance to Jews in Palestine, the organization quickly widened its scope to assist Jewish humanitarian needs globally. Mirroring the federation model and drawing upon the European precedents, the JDC coordinated *landsmanschaftn* and other small-scale Jewish organizations, and it rapidly developed into the most prominent and well-coordinated international nongovernmental organization serving global Jewish needs.[32]

Through their centralization and consolidation over the late nineteenth and early twentieth centuries, American Jewish philanthropic organizations gained heft and trendsetting power that far outweighed the small size of the Jewish population, never more than 4% of the American public. In a 1923 report, the National Conference of Jewish Social Service, an organization established in the late nineteenth century that steadily sought to professionalize and coordinate Jewish social work, praised the proliferation of the federation structure within the Jewish community for "improving the financial methods of our communal agencies" and achieving "a more intelligent, just and efficient distribution of the funds thus realized." The Jewish social work organization believed that the services its members provided to individuals could be no better than the mechanisms that funded those services.[33]

Through categories of tax exemption and deduction, the government subsidized, though often quietly, a growing number of individual donors and philanthropists who divested themselves of some of their personal capital in the interest of the public good. Yet in the early decades of the twentieth century, American Jewish philanthropic organizations did not have their eyes on the role that state bodies played in enriching and regulating associational life. Similarly, few imagined requesting state entities to step in and fulfill some of the most pressing needs that their organizations sought to address. The 1923 Jewish social service report put the blame for insufficient social services on Jewish federations' inability to raise money through "cooperation and active participation of all the elements making up the Jewish body politic."[34]

Here as elsewhere, the language of individual sacrifice and altruism (or, in this case, the lack thereof) took center stage, even as the instruments of the American state to regulate and manage American life were fast developing. The individual face of philanthropy—the donor who would feel moved by generosity and obligation to support a cause or organization—continued to overshadow the role of the state. Yet not only did philanthropic associations exhibit the same transformations occurring in American government, including its centralization and consolidation of power, but they also were coming to depend on the state, especially its new tax regime, to support them.

———

As federated institutions became a core manifestation of American associationalism in the Progressive era, they existed alongside—and sometimes in conflict with—a seemingly divergent associational model: the philanthropic foundation. Whereas federations dealt in masses of people and property, collecting and allocating capital on behalf of the group, philanthropic foundations appeared far more individually oriented. Yet to regard Progressive-era philanthropic foundations as primarily individual forms ignores the fact that they, too, were structured by the nascent regulatory framework of state-based laws and policies governing associations. Through incorporation and tax law, state legislatures regulated foundations, mandating they maintain boards and making claims on their property. Thus, although they took different forms with different histories and arrangements of power, both federations and foundations were shaped by the American state's efforts to balance democracy and capitalism through the strengthening of its own regulatory tools.

Private endowments, with legal instruments specifying how their assets should be spent, predated Progressive-era America, but modern philanthropic foundations emerged in the early twentieth century only with the creation of a legal apparatus to name and govern them. Unsurprisingly, the earliest modern American foundations had their origins in the late nineteenth and early twentieth centuries, when states and, then, the federal government modernized incorporation and tax law to manage new stores of publicly purposed capital spun off from the fortunes of phenomenally wealthy industrial capitalists. The founders of America's first modern foundations formed them by transferring their capital holdings into uniquely incorporated accounts that could exist in perpetuity so long as the custodians of those accounts adhered to the stated public purpose of their creation. For example, although John D. Rockefeller and Andrew Carnegie incorporated their foundations during their lifetimes, both expected the property in their foundations to last beyond their lifetimes. They attempted to guarantee the perpetuity of their foundations by creating a corpus for investment and spending only the income from investment, not the corpus, on their foundations' missions.

Political theorist Rob Reich writes, "The modern philanthropic foundation is perhaps the most unaccountable, nontransparent, peculiar institutional form we have in a democratic society." In federated philanthropy, the structuring power of the democratic ideal was more readily apparent: a mass of people centralized its money in the hands of a single body that then allocated funds annually in the name of the people. The people could express its support or censure for the allocation process by deciding to give or not the following year. Foundations, however, appeared far more remote from democratic control, amassing capital in a permanent fund to be allocated according to the wishes of a board of trustees often designated by the very same individuals who had placed their capital in a foundation.[35]

Foundations were, nonetheless, structures of the modern American state—or in Reich's terms, "artifact[s] of the state." By the early decades of the twentieth century, private foundations and federated charities were the two primary "technologies" of American philanthropy. Both applied particular forms of knowledge and capital strategies to the problems of their time. These technologies extended and reshaped American associations by providing new methods for collectives and individuals to organize themselves and their property in the name of the public good. As these forms developed, in order to keep up with their growth and changing practices, American state bodies likewise devised their own new technologies to regulate and control them in the name of the same public good.[36]

———

Between the 1870s and early decades of the twentieth century, modern American philanthropy was born. Without the much longer history of state-by-state experimentation with political frameworks intended to flexibly accommodate collective interests, while structuring and managing their growth, modern American philanthropy could not have emerged when and how it did. However, only in the late nineteenth century, alongside the rebirth of a federal government faced with the daunting task of re-forming a national union, can we identify the origins of modern American philanthropy. Better, in fact, to identify the twinned birth of modern American philanthropy and the modern American state in these years. More than parallel developments, the two emerged in tandem as American elites sought to figure out how the fruits (or spoils) of modern capitalism could best advance a democracy made fragile by its diverse and often warring publics, its vast social and economic inequalities, and its underdeveloped federalized apparatus.

Throughout the nineteenth century, American Jews shaped their collective efforts to meet the requirements of state and federal law, and they also adjusted the apparatus of associationalism to meet their needs. It is hardly a coincidence that Jews were some of the first exponents of federated charitable giving, as they felt pressed to attend to the needs of a burgeoning Jewish immigrant population throughout the second half of the nineteenth century. As they did so, they drew on their historical experiences coordinating and provisioning for communities across geography and navigating power structures not of their making. At the same time, the political economy of the American state and its associational form delimited the possibilities for how American Jews might organize their collective lives.

Through its associational apparatus, the American state—including state-level and federal legislative bodies, courts, and agencies—made Jewish collective life visible to it. From historians of American Jews, we know a great deal about how Jews adapted to and reshaped American cultural norms. The framework of an American Jewish synthesis has dominated the field, echoing the pronouncements that American Jews themselves have made across time about the perfect fit between Jewish and American life (so much so that one historian has characterized this synthesis as a "cult"-like obsession for American Jews). But far less thoroughly examined are the structural features of American political economy that were grafted onto Jewish life, not as an act of synthesis but rather as the policies, laws, and economic modes that authorized collective Jewish life. Jews became visible to the American state within a formal structure of associationalism. This structure did not differentiate Jews as Jews, but rather allowed their collective enterprises to gain recognition, protections, and benefits in return for abiding by its regulations.[37]

Jews joined a vast array of other American groups, similarly operating in the sinews of an associational structure that attempted to lash together democracy and capitalism by designating certain forms of private property and behavior as ipso facto accruing to the public benefit. Through its policies regulating associational life, the American state enforced structural uniformity, while allowing substantive diversity. In broad strokes, Jewish and non-Jewish collective pursuits resembled one another by the early years of the twentieth century because they were regulated by similar instruments. But this is not the same as asserting that American governing forces did not regulate or could not distinguish Jewish collective endeavors. A core American freedom to organize collectively came with rules and discipline that allowed the American state, at its multiple layers, to see Jews as a collective, not solely as individuals.

As fields, American history and American Jewish history have long been oriented around a narrative of progress. Associationalism, voluntarism, and philanthropy have played leading parts in that story, each exemplifying the conjoining of democracy and capitalism to steadily improve the human condition. Yet in excising the role of the state, its structures of management, and its systems for exercising financial and legal power from the story, historians risk overstating progress as an engine of change, as if human improvement were inevitable and unique to the social alchemy of the United States, interrupted only by anomalous or aberrant forces. Regulation and incentive, discipline and freedom, democracy and capitalism were all stitched together, imperfectly and never with a sense of finality, as the American state developed and redeveloped its regulatory infrastructure.[38]

2

Regulations

IN JANUARY 1915, Samuel Untermyer, a Jewish lawyer from New York City, appeared before the US Commission on Industrial Relations, a Senate-appointed body to investigate concentrations of industrial power. Precipitated by a fatal labor conflict at a Colorado coal mine owned by John D. Rockefeller, the investigation quickly turned to scrutinizing Rockefeller's charitable activities and their relationship to philanthropic foundations more generally. Before addressing the commission's questions, Untermyer offered a preamble: "Notwithstanding its injustice and many other shortcomings, I believe in the capitalistic system as our only present solution. Socialism is a beautiful, iridescent dream. It is useful mainly as a protest against the cruel inequalities of existing social conditions. . . . But it does not work out as a practical, constructive policy of government." Although he had made his career pressing for state regulation of large corporate entities and seeking to limit the influence of big finance on government, Untermyer also believed solutions to the problems of capitalism could be found within the capitalist framework itself, particularly in the form of philanthropy and its regulation.[1]

In his testimony, Untermyer mounted a robust defense of philanthropy, setting his voice in opposition to the tenor of the investigation and Congress's refusal to grant large corporate families—the Rockefellers, the Carnegies, the Sages, and so on—charters for their philanthropic foundations. He understood that many members of Congress harbored deep suspicions that these families were trying to cloak their rapacious capitalism in shallow acts of benevolence. Untermyer, however, saw things differently and elaborated, "I believe [these foundations] to be prompted by the highest ideals of patriotism and unselfish public spirit. They are magnificently managed by the best intellect of the country—far better than would be possible with any public institution. The genius and resourcefulness to which their founders owed their material success have been unselfishly expended by these men upon these foundations, which are to be monuments to future generations of their useful-ness to society. They are doing incalculable public good and no harm." More than a superficial gesture, philanthropy could tie the very best of capitalist vitality to a democratic vision.[2]

Ever faithful to the necessity of regulation, Untermyer nonetheless sug-gested that philanthropy, much like capitalism, would advance human pro-gress only if state organs took active roles in shaping it. One after another, he ticked off the policies that would balance the capitalist impulses and demo-cratic aspirations of philanthropy: oversight of board appointments; time-bound charters to avoid perpetual power; and limitations on the assets held and accumulated. Instead of operating as a shadow state or an instrument of capitalism, philanthropy, properly regulated, could blend the ideals of democ-racy and capitalism into a third enterprise that proved the value of each.[3]

Hardly an accepted feature of American statecraft at the time, the regula-tory measures Untermyer suggested required the American state to regard its power in new ways. Although over the course of the nineteenth century, indi-vidual states' governments had constructed the framework of incorporation and tax law as a means to regulate associations of private citizens, and by the turn of the century, these legal tools had helped the federal government ex-pand its regulatory apparatus, the federal government was still new to the busi-ness of private regulation.[4]

By the time he testified, Untermyer had already helped shape an expanded vision of regulatory government by assisting in the 1913 establishment of the Federal Reserve Bank, a semi-centralized, federally backed system to safeguard the economy from financial panics. Additionally, Untermyer worked with the US Treasury Department to craft early interpretations of income tax legisla-tion and was active in Democratic party politics, serving as a delegate at its national conventions throughout the early decades of the twentieth century.[5]

Related to his broad efforts to help create a regulatory financial state was Untermyer's own background. Born in 1858 in Lynchburg, Virginia, to German-Jewish immigrants, Untermyer's family had moved to New York City after his father's death as a Confederate lieutenant in the Civil War. He attended City College and then Columbia Law School, and built a law practice—and, even-tually, a substantial fortune—around the parade of late-nineteenth- and early-twentieth-century corporate mergers. His wealth gained him access to chan-nels of American power and, also, to emerging Jewish institutions that held communal power. But, as noted in his front-page *New York Times* obituary in

FIGURE 2.1. Portrait of Samuel Untermyer. Courtesy of the Jacob Rader Marcus Center of the American Jewish Archives, Cincinnati, Ohio, at american-jewisharchives.org.

1940, his elevated station had not stopped him from defending those who challenged the terms of American power: "Although an avowed opponent of socialistic theories, Mr. Untermyer's political philosophy was so liberal that he did not hesitate to defend individual Socialists and radicals when he believed that their rights had been attacked unjustly." The particular features of Untermyer's biography—a man, a lawyer, affluent, and Jewish—landed him in a position from which he could both extol the virtues of capitalism and warn of its dangers to democracy were it not properly restrained.[6]

Despite the Commission on Industrial Relations' mistrust of foundations, philanthropic foundations with substantial holdings grew quickly in the early decades of the twentieth century, from just a dozen or so in 1915 to more than two hundred by 1930, growth that paralleled the expansion of federated charities. In these years, the American state imprinted itself on philanthropy in deeper ways than ever, extending its practices of regulating and incentivizing associational life into new laws, policies, and financial arrangements. As in the past, the inducements state bodies offered private actors served as rewards for their adherence to new forms of governance. Citizens and groups that requested state consideration, whether in the form of incorporation rights, tax exemptions, or both, continued to make themselves visible to the state, but in the twentieth century, the regulations they faced and the incentives they gained expanded considerably.[7]

Faith in regulation, expressed so passionately in Untermyer's testimony to the Commission on Industrial Relations and echoed in the practices of Jewish institutions and the voting behavior of Jewish individuals, embedded the structures of American Jewish collective life more firmly than ever in state structures built to balance capitalist growth with a democratic vision. Eventually that faith would start to cave in on itself, as midcentury policymakers joined with business leaders to reform state regulatory practices with an eye toward market freedom and state-subsidized capitalist growth. Jewish philanthropic institutions, creatures of the American state, would likewise embrace and even help shape this shifting balance of state and market power, but not before they learned to function and thrive within the regulatory structure of the American state.

———

Sharing in the federal government's suspicion of the fortunes amassed by the titans of industry, Jewish federation leaders across the country oriented their institutions around the immediate distribution of the money they collected. New York City's federation, incorporated in 1917 to coordinate domestic philanthropic efforts for the largest and most concentrated Jewish population in the United States, offers a window into the distributive logic that governed Jewish philanthropy from World War I until the post–World War II decades. Its leaders valued philanthropic capital by the immediate needs it could fulfill and worked to make the process of collection and allocation as efficient as possible, as if moving funds through a revolving door. These leaders assumed that donors would be convinced to renew or, better yet, increase their contributions only if they saw the money they donated being used to meet urgent needs. The organization's bylaws clearly stated, "The Federation shall discourage the making of legacies and devises [bequests of real estate]. . . . The Federation shall not accept legacies and devises by which the principal is to be held in trust by Federation and only the income is to be available for distribution." Any legacies it happened to receive were to be distributed within three years, and its "Emergency Fund"—that is, money held and not distributed—was capped at $1 million.[8]

In a parallel fashion, Catholic Charities, which formed a federated association in the 1920s to consolidate its charitable work, sought to match its revenue intake with its distribution, pursuing a similar logic of revolving-door philanthropy, from collection to allocation. An early director of Catholic Charities explicitly noted his effort to imitate Jewish philanthropic practices in moving money efficiently to satisfy material needs. In common with many Jewish federations, Catholic Charities' bylaws prohibited holding back funds for savings or endowment. Jewish and Catholic philanthropic institutions regarded their yearly fund-raising as a mandate from the people, and their quick distribution of those dollars to meet material needs served to legitimate the following year's campaign.[9]

Limited resources surely dictated early-twentieth-century Jewish and Catholic eschewal of endowment-building, yet the practical constraints also reinforced an ideological case for distributing, as opposed to accumulating, charitable resources. In the wake of the Gilded Age, which saw the rise of striking inequality, many Americans maintained a distrust of stockpiled wealth. Even Andrew Carnegie, the consummate industrial capitalist, denounced the practice of holding vast fortunes in perpetuity, and in his famous late-nineteenth-century essay, "The Gospel of Wealth," he argued for the return of wealth to society through philanthropic distribution. During his time in office, Theodore Roosevelt amplified Populist and Progressive concerns about wealth concentration and began to advocate a federal inheritance tax. In 1916, on the heels of the Commission on Industrial Relations' report that drew attention to the extent of American economic inequality, Congress passed the tax into law. If left unregulated, inheritance served much like a trust or endowment to concentrate capital and restrict its flow.[10]

The men who guided the early work of New York's federation came from the worlds of business and banking and were not averse to capital accumulation, trusts, or power. The founding president, Felix Warburg, was the scion

of a German banking family and shared a profile of wealth, German or Central
European heritage, and business experience with the other founders (and with
Samuel Untermyer). Yet the federation's bylaws revealed its founders' belief
that a regulatory framework that constrained capitalist growth would best advance charitable work. In part, this reflected the fact that they had to sell their
model to agencies throughout the city. Should they have been perceived as
accumulating capital without releasing it, those agencies, numbering ninety-
two by 1918, likely would not have agreed to compromise their fiscal autonomy
in return for centralized fund-raising. But their embrace of regulatory policies
also echoed public distrust of unbridled capital accumulation. Far from regarding the concentration of wealth as a civic virtue, policy proposals and
popular voices made the case for just the opposite, castigating charitable trusts
for pandering to the interests of the wealthy under the guise of advancing the
public good.[11]

Nonetheless, with Warburg at its helm, the board of New York's federation
gradually began to question whether its decision to preclude endowment
growth came at the expense of its ability to fulfill its mission, which would
ultimately prove untenable in the absence of reliable access to funds. In late
1921, Warburg charged a committee with revising the bylaws to address the
problem of a prospective donor who might feel entitled "to leave this money
as he wished . . . and some way must be found whereby these persons could
make gifts or legacies in the way which they desired." Shifting the discussion
of endowment from the problems of capital accumulation to the desires of
individual donors, Warburg provided a way for reluctant trustees to understand that overly draconian regulations against holding funds in trust might
lead the institution to squander its access to certain kinds of donors, especially
wealthy ones who would expect some say over how their fortunes were used.[12]

The potential conflict between the will of individual donors and the federation's prohibition on long-term trusts was hardly theoretical. In the fall of 1920,
Jacob Schiff, a German-born banker who financed loans to several countries
in the early twentieth century and was a prominent supporter of New York's
Jewish, cultural, and educational institutions, died. Schiff, it happened, was
also Warburg's father-in-law, so Warburg knew—along with careful readers of
the *New York Times*, where Schiff's will had been printed in full—that the
deceased had left a $500,000 bequest to the New York federation. In his will,
Schiff had written that while he understood that the federation's bylaws prohibited accepting legacies to be held in trust, "I am, however, convinced that
it will be in the interest of the Federation to repeal this provision of its by-laws

so that it may receive legacies or devises to be held by it in permanent trust." And though he claimed to have "no desire to exercise any pressure" on the federation, his promised bequest certainly put a thumb, if not a dead hand, on the scale in favor of amending the bylaws.[13]

Even with half a million dollars on the table, the trustees fiercely debated whether and how to modify the bylaws whose regulations of endowment seemed essential to the federation's model for serving the Jewish communal public good. A 1917 manual on the "principles and methods" of Jewish philanthropy instructed, "With the growing demand upon charitable activities, there is a strong sentiment to designate charity bequests for immediate actual needs rather than to transfer them into permanent sources of income." Endowment funds might help ensure a financially stable future, but, according to the manual, they too often constrained spending, committing institutions to causes that had become obsolete or releasing only small amounts of their holdings despite the gravity of social problems, all the while signaling to community members that their own donations were unnecessary.[14]

Arguing in favor of maintaining the restrictions on the federation's endowment, Leo Arnstein, a Jewish businessman and founding federation trustee representing Mount Sinai Hospital, a federation-funded institution, noted, "There has been a good deal of legislature [sic] against such sums in perpetuity because it cannot be foretold what will happen to them." In fact, Congress had not passed any of the measures to limit charitable perpetuities that Untermyer and others had suggested during the Commission on Industrial Relations investigation, though Arnstein was correct that Congress had contemplated such actions. He strongly encouraged the group to stick to its original purpose "as a collecting and distributing agency" and not enter the business of endowment-building. Other federation leaders, however, worried that if they checked their business acumen at the door when they organized Jewish collective life, they would imperil its future security. One reminded the group that no respectable business would operate with a $3 million spending budget and "without a single dollar of reserve whenever an emergency arises." He warned that this financial practice left the federation unable to plan for its future.[15]

At Warburg's instruction, a committee of trustees proposed a revision to the bylaws that would allow for a slightly more permissive attitude toward endowment-building, while still, in the committee's words, "allay[ing] any fears, however unwarranted they may be, that . . . Federation [might] amass funds without limit, thereby creating for itself a position of power that might make for evil in the community" or "become a menacing, all-powerful 'charity-trust' so called." The committee modestly suggested softening the word "discourage," which presently served to stymie any endowment-building, with the more neutral language that "the Federation shall neither solicit nor encourage" the collection of endowments. Additionally, the amendment released the board from its earlier pledge to spend reserve funds after three years, instead freeing it to hold funds without a time limit in the case of extraordinary circumstances, such as explicit instructions in a will. Approved by the vast majority of board members (with only eight out of seventy members objecting) in December 1921, the new measure took effect immediately. Without a break in its business, the board then turned to approve the receipt of a $500,000 trust from Schiff's bequest, permissible now thanks to the amended bylaws.[16]

Over the next two decades, New York's federation would seek to regulate its capital growth through a commitment to distribution, while also blunting the force of its own regulatory practices by increasing the limits it placed on reserve funds, approving new accounts to hold trusts and legacies, and establishing investment policies to manage property and securities held in nondistributive funds. Still, at each turn, it approached these new financial decisions by reiterating its primary commitment to buttressing the annual campaign and its distributive logic. Jewish federations across the country acted similarly, gradually placing more funds in trust and developing strategies for capital accumulation, while treating those funds as tangential to their mission and apart from their general philosophy.[17]

————

Throughout the 1920s, the trustees of New York's federation confronted the realities of capital expansion. Their commitment to raising and distributing funds in the span of a single year remained central to the organization's philanthropic practices but could not keep pace with the new sources of capital, in the forms of legacies, bequests, and investment returns, that now appeared monthly in budget reports. Shortly after the trustees had amended their bylaws to reflect a more neutral position toward accepting the terms of bequests, they were faced with the task of managing several new substantial gifts, many with their own terms and conditions. In the prosperous 1920s, it was almost as if capital growth afflicted Jewish philanthropy, despite its leaders' best regulatory intentions.

Pressure to adapt to a new capital climate continued to build from within the federation. In January 1922, Warburg announced that to mark the birthday

FIGURE 2.2. Portrait of Felix Warburg. Courtesy of the Jacob Rader Marcus Center of the American Jewish Archives, Cincinnati, Ohio, at americanjewisharchives.org.

of his late father-in-law, Jacob Schiff, he intended to donate more than $500,000 in securities from his own banking firm. The minutes recorded "great applause" following the announcement and noted that Warburg "added a brief word to the effect that since the change in the By-Laws making it possible for Federation to accept such funds has been made, the principal of it is to remain invested as the Finance Committee of Federation sees fit, and the interest is to be used for the purposes of Federation." With his gift, Warburg pushed the federation farther down the path toward the normalization of capital accumulation as a philanthropic strategy.[18]

The complex terms of Warburg's gift demanded new philanthropic practices and forms of financial expertise. His donated securities would serve as the federation's investment property, generating income on an annual basis. He committed these earnings, topped off by a gift he would make out of pocket to fulfill his annual pledge, to the federation's routine purposes. It could treat this investment income as an annual gift and distribute it according to standard protocol. But the investment itself, the principal, was marked as standing outside of the revolving door of dollar intake and distribution. Instead, its purpose was to grow investment capital, which could not occur if the principal were either disbursed or invested poorly.[19]

In donating securities to the federation, Warburg relinquished his private control over them and their earnings, but he exercised power over the federation's financial practices. With a gentle hand, Warburg allowed the organization time to develop and acclimate to a new financial model geared toward capital growth. His decision to augment the earnings from the securities he donated up to a fixed amount equaling his annual fund pledge insulated the federation from risk and allowed the organization to continue to perceive itself as committed to distribution, not capital accumulation, even as it now held a more significant sum of perpetual funds. In the process, federation leaders started to learn how to think about their philanthropic practices through the lens of investment. At future meetings, the Finance Committee offered detailed reports of its investment decisions and earnings, training the board to understand how capital growth—as opposed to annual gifts—could meet some present needs through its income, while also laying the foundations for a secure philanthropic future. Federation leaders would learn how their organization could participate in the growing American "investors' democracy," a product of business and governmental efforts to convince middle-class, predominantly white Americans that investing their money in securities was good for their own pocketbooks and for their country.[20]

Nonetheless, even as investment became a more common American financial practice, federation leaders still worried about appearing to stockpile capital at the expense of immediate needs. When, for example, a board member suggested writing local estate attorneys to educate them about the best way of designating the federation in their clients' wills, the board voted down the motion, persuaded that doing so would "only stir up a controversy." Whether they saw this as a matter of substance or merely appearance, the federation leaders were anxious about stepping into a culture of capital accumulation and growth at a time when donors and community members would have seen immediate needs almost everywhere they looked. Joined to these concerns was the practical danger of wading into ill-defined legal waters.[21]

In the 1920s, American charitable law, the offspring of legal precedent from British common law and individual states' practices, was in its infancy. Legislators and bureaucrats were just beginning to develop policy and enforcement mechanisms that would influence new federal tax legislation. In 1923, the Bureau of Internal Revenue, established just a decade earlier with the passage of the federal income tax, investigated the New York federation's tax-exempt status on the grounds that some of the agencies it funded did not meet the requirements of exemption. According to the Revenue Act of 1918, tax-exempt entities included "Corporations organized and operated exclusively for religious, charitable, scientific or educational purposes, or for the prevention of cruelty to children or animals, no part of the net earnings of which inures to the benefit of any private stockholder or individual."[22]

The lawyer who chaired the federation's law committee cited the immaturity of federal tax law as a defense against any potential charges. He noted that the courts had not yet "had an opportunity to define the exact meaning" of exempt status or behavior, which tax legislation had defined in only a legally minimalist way. Nonetheless, he offered assurances that federation agencies were all acting within even the strictest interpretation of the law's definition of qualifying charitable activity. In the meantime, working through New York federation networks, the lawyer tapped a former member of the Bureau of Internal Revenue's Legal Division to help him navigate the investigation and prepare for a hearing in Washington, DC. A few months later, the chair of the law committee happily reported that the Bureau had concluded its investigation after the hearing and found in favor of the federation. The experience, however, foreshadowed deepening entanglements between Jewish federations and the American state's regulatory apparatus.[23]

In defining tax-exempt entities, Congress had specifically prohibited private enrichment from exempt purposes. If an individual directly gained from a tax-exempt purpose, the rationale for exemption—that an activity fell on the public side of the government's ledger and thus should not be taxed—would fall apart. Yet, as the Bureau of Internal Revenue experimented with its enforcement power, seeking to determine how it could identify and punish private inurement, Jewish federations experimented with new financial mechanisms that prioritized the desires and freedoms, if not the direct private benefit, of the individual, even as they attempted to maintain the spirit of their own and the state's regulatory measures against undue private control over philanthropy.

In 1925, New York's federation debated a proposal to allow individual donors to designate the specific agencies or causes they wished to support
through bequests. Warburg, a partial defender of donor autonomy, bridled at
giving donors this level of control. He viewed the federation's role as a unifying
one, possible only if donors evinced "an understanding of and sympathy for
the charitable philanthropic requirements of the community as a whole." A
contrary view, however, had started to develop within the ranks of the board.
Warburg's detractors maintained that the federation had already compromised
any case it might mount in favor of total community control over finance. In
opening its doors to bequests and other large gifts, it tilted the balance, even
if just slightly, toward capital accumulation over distribution and, thus, toward
the empowerment of donors whose capital the federation had agreed to hold
in trust. Furthermore, supporters of expanding donor autonomy argued that
as the federation permitted itself to hold more capital in endowment funds, it
lost standing to justify stripping donors of their control on the count of urgent
community needs that might go unfulfilled if donors were allowed to choose
how to earmark their gifts. Indeed, it would be an act of bad faith to tell potential donors that their bequests were needed for urgent purposes when, in reality, those bequests were going to sit in capital growth funds that, at most,
would spend only a portion of their investment income.[24]

Above all else, however, proponents of extending donor control over bequests simply believed that the federation's regulatory framework was, in the
words of one, a "blow at personal liberty." Mounting a case for individual freedom over collective regulation, this same supporter, a prominent businessman, explained that he "could not conceive how any group of men or institutions could assume the right to dictate to any individual how he should dispose
of his own funds, nor how any group could say to an individual who wished
to benefit one particular type of activity that he could not do so, but that he
must leave his money so that varied activities or institutions, possibly some
whose work he was unsympathetic toward, must derive the benefit of his
generosity."[25]

The proposal to allow restrictions and gift specifications on bequests failed,
but its sponsors had mustered a full third of the board's support, indicating
what would be a steady waning of its fealty to regulatory measures—from caps
on endowments to the refusal to accept donor restrictions—over individuals'
donated property. Although Warburg and others would maintain that once
donors ceded their property to a philanthropic cause, they should lose control
over its designation, the case for collective power and regulation would not

hold up well in the face of the federation's capital accumulation and would echo tensions in American political and economic circles over the extent to which the government should regulate, whether through taxation or other means, people's private holdings.[26]

Heightened possibilities for capital accumulation caused federation leaders to reassess, if not necessarily reform, their regulatory structures and also slowly precipitated the introduction of new tools to manage capital. The approximately sixty federations that existed by the mid-1920s in the United States had total budgets of $13.5 million. Jewish federations kept pace with community chest campaigns (forerunners of the United Way), raising on average slightly more per federation than the average intake of each of the 308 community chests in those years. In all cases, however, budgets had grown sharply throughout the 1920s, reflecting both the economic prosperity of the times and the broader purview of these organizations. As budgets increased, charitable institutions focused on creating more efficient mechanisms for fund-raising that embraced modern forms of knowledge and expertise.[27]

New York's federation, with an annual budget of $4.4 million by the mid-1920s, making it the largest of any federation, sought to modernize its financial strategies. For example, a group of businessmen suggested hiring a "rating statistician" to ascertain individuals' giving potential, with an eye toward equipping fund-raisers with more knowledge. Reacting against what one report for New York's federation characterized as "Schnorrer Methods" (which, according to the report, used the technique of "the proverbial old school Jewish beggar"), the businessmen sought to modernize the practice of fund-raising. Only through a scientific approach—dividing givers into classes by wealth and profession, employing professional fund-raisers, and becoming well-versed in modern finance—could the federation avoid the indignities of begging.[28]

Although one way that many federations showed their modern colors in the 1920s was to assert regulatory control over community capital, in other ways they worked against regulation by pursuing a nascent model of freeing capital from restriction—that is, of market freedom. When it came to large gifts, the leaders of New York's federation throughout the 1920s clearly felt opposing pressures to conserve their institution's commitment to immediate allocation through one centralized process, and to accept gifts with whatever stipulations, from long-term trusts to donor control, that might come with them. Over the decade, as New York's federation experimented with endowment-building, using the language of reserve and emergency to justify the importance of withholding some capital from its annual distribution cycle, it tiptoed around a new logic of collective Jewish philanthropy oriented around accumulation, not distribution, that would transform the communal landscape.

———

In 1927, after vigorous debate, the board of New York's federation decided to raise the cap on its emergency fund from $1 million to $3 million. Still, the federation's leaders could hardly imagine approaching that limit. The chair of the board, a lawyer named Sol Stroock, chided the reluctant trustees, "We have been talking here as if legacies have just rained upon us and as if we are getting so much money that we would not know what to do with it." In total, the federation held $135,000 in its reserve fund, a laughable sum compared to the hypothetical riches of the debate. Stroock continued, "I would like to see this reserve fund not $3,000,000 but $10,000,000 and ultimately $30,000,000 because it is a real necessity . . . if we are to make of the various institutions something approaching what they ought to be in capacity of serving this community." By the end of the century, his hyperbole would sound modest.[29]

Although leaders of New York's federation pitted themselves against "charity trusts" as they sought to prove their fundamental commitment to distributing capital quickly to serve immediate public needs, their simultaneous experiments with endowment-building and capital growth revealed a much more complicated philanthropic landscape. Indeed, the line between charity trusts, a shorthand for private philanthropic foundations that had emerged in the late nineteenth and early twentieth centuries from the massive holdings of industrialists, and federated charities was hardly so stark. The same 1917 manual that had admonished federation leaders against the seductions of endowment-building had also praised Julius Rosenwald, the Chicago-based part owner and president of Sears, Roebuck and Company, as an exemplar of good philanthropic practice. Seemingly one of those business magnates whose astronomical earnings had been parked in a charity trust, Rosenwald instead was the poster child for responsibly self-regulated philanthropy.[30]

A Jewish man born to parents who had left central Europe in the middle of the nineteenth century, Rosenwald chartered the Rosenwald Fund in the state of Illinois in 1917 to serve "the well being of mankind." Here was a man who could have established a perpetual foundation just as Rockefeller or Carnegie had, intent upon their names and desires living eternally. Instead, Rosenwald did the opposite: he created a fund governed—indeed, regulated—by the logic of capital distribution, not accumulation or immortality. As federation leaders gradually moderated their stance against endowment and capital accumulation, Rosenwald only became firmer in his resolve against creating a perpetual endowment fund.[31]

In the early twentieth century, Rosenwald had begun to designate a portion of his fortune to philanthropic endeavors, choosing a number of Jewish and African American organizations as the earliest recipients of his largesse. But so large was his fortune and so small were many of the organizations he wished to support that he quickly realized he would need to build a strategy to deploy his philanthropic capital effectively. As he tested his ideas, Rosenwald turned to the Associated Jewish Charities, Chicago's federation, where he served as president, to see if he could develop a method to help organizations build the capacity to absorb large gifts and to involve a broad community in the process. To mark his fiftieth birthday in 1912, he pledged $50,000 to the federation on the condition that it raised an additional $300,000 from other sources that year. In a precise gift agreement, he also granted the federation the right to place a portion of his gift in an endowment with the stipulation that the fund be depleted within twenty-five years. Had New York's federation leaders been faced with the same gift (and had their federation been around in 1912, which it was not), they might have had to walk away from it, since their earliest by-laws committed them to an annual distribution cycle with no more than a three-year lag between the receipt of a gift and its expenditure. Still, if Jacob Schiff's posthumous sway over New York's federation was any indication, one can imagine that wealth and leadership might have commanded expedient policy reform.[32]

Five years later, when Rosenwald incorporated his own foundation with an initial corpus of $10 million, his earlier experiments in philanthropic giving had developed into a full-fledged philosophy of releasing philanthropic capital quickly and using it to leverage gifts from recipient communities. As an expression of his commitment to this philosophy, Rosenwald mandated a twenty-five-year spenddown for his entire foundation, echoing the gift agreement he had created with Chicago's federation.[33]

Driven by a desire to spread his philosophy and gain respect for it, Rosenwald described his method of self-regulated philanthropy for all of America to read in a 1929 issue of the *Saturday Evening Post*. All too often, he argued, wealthy people allowed their basest impulses for power and immortality to drive their philanthropic behavior. As a result, "Millions—soon it will be billions—of dollars are lying idle, or almost idle, because the purposes for which they have been endowed have largely disappeared. From being a boon, as their well-meaning founders intended, these endowments have become a burden to posterity." Wise and modern philanthropists, such as himself, would embrace the limitations of mortality and employ a judicious measure of self-regulation to ensure that their wealth quickly entered into charitable circulation so that it might address current problems and not indebt the future to the past.[34]

The slogan "Give While You Live," coined by Rosenwald's friend, a newspaper editor who had assisted him in making his birthday gifts in 1912, encapsulated his strategy against what legal theorists called the *mortmain* or the "dead hand" of the donor. Not mincing his words, Rosenwald explained, "I consider, therefore, timeliness one of the basic prerequisites of worthwhile philanthropy." Characterizing endowments as "perpetuities," he dismissed them as vain and wasteful. Although he suggested that a levelheaded philanthropist would regulate his own practices, he also lambasted the legal structure that protected "the perpetual endowment pulmotor operated by a dead hand," even after an endowment had long outlived its purpose. The hubris to assume that wealth gave individuals the gift of prophesy and the right to bind the future, Rosenwald averred, must give way to a humble awareness "that the needs of the future can safely be left to be met by the generations of the future."[35]

Rosenwald remains best known for establishing primary schools, often referred to as "Rosenwald Schools," for African American children in the South. These schools enacted his philanthropic philosophy of releasing large-scale capital to serve immediate needs and leveraging large gifts to stimulate financial support from other quarters, including recipient communities and the government. By 1929, more than four thousand schools had been established at a cost of $19 million. As Rosenwald calculated, "[T]he colored people themselves have raised nearly four million dollars, white folks one million, while public funds furnished more than $11,000,000." He noted with satisfaction that his contribution was only $3.5 million, not even a fifth of the total dollars raised.[36]

By the time the Rosenwald Fund spent its last dollars and shuttered its doors in the late 1940s, its strategy of capital distribution appeared locked in an ultimately losing battle against a very different philanthropic philosophy: that of capital accumulation and perpetuity. Although Congress had periodically returned to the subject of philanthropy after it closed the Commission on Industrial Relations investigation, by the late 1940s it had not passed any significant regulations on philanthropic endowments, their growth, or their distribution. One could speculate that had the Great Depression not interrupted the post–World War I period of relative American prosperity, then Congress might have turned its regulatory energy on philanthropic endowments. However, beyond the exercise of a counterfactual, what we do know is that the Great Depression changed the way Americans thought about wealth and its regulation. A surge of legislation passed during the era of economic turmoil empowered the federal government to better control and redistribute capital in the service of the public good. The relative freedoms preserved for philanthropic endeavors reflected a countervailing impulse to protect individualism and what industrial leaders began to call "free enterprise" from the heavy hand of government regulation. At the same time, the stock market crash so crippled the American economy that members of Congress would have been hard pressed to justify new regulatory measures on philanthropy.[37]

As New York's federation slowly permitted itself to hold larger and larger funds in endowment throughout the 1920s, it justified its actions not only through the sanguine acknowledgment that Jews had greater access to capital resources than in the past, but also through a much darker prediction that days of bounty would inevitably be followed by times of scarcity. Emergency funds anticipated periods of emergency, and in the fall of 1929, just such crisis occurred, in the form of the stock market crash and the start of the Great Depression. The following March, as the board considered its budget for the coming year, one of its members sought to put in perspective the past and what the future could bring. "Last year we were in the flood-tide of prosperity," he began. Dollars were flowing in faster than ever, and the ambitious $2 million campaign goal seemed a sure thing. Until all of it, from pledges to payments to prosperity, froze. "We have a different situation this year," the board member continued grimly. "Therefore, I think we ought to recognize the fact that we shall very likely have to go into the reserve funds of Federation." Holding out hope that the economic crisis would pass quickly, the board approved a budget that did not trim allocations but balanced its optimism with a recognition that it was putting its reserve funds on the line.[38]

By 1932, New York's reserve funds had been completely emptied. Judge Joseph Proskauer, a justice for the New York State Supreme Court and president of New York's federation in the 1930s, took responsibility for the institution's spending policy: "We have distributed to the societies every dollar of available surplus which we have had and the obloquy of that, if that be obloquy, will fall on my administration, but I have counseled it with my eyes open, with a complete loyalty to the ninety-one institutions and their needs, and with the belief that in times of emergency like these Federation should take every chance in order to keep the ninety-one institutions functioning." Nevertheless, as the Depression wore on, federations across the country could hardly keep up with the demands being placed upon their agencies. A 1933 report found that over the last two years, reversing a trend of consistent federation growth across the country, federations' incomes had declined by approximately 30% each year.[39]

In the face of persistent economic crisis, philanthropic bodies faltered and government grew. Julius Rosenwald had insisted that philanthropic dollars alone would not ameliorate the broad sweep of social problems, and starting in the 1920s, he sought government funding for many of the health and education projects he initiated. He used his own wealth, paltry in the face of the government's resources, to try to encourage public spending. Already, his own philanthropic spending carried a level of public subsidy through tax deductions and exemptions, but he aspired to train government, through partnerships with his philanthropic work, to invest more in social welfare and rely less on private sources of funding to ensure its citizens' basic needs were met. The Great Depression provided a crash course in government spending, as philanthropic entities, including the Rosenwald Fund, watched their investment income plummet and as solicitations from mass charities like federations went unanswered.[40]

In the fall of 1933, New York's federation went on the record endorsing a proposal for the state of New York to issue a $60 million emergency bond for unemployment relief. Charitable entities knew firsthand that social welfare needs, once fulfilled by their allocations, would go unmet absent state assistance. A 1929 study of 116 American cities had found that private charities covered roughly a quarter of all public relief; by 1935, private charities' contributions had dipped to 1.3%. Not only had the needs of American citizens increased due to the economic crisis, but philanthropy, compromised by that same economic crisis, had proved itself ill-equipped to keep pace with its own prior levels of social welfare support.[41]

At the first meeting of the Council of Jewish Federations and Welfare Funds (CJFWF), a body organized in the early 1930s to coordinate federation activities across the country, a researcher identified a series of "conditioning factors" that threatened the federation system, including "the development in the United States during the depression of an elaborate program of public social work, particularly in the field of relief," and "the launching or promise of various socio-economic measures under the Roosevelt administration that aim both to bring recovery and to lay a foundation for a stable economic life and a decent standard of living." A state called into action by the failure of private institutions to meet the needs of its citizens offered a solution in the form of a robust social democracy. Yet the welfare state also posed a challenge to those very same private entities and their interests, by threatening to render many of their associations (or agencies) superfluous and endangering the fund-raising model that supported them.[42]

As most students of history know, American Jews supported Franklin Delano Roosevelt and his New Deal programs with loyalty unmatched by almost any other American ethnic group. Yet it was hardly clear that a strong, centralized state was in the interest of American Jews. Strong states tend to rely on nationalism to create a sense of coherence and obligation, and, historically, fervent nationalism has often been corrosive of political structures that safeguard minority rights. Without a doubt, the growth of American state infrastructure—from new agencies and programs to laws and policies that gave it greater power over its citizens' lives—introduced a measure of risk to American Jews' communal structures. Would a strong state continue to rely on and enrich associations? Would private donors continue to feel moved to support collective associations when the state seemed capable of meeting the needs of its citizens? And, finally, would an expanded state, more willing than ever to involve itself in its citizens' private lives, make demands that might challenge the terms of Jewish life in the United States?[43]

The researcher who presented at the first meeting of the CJFWF offered a vision for how Jewish federations might tame the potential threats of American state growth while still endorsing it: "[W]here public social work and the protective devices of social legislation can be made to operate, Jews will participate as citizens in the general community," and, thus, "by freeing Federations of primary relief demands, [we can] release funds toward the support of adjustment projects for the economic and social welfare of the Jewish group, and for distinctively Jewish communal activities." Anticipating the massive transformation of Jewish philanthropy that would occur after World War II from material-needs philanthropy to Jewish-identity philanthropy, the speaker suggested that philanthropic institutions could cede the ground of general social welfare to the government and carve out new and, in the case of Jewish federations, specifically communal aims.[44]

Whether by coincidence or prescience, the 1934 presenter rightly implied that New Deal programs could stitch democracy to capitalism more tightly than ever, despite the rupture that many anticipated. A social welfare state could preserve the logic of capitalism, in part by continuing to empower private philanthropy to meet all but the public's most basic and pressing needs. As historian Kim Phillips-Fein explains, "The New Deal did not mark a break with capitalism; on the contrary, Roosevelt always believed that he was acting to save private property." Intended to harness the power of the state—its bureaucracy, infrastructure, and citizens—New Deal programs established a dizzying variety of ways for public and private interests to coexist, whether through social welfare programs mandated and funded by the state but delivered through private entities or through a whole range of public-private partnerships that guided real estate development, financial services, the defense industry, and the arts and culture sector. Private dollars, philanthropically earmarked or not, remained essential to the developing social welfare state.[45]

———

Property—cash and noncash assets, including real estate—served as a fulcrum point, at which the interests of a private individual or entity could meet the interests of the state. Tipped toward the state, property became a public good to be taxed and redistributed; tipped toward the individual or business, property became a private asset to be protected, risked, or grown for one's own benefit. But balanced in the middle, upon the association, property might be regarded as a private asset that operated in the public interest. During the New Deal era, policymakers and private industry leaders joined to fashion capitalism in just this way, as a source of broad public good whose regulation, much like the regulation of an American citizen, always had to be balanced with respect for its freedom.

An enlarged American state, made all the stronger in the following decade by its wartime expansion, flexed new regulatory muscles, while also forging closer bonds than ever with private industries and associations over their shared expansionist aims. Yet, far from being purely harmonious, the process of state-building and corporate growth poked at fundamental conflicts over who controlled property and to what ends. Starting in the 1950s, Congress would embark upon a two-decades-long interrogation of philanthropy's propertied logic, an effort that emerged from long-simmering tensions about whether private actors' property, even when bundled in associations, was best suited to meet public needs—that is, about whether capitalism created or solved the problems of democracy.

For American Jewish philanthropic bodies, World War II and its aftermath put the question of Jewish property front and center. Global demands on American Jewish property spiked, all framed by the psychological trauma wrought by the Nazis' expropriation of Jewish property and their genocidal policies that led to the murder of the vast majority of Jews living in Europe. Although American Jewish property could not undo the losses, the status of property—as a point of intersection with American state power and an instrument for communal stability—mattered incredibly to how Jewish leaders and institutions imagined building a viable Jewish future in the United States.

3

Property

IN THE SUMMER OF 1942, as the Nazis stripped thousands upon thousands of European Jews of their homes, possessions, clothing, gold teeth, and hair, and then murdered them, Jewish historian Salo Baron reappraised the role of property in Jewish history and "Jewish fate." Writing in the pages of the *Menorah Journal*, a Jewish intellectual journal begun at Harvard University in 1915, the Columbia historian judged the historical development of capitalism— when currency and "money trade" replaced land as the "main factor of economic, social and even political life"—as initially beneficial to Jews. He explained that "through long processes of medieval discrimination, [Jews] had been practically forced off the land and driven into trade." Throughout the nineteenth century, European Jews had relied on their "possession of a relatively larger share of floating capital" than other groups to secure their protection within new national arrangements. Yet, according to Baron, for however much Jews had benefited from capitalism, its returns had diminished over time. By the early twentieth century, the onset of "late capitalism" challenged "the very survival of the Jewish people even more menacingly than had the antagonism and large-scale extinction of the previous feudal system."[1]

Baron believed that the wealth concentration and inequality that he attributed to late-stage capitalism endangered Jews in two contradictory ways. First, those Jews who gained control over significant amounts of capital became the visible targets of animus and conspiracy theories from the growing population of the disenfranchised, a constituency that populist leaders could easily rally on the basis of antisemitic sentiment. Second, in their pursuit of individualist capital gain, many Jews had abandoned their communal structures and institutions, leaving individuals alone and vulnerable to the allure of overly radical ideas once capital rewards fell, as they inevitably did. Hitler loomed large in the historian's analysis. The Nazi autocrat reviled Jews for embodying both extremes of this historical progression—as hoarding private property and seeking to destroy it—"unperturbedly lumping communism together with capitalism" as "mere instruments of Jewish world domination." Hitler did not invent these core antisemitic allegations, but he wove them into an ideology that demanded the full liquidation of Jews and their property as the only means for thwarting Jews' conspiratorial aims.[2]

Baron concluded that the world was, indeed, witnessing the final blows to capitalism, but its demise would not destroy the Jewish people or fulfill any such "lachrymose" fantasies. Instead, Jews would emerge from the cataclysm with an opportunity to engage in "creative readjustment" to whatever political and economic order might arise in capitalism's place. (Baron speculated "social democracy.") Understandably incapable of imagining the full extent of the deprivation Jews would suffer at Hitler's hands, he suggested that Jews could embrace a new vision of property to supplant the capitalist one.[3]

No matter how far short his view of Hitler's threat to Jews fell, Baron was correct that property, through the territorialization of Jewish life in the State of Israel, would rest at the heart of one of Jews' primary responses to destruction. But Baron's predictions about the end of capitalism proved well off the mark. Not only did capitalism survive into the post–World War II era, it also became one of the poles of a geopolitical divide definitive of that era. The struggle between capitalism and communism seemed only to harden each into full-fledged worldviews. Policymakers, world leaders, and cultural producers transformed theories about the distribution of property into visions for human progress and humanity itself.[4]

The most specific refutation of Baron's predictions, however, came in the form of American Jewish institutions' deepening commitment to capitalism after World War II. The historian had hoped to convince his readers that "the survival of the Jewish people is by no means contingent on the survival of the present structure of our civilization," and he judged the "identification of modern capitalism with 'the spirit of Judaism'" as a "tragic irony." Yet, to the contrary, American Jewish institutions after World War II strengthened their commitment to a capitalist vision of growth and security through the accumulation of property.[5]

A post–World War II transformation in Jewish philanthropy toward a firmer embrace than ever of capitalist logic aligned with similar transformations in American political economy. In the decades after World War II, the rules and regulations governing property ownership in the United States were suddenly enlisted in a battle for American global power. The fact that

Americans had private property rights and that the democratic state could provide for its citizens' needs without abrogating their privacy or freedom stood to distinguish "the American Way" from communism and totalitarianism. Yet even when packaged together, democracy and capitalism would continue to exist in tension with one another. To the dismay of policymakers who sought to present capitalism and democracy together as the source of American superiority, core social debates in the United States hinged on the question of how much control over property—homes, neighborhoods, schools, religious institutions, cities, bank accounts, and bodies—should fall to individuals and private groups versus the state.[6]

The World War II era and its immediate aftermath represented a high mark for American state policies that mandated capital redistribution through taxation and through social welfare programs. During those very same years, however, a counterpoising movement to protect capital from state control began to assert itself through the expansion of philanthropic institutions and the emergent language of market freedom.

American Jewish philanthropic organizations displayed their fervent hope, against the poor odds that Baron had forecasted, that capitalism could serve as a guarantor of the Jewish future. By paying close attention to how American Jewish leaders learned to think of their philanthropic institutions as property- or capital-generating instruments, we can see the earliest roots of the massive transformations in the American political economy usually traced only to the 1970s, when observers and regular citizens began to notice the disturbing political and economic ramifications of policies that had allowed private capitalist growth to supersede democratic aspirations.[7]

———

By 1944, Jacob Schiff's half-a-million-dollar bequest, which in the 1920s had convinced leaders of New York's federation to amend the organization's by-laws, now comprised just one-eighth of the total value of funds held in trust there. As anticipated by federation leaders, Schiff's gift had inspired others to designate the institution in their bequests and, despite the severe economic crisis of the 1930s, the federation had amassed substantial property in trust. The growth of these funds depended almost entirely on new bequests. Constrained by a New York state law limiting the range of securities in which charitable funds were permitted to invest, the custodians of the federation's endowment had given little thought to crafting an investment strategy until 1940, when "an exhaustive inquiry" into the practices of other "large charitable trusts" convinced the board that its adherence to the law was overly punctilious. The Finance Committee, described in federation minutes as "a group of men experienced in investment matters," quickly changed course and resolved, "Our policy is to get the largest return in interest and dividends compatible with our conception of safety and capital."[8]

What had been the purview of no more than 1% of the American population at the turn of the century, stock ownership expanded to roughly one-quarter of the population just three decades later, as more and more Americans learned to regard investment and capital growth as crucial to their own and the nation's productivity. Employing strategies from their day jobs and, likely, their personal investment affairs, federation leaders diversified their funds' investments to include common stocks, real estate mortgages, and a range of debt-based securities in order to balance risk with capital growth. Initial returns were modest—in 1943, the Finance Committee recorded a 3.6% rate of return—but the shifting expectations for philanthropic capital growth would have profound effects.[9]

By the 1940s, a growing number of American Jewish communal organizations began to reassess the overwhelming priority they had given to the distribution, as opposed to accumulation, of philanthropic capital. In part, this reflected the simple fact that more American Jews controlled more property, whether in cash assets, real estate, or other investments, than in earlier decades. A feeling of present plenty allowed Jewish organizations to plan for a future of imagined scarcity, all the more imaginable in the wake of the Great Depression. American Jews also began to confront, in fits and starts, the depths of devastation that European Jews were experiencing at the hands of the Nazis. As the war continued, fund-raising drives with massive publicity campaigns, dinners where individuals publicly pledged donations, and newspaper announcements, plaques, and galas to honor high-level donors all affirmed American Jewish vitality, in contrast to the reported destruction that European Jews were facing. American Jewish leaders, who had earlier expressed reluctance to build endowments and had given little thought to investing philanthropic capital in the market, more readily than ever before embraced a new valuation of Jewish property premised upon its future worth, as they came to understand how much of the Jewish future now rested in their hands. The present value of Jewish property—the agencies or causes it could fund and the trauma it could heal—paled in comparison to the future its growth could secure.[10]

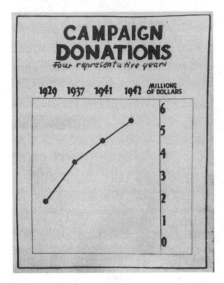

CAMPAIGN
DONATIONS
Four representative years

1929 1937 1941 1942 MILLIONS OF DOLLARS

6
5
4
3
2
1
0

FIGURE 3.1. Graph of New York Federation campaign donations, 1929–1942, Minutes of the Board of Trustees, March 8, 1943, Subgroup I Federation of Jewish Philanthropies, Series 1, Subseries A, subsubseries i in the UJA-Federation of New York collection (I-433). Courtesy of the American Jewish Historical Society at the Center for Jewish History, New York, NY.

In the early 1940s, New York's federation completed its most successful run of annual campaigns ever, reporting unprecedented numbers of volunteers, of individuals who showed up at meetings to make public pledges, and of dollars raised. During this period, each year's yield exceeded the prior ones many times over. Having weathered fiscal crises and dealt with the pressures of meeting the rising costs of keeping agencies that depended on it afloat, the New York federation approached its new financial abundance with caution. Chaired by a man named Norman Goetz, a New York–born lawyer who had served in World War I, New York's extraordinarily successful campaigns might have proved that the federation was on the right course. Jews were enthusiastically donating money on an annual basis, showing their faith in the federation and the agencies it funded. Instead, Goetz interpreted the success of the campaign, which in his estimation "raised the largest sum of money ever secured for a sectarian charity in the history of the City of New York, and that probably means anywhere," as occasion to think differently about philanthropy. "In times of prosperity," he explained, "we can afford to take stock of ourselves."[11]

Even before the conclusion of the 1943 campaign, which would raise more than $8 million, Goetz suggested supplementing the federation's financial distribution model with one focused on accumulation and, presumably, capital growth: "What we should do is to create for ourselves reserves of $12,000,000 so that in case of adversity, Federation could go along for two years, even if it did not take in a nickel." As much as Goetz and his fellow federation leaders in other cities celebrated the present-day abundance of their institution, they also betrayed their anxiety about the future, not only for their institutions but for the Jewish people more generally.

In Boston, the executive director of the federation straightforwardly credited "Hitlerism" with the spike in fund-raising "on a scale unequalled by any
group in the history of private philanthropy." Not mincing his words, he described American Jews' dollars as their weapons in a "battle for survival." As
Jews across the country heard reports about the transfer of Jewish communities into ghettos, the confiscation of Jewish property, and, eventually, the bru-
tal murder of Jews, some wondered how to make the best use of the millions
of dollars that now flowed into federations on an annual basis. A different
approach to Jewish philanthropy might offer some succor and help American
Jews feel as if they were doing something to safeguard the Jewish future.[12]

The battle for Jewish survival, a fight and a rhetoric that would determine
the contours of Jewish collective life for many decades to come, included a
transformative economic vision that slowly shifted the time horizon and capital logic of American Jewish philanthropy. To believe in Jewish survival and a
Jewish future: this may have been a matter of faith. But to capitalize for and on
Jewish survival was a matter of transforming the financial strategy of Jewish
philanthropy and, most important, the story that American Jews told about
why and how they divested themselves of their property. New York's Goetz,
who eventually assumed the presidency of the federation in 1945, helped re-
fashion this narrative, shifting the perception of philanthropy's value from
immediate needs fulfilled to a far more existential calculation of the future it
could guarantee.

In advance of the 1943 annual campaign and anticipating yet another ban-
ner year, the board granted Goetz permission to raise special funds that would
not be distributed in the typical federation allocation process. Unsure of how
to refer to the money—"reserve funds, insurance, stockpile, rainy-day fund"—
Goetz described these excess funds as "sacred," representing the community's
faith in the federation to maintain them until "the day when the emergency
needs that they were designed to serve will have presented themselves." Using
religious language and depicting a vow of trust between donors and federations, Goetz bolstered the narrative of a Jewish community prepared to view
capital accumulation as its duty, and the minutes recorded that he "received
prolonged and impressive applause" from the board after presenting his case.[13]

Goetz, alongside Joseph Willen, the executive vice president who served
from 1941 to 1967 and helped raise more than $1 billion for the New York fed-
eration, portrayed American Jews as maturing into the ability to see beyond
the needs of their present moment. They amassed evidence to show the board
that more donors than ever appreciated why the rapid circulation of their

philanthropic contributions might not always be the best path forward. In 1944, Willen shared his observation that, in the short time since he had joined the organization, he had witnessed donors who in the past had not been "ready to give today for tomorrow's troubles" start to inquire about opportunities to contribute for the future. This, to him, indicated a rising "degree of communal interest" in long-range giving. Playing both ends, Willen suggested the federation follow the trend, but also encouraged the board to be trendsetters, noting that he had met with "potential givers, economists, Federal tax officials" and others to explore new ways of holding philanthropic capital in reserve for future crises.[14]

Even as they crafted a story to normalize capital accumulation as a legitimate philanthropic practice, Goetz, Willen, and other federation leaders continued to run up against the counternarrative of immediate capital distribution, enshrined in the institution's bylaws. These legal documents still capped reserve funds and, even more damning, communicated a censoriousness toward capital accumulation, as if holding back funds from present distribution signified unredeemable avarice. Extending trends from the 1920s, the New York federation had steadily raised the ceiling on its endowment funds and freed itself from constraints against soliciting legacies in the 1940s, but it struggled to make a positive case for doing so that would have justified a quicker pace of change. Only in emphasizing the future risk against which these funds would hedge could leaders convince themselves and their donors to embrace a nondistributive logic.

The slow pace of deliberation over shifting the balance from philanthropic distribution to philanthropic accumulation revealed just how close to the core of federation and Jewish philanthropy a change in financial practice cut. In the fall of 1946, at the behest of Goetz and the federation's powerful Business Men's Council, a group comprised of the majority of the federation's top donors who were at the time generally independent, self-employed businessmen, the board considered passing another incremental change to its bylaws to give it more freedom to solicit legacies and build up nondistributive funds. Goetz, clearly a proponent of the plan, nonetheless cautioned against any rash shift in policy. He noted that, although he did not share the concern, "many genuine friends of Federation did not believe it sound for Federation to accumulate large sums which were not distributed." Chief among those friends were the heads of agencies reliant upon annual grants from the federation to support their work. Should the trustees pursue a future-oriented, accumulation-based financial model, then the agencies might feel that their access to resources was

FIGURE 3.2. Map of New York federation agencies by Nora Benjamin Kubie, approx. 1950s, Subgroup I Federation of Jewish Philanthropies, Other Departments: Public Relations in the UJA-Federation of New York collection (I-433). Courtesy of the American Jewish Historical Society at the Center for Jewish History, New York, NY.

being choked by the federation's capital ambitions. For example, Alfred Rose, who sat on the board as a representative from Mount Sinai Hospital, noted that some of his fellow board members "urged the utmost caution" in supporting any change that allowed the federation to amass resources without distributing them.[15]

As debate about expanding nondistributive funds continued into the next year, a generation gap appeared between the founding trustees, a dwindling group, and younger trustees. When Emil Goldmark, one of the men who had signed the federation's original bylaws, looked around the room in January 1947, he recognized only one other founding member in attendance. Moved to instruct the assembled group in its history, Goldmark explained that early leaders had taken a "moral pledge" to use federation dollars exclusively in the support of its constituent agencies. Therefore, they had steered the organization away from collecting legacies and had permitted only a very modest emergency fund to accrue. Certain this history remained relevant, Goldmark turned to his younger counterparts and accused them of treating the founding generation as a mere "dead hand," unfairly restraining them for their desires, when in truth the wisdom of those founders remained a "live fist," ready to strike against accumulative practices that would bind the future and deprive the present.[16]

Whether dead or alive, the will of the founders and their historical circumstances animated the federation's institutional culture and compelled the current leadership, even those seeking a change, to pursue a course of gradualism. As of 1947, the board approved a modest expansion of the federation's endowment potential, by allowing endowment funds to build until they exceeded the sum of the prior two years' distributions. Even with the passage of this revised bylaw, the New York federation had only about $5 million in its endowment fund by the late 1940s, a far cry from the $20 million that would necessitate a spenddown. Nonetheless, the eventual movement toward capital accumulation and growth could be anticipated in the narratives and counternarratives that federation leaders fashioned in the 1940s. The conservative impulse to stay the course and continue to abide by a policy of annual intake and distribution would not so easily be unseated, but a formidable challenge to it arose in the form of an equally conserving logic for using capital growth to anticipate future emergencies. Property properly accumulated and invested could assure post-Holocaust American Jews that a stable Jewish future was ahead.[17]

However, the most powerful force pushing American Jewish philanthropic institutions to abandon their fealty to distribution and instead embrace accumulation came from the policies of the American state. Just as American legal and financial structures had shaped earlier versions of Jewish communal life, they would continue to draw Jews into the shifting tides of the American political economy. By the middle of the twentieth century, the federal government in particular had expanded its apparatus for regulating and incentivizing private property channeled into public purposes. As the American state grew, its power to shape American life likewise expanded. For American Jews and their communal organizations, state growth changed the ways in which they regarded their property and its present and future capacity to serve the public good.

———

In celebrating the success of the federation's fund-raising, executive vice president Willen told the board, "The story of the 1943 campaign is the story of a very generous city, richly proud of a century of great institutional work, benefited by a tax law and great accumulations of profit." Hardly a sideshow, changes in tax law had occupied federation leaders' attention as they crafted their fund-raising strategy. Goetz explained that in soliciting gifts, he and his annual campaign committee had calculated the maximum sum an individual could contribute based on his "personal prosperity and the rate of Federal taxation to which he might be subjected." Their goal was to show donors that a larger gift could carry tax benefits that outweighed the difference between it and a smaller gift. Furthermore, in determining to raise funds specifically to put into reserve, the campaign committee had spoken with "Federal tax officials" to gain specific approval for extending tax benefits for gifts earmarked for endowment. Tax policy promised rewards to those who knew how to use it and its exemptions.[18]

Tax generation took in property to fund public goods, but tax expenditures, in the form of deductions and exemptions, released property from public claims on the grounds that property assigned to certain purposes inherently served the public good. Over the course of the 1940s, the dynamic system of tax generation and expenditure grew to encompass a greater number of Americans and their collective entities than ever before. In 1939, the federal government had taxed the incomes of only about 3.9 million Americans, but by 1945, its reaches had grown to encompass the incomes of 46.2 million Americans, boosting the amount of revenue generated by sixteen times. In addition to instituting a broad-based income tax, the federal government also increased the progressivity of the federal tax scale. By 1945, the wealthiest 1% of Americans accounted for 32% of the total dollars collected through the income tax, and that year, the top marginal tax rate stood at 94% for all dollars earned above $200,000; 93% for over $150,000; 92% for over $100,000; and so on, resulting in a high effective tax rate for the biggest earners.[19]

While still protecting private property ownership—a political necessity after World War II and during the Cold War—the growth of the federal income tax nonetheless expanded public claims on revenue-generating property. Some portion of the income earned from one's labor and holdings belonged to the government to distribute according to the public will. But in determining what kinds of earnings would be classified as income and what percentage of that income was the rightful property of the state, lawmakers were delineating the very boundaries between democracy and capitalism. The amount of resources the government needed to run depended on the work it did. To fight a war and secure a nation's borders, to provide benefits to veterans or homeowners or senior citizens, to support research, to build highways: all of these projects demanded that private property be apportioned to governing bodies and agencies. At the same time, the state could release some income from its control by designating certain forms of private property as acting in service of the public good.[20]

As the American lawmakers expanded the income tax, they likewise expanded the circle of exemption while also, and rather contradictorily, expressing suspicion of exempt entities. Designating some exempt entities as deserving and others as less so, Congress's power of taxation generated a new body of legal interpretation regarding the status of property. Those who could prove they deserved exempt status gained substantial rewards from the expanded tax system, while those who could not became subject to greater discipline and regulation. Addressing Congress in early 1950, President Truman explained, "A tax concession to a favored few is always unfair, but it becomes a gross injustice against the rest of the population when rates are high," as they were under his watch. He charged Congress with closing what he characterized as "loopholes" that threatened to turn the income tax into a system that perpetuated instead of mitigated inequality.[21]

Contrary to Truman's analysis, however, tax loopholes and exemptions were core policy levers of the American income tax that Congress pulled to engineer behavior. As a staff attorney for the Internal Revenue Service (the new name for the Bureau of Internal Revenue as of 1953) would argue in the late 1950s, tax exemption "differs only in method from a disbursement of government funds. It therefore cannot be sustained as law except when the public interest is served in much the same manner as when public funds are properly expended." In other words, exemptions and tax loopholes could be just as sound public policy as any other facet of the tax code if they enacted state goals. In the coming decade, the spokespeople for exempt organizations, including executive directors, board members, and attorneys, would learn to make the case for their exemptions by highlighting the public policy interests they purportedly served. What one observer might identify as a loophole could be reframed as a state goal pursued through nonstate channels.[22]

The expansion of the federal income tax went hand in hand with the expansion of charitable organizations in the United States. From the early 1930s through the end of the 1940s, more than two hundred new Jewish federations were established, serving Jewish populations across the country and mirroring similar growth trends among nonsectarian community chests and myriad other religious and ethnic charitable associations. However, when President Truman threw down the gauntlet to Congress to close its tax loopholes, his ire was almost surely not directed at mass-based charitable federations. Rather, Congress understood his charge to refer to private stores of wealth that found shelter from taxation in charitable foundations and other exempt purposes, and it oriented its investigatory work and, eventually, legislative agenda around identifying and thwarting abuses within this system.[23]

By 1949, roughly five thousand foundations were incorporated in the United States, with one-tenth of them controlling assets of more than $50,000 each. The Ford Foundation, established in 1936, had become the largest American foundation in 1947, when the estates of Henry Ford and his son, Edsel, were both bequeathed to it, thus dwarfing Rockefeller, Carnegie, and the endowments of Harvard and Yale by hundreds of millions of dollars. By entrusting the bulk of its assets to the foundation, the Ford family avoided the 70% inheritance tax levied on estates exceeding $50 million, and the Ford Foundation became the majority shareholder of the Ford Motor Company, holding 90% of the company's nonvoting stock. Even less spectacular charitable foundations tended to relate differently to the property they controlled than did charitable federations. Foundations did not engage in mass fund-raising appeals, rarely employed rapid distribution models, and were usually directed by earners or their descendants. Nevertheless, despite all of these differences, charitable foundations were not yet subject to unique statutory definition or treatment.[24]

———

Aside from Julius Rosenwald's foundation, which gained national prominence and remains historically noteworthy despite its rapid spenddown, very few midcentury American Jews established significant charitable foundations. The strength and ubiquity of the federation system likely deterred some who might have otherwise thought to do so, and, although some Jews had become strikingly wealthy by the middle of the twentieth century, they were far fewer in number than they would be later in the century, when Jewish private foundations proliferated. Nonetheless, by examining a particularly successful, large, and long-lasting American Jewish foundation—the Crown family foundation—that was established in these years, we can observe how new financial strategies, validated by state practices, made their way into Jewish communal life and helped achieve the broad transformation from capital distribution to accumulation in Jewish philanthropy.

In 1947, five men, the children and grandchildren of Jewish immigrants to Chicago from Lithuania, incorporated the Crown Foundation in the state of Illinois. With earnings from the family's business, a company that supplied building materials, the foundation set forth its purpose in broad terms: "To engage in works of public charity . . . to promote education . . . to promote religion and religious education . . . to distribute the moneys or other property of this corporation . . . to other charitable corporations carrying on works of public charities." As the foundation grew, changing its name almost immediately to the Arie Crown Memorial Fund (and then in 1959 to the Arie and Ida Crown Memorial Fund) to recognize the immigrant progenitors of the family, it funded a range of Chicago-area organizations, from the local Jewish federation to Jewish social welfare agencies to synagogues and, even, nonsectarian and Christian institutions such as the American Red Cross and Loyola University. In its early years, only a very few grants traveled beyond Chicago, supporting a Jewish hospital in Denver in one case and aiding two different American Zionist organizations in another. But over time, the grant-making horizons of the Crown Foundation expanded, channeling dollars across state and national lines, especially to purchase bonds issued by the newly established State of Israel, and funding secular and some Christian organizations, including hospitals and charitable agencies.[25]

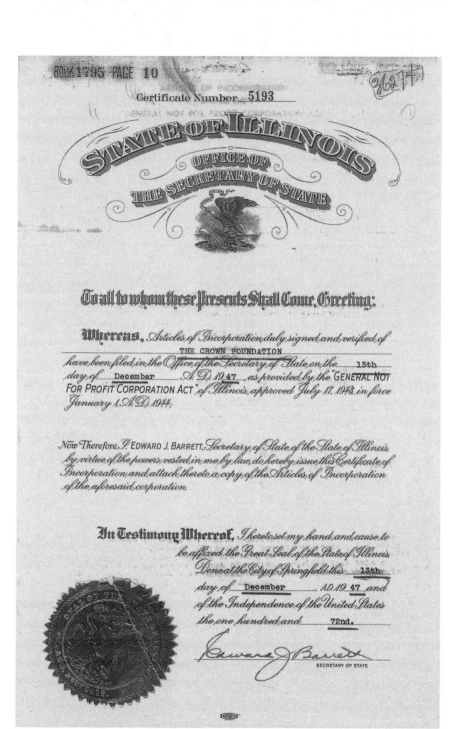

Certificate Number   5193

ARTICLES OF INCORPORATION

GENERAL NOT FOR PROFIT CORPORATION ACT

STATE OF ILLINOIS

OFFICE OF
THE SECRETARY OF STATE

To all to whom these Presents Shall Come, Greeting:

Whereas, Articles of Incorporation duly signed, and verified, of
THE CROWN FOUNDATION
have been filed in the Office of the Secretary of State, on the   13th
day of   December   A. D. 19 47, as provided by the "GENERAL NOT
FOR PROFIT CORPORATION ACT" of Illinois, approved July 17, 1943, in force
January 1, A. D. 1944;

Now Therefore, I, EDWARD J. BARRETT, Secretary of State of the State of Illinois,
by virtue of the powers, vested in me by law, do hereby issue this Certificate of
Incorporation and attach thereto a copy of the Articles of Incorporation
of the aforesaid corporation.

In Testimony Whereof, I hereto set my hand, and, cause to
be affixed the Great Seal of the State of Illinois.
Done at the City of Springfield this   13th
day of   December   AD. 19 47 and
of the Independence of the United States
the one hundred and   72nd.

SECRETARY OF STATE

FIGURE 3.3. Articles of Incorporation of the Crown Foundation, 1947. Courtesy of the Crown Family Philanthropies, Chicago, Illinois.

The Crown Foundation's financial model relied upon the growth of its corpus through wise and, sometimes, risky investments. Although periodic cash gifts helped build the corpus, shares of stock donated from family members appear far more significant to the expansion of the foundation in its early records. A board of directors, comprised of family members as well as an attorney and an accountant with strong ties to the family's business interests, managed all financial decisions. According to the foundation's bylaws, all grants had to be approved by the board, but an amendment in 1949 authorized the president's unilateral power to "sell on the open market any and all securities from time to time owned by this corporation," as long as proceeds were reinvested in the foundation. Periodically, the board would still advise the president to sell some of the foundation's shares, presumably when the value of these shares was high or when the foundation needed liquidity.[26]

By accumulating securities donated from family members' holdings, the Crown charitable foundation expanded alongside the family's growing business empire. Its building supply company, valued at $58 million by the 1950s, served as a springboard for an array of investments, including significant shares in the Hilton Hotels Corporation, the Chicago, Rock Island and Pacific Railroad, and, most famously, ownership of the Empire State Building. In 1951, Henry Crown, the third of Arie and Ida's children, initially secured a 25% share in the building and then quickly received offers from other large investors to purchase their shares in it. Within a matter of months, he controlled the Empire State Building Corporation. The comptroller of the family's building company, who also served as one of the few nonfamily members on the foundation's board, helped arrange the deal. Records indicate that shortly after completing the transaction, Henry gifted a portion of his shares in the building to his family's foundation, where they were sold and folded into the foundation's corpus.[27]

An article in the New Yorker chronicling Henry Crown's "Big Purchase" credited Henry with writing to a friend, "Accumulation of money in itself is not the yardstick for success." Although in the long run, Henry and his family's foundation accumulated substantial capital, he steered his family fortune in the direction of investment and capital growth, never content to see capital simply sit. With particular verve, Henry bought and sold real estate, often looking for the next investment opportunity. Just a decade after his "Big Purchase," Henry sold the Empire State Building for a reported $32 million profit. Furthermore, as the Crown family's business holdings expanded, its foundation also served as a release valve for accumulated capital, a place where family members could transfer wealth and investments to serve the public good. The foundation's corpus grew as it absorbed property transfers and generated income from its investments, with only a percentage of that income distributed through grants. Thus, the Crown family's holdings across its business and philanthropic concerns consistently increased and diversified as the foundation's long-term growth exceeded its charitable grants.[28]

Although the Crown Foundation's avowed mission was to serve the needs of "public charity," its activities simply could not be separated from the accumulation of property and its profitability through investment. The foundation's charitable work distributed profit gained from the Crown family's business holdings, but as a charitable vehicle that both absorbed donations and held investments, it generated more capital than it expended. Crown was not unique. Perpetual foundations, which unlike the Rosenwald foundation never pledged to distribute all of their holdings and shutter their doors, simply operated in this way.[29]

Because the number and size of charitable foundations were on the rise in the 1950s, and because many of them made income through investments and engaged in financial transactions with economic and political ramifications yet did not carry tax liabilities, members of Congress began to regard foundations' tax-exempt status as worthy of concern. Already in 1950, when President Truman instructed Congress to reform aspects of the tax code that gave individuals more benefits than their exempt activities provided for the public, his directive gestured toward these charitable organizations. But even as Congress set its sights on charitable foundations, it often did not know what it was looking at—or looking for. In order to investigate, let alone regulate, charitable foundations, Congress would first need to define them. Yet charitable foundations appeared to evade precise classification. Politicians, lawyers, and accountants tended to lump them together with charitable federations and other organizations as public-benefit exempt entities, even as they recognized that this convenience occluded substantive differences among charitable vehicles. Writing in the *Virginia Law Review* in 1949, a lawyer who specialized in taxation noted that "the most amazing aspect of foundations is that so little information is available concerning them," and continued that if tax lawyers were befuddled by the subject, "to the general public . . . the subject assumes the aura of a mystery."[30]

In 1950, Congress began a slow process of determining how to distinguish charitable foundations from other philanthropic entities. As it did so, it started to build a case for the differential treatment of foundations. In its 1950 Revenue

Act, Congress took the modest step of imposing regulations on only certain types of philanthropic property. Schools, churches, hospitals, and religious organizations gained immunity from these new regulations because Congress did not believe they needed to prove their public benefit. But other philanthropic entities, such as private foundations, stood to lose their exempt status if they engaged in prohibited activities, from deriving personal benefit from charitable work to engaging in business activities that were wholly unrelated to their mission. In order to implement these regulations, Congress instituted new reporting requirements for all charitable entities, except those it had categorically excused. Still, it opted not to create a clear statutory definition of private foundations or other kinds of charities.[31]

———

When New York's Norman Goetz had celebrated the success of the 1943 annual campaign, amidst fighting in Europe and Jewish deaths far more horrific and numerous than the press reported, he commended the federation for standing "above the battle, and as gathering in its broad tent—Jews of every form of political, economic and religious view." While the ability to raise charitable dollars from a broad group of American Jews and allocate them to support a range of Jewish communal agencies might indicate the vitality of a "broad tent" Jewish community, the possibility of accumulating Jewish charitable capital offered a strikingly new calculation of how individual property could offer salvation and serve as the key to Jewish survival, in defiance of Hitler's plans.[32]

Contrary to Salo Baron's expectations, the new world order set into motion in the wake of World War II did not unseat capitalism. Quite the opposite, across global contests and movements, capitalism captivated new attention, not only as an economic ideology but as a mode of governance that would fuel the reconstruction of an international order. As the United States emerged from the war, its political leaders reoriented the country around capital growth. Although certain political thinkers and policymakers made calls to free the market from state interference in the interest of unfettered capital growth, the more dominant forces embraced a state-assisted or "subsidiarity" model of growth. Built upon New Deal–era experiments, state-assisted capital growth in the post–World War II years flourished, thanks to a prosperous American economy. A new infrastructure of state regulations and incentives defined the channels of state-subsidized capital growth, allowing the state to collect more revenue and to apportion it to private actors in new ways.[33]

Philanthropic property straddled the line between public and private, be-tween the state and the individual, and between democracy and capitalism. This was the nub of Congress's clumsy efforts to define and regulate it. In its deliberations over the 1950 Revenue Act, for example, it focused on "unrelated business activity" as a possible stark line of differentiation between exempt and non-exempt philanthropic behavior. But far from offering a clear-cut stan-dard, the invocation of business activity and income generation raised the thorny matter of philanthropic entities, from Crown to Jewish federations and thousands of others, that invested their holdings in securities and generated income—surely a business activity. Accumulating property and investing it for income therefore could not be prohibited activities that would disqualify an organization from tax exemption. Rather, the prohibition would have to focus on future intention. Philanthropic entities had to express their intent to devote the entirety of their property holdings to the public interest. Congress indicated that some entities' purpose—to educate, to heal, or to worship—confirmed their public-facing aims, while others had to meet a higher standard of proof of intention.

The intentions motivating how property and its capital growth would be used became the standard to which Congress held tax-exempt philanthropic entities. Tests of intent brought the future into bold relief as the arbiter of philanthropic good. How one had generated philanthropic capital or had dis-tributed it in the past did not matter nearly as much as how one planned to use it in the future. The intent to serve the public had no deadline and demanded no immediate release of capital. Intent justified capital accumulation and growth, because the opportunity to realize it might always lie a few steps be-yond the present and might always benefit from still deeper pockets of reserve.

In the 1950s, Congress gradually confronted the fact that its system of taxa-tion and, specifically, exemption from taxation, created a web of public policy that spun well beyond state revenue generation. It appeared to be standing on the edge of a deep regulatory abyss, nervously toeing the edge of reformist proposals that might fill it. Those with considerable investments in the phil-anthropic system, including American Jews who by the immediate post–World War II years controlled well-resourced communal organizations depen-dent upon philanthropy and who also relied on philanthropy for their legal standing as a collective deserving of state benefits and protections, could not afford to stand on the sidelines of debates about the tax status of philanthropic property. The stakes were simply too high.

4

Taxation

IN NOVEMBER 1952, Norman Sugarman appeared before Congress. Thirty-five years old, a lawyer and an assistant commissioner for the Bureau of Internal Revenue, Sugarman had prepared a statement to enter into the record of the recently formed House Select Committee to Investigate Tax-Exempt Foundations and Comparable Organizations. Chaired by Edward Cox, a segregationist Democrat from Georgia, the committee was formed to assess whether charitable organizations deserved the special tax treatment they received and, as the authorizing resolution put it, "especially to determine which such foundations and organizations are using their resources for un-American and subversive activities or for purposes not in the interest or tradition of the United States."[1]

In his testimony, Sugarman communicated the central article of his professional faith: that tax law, when applied "fairly and evenly," served the interests of American democracy and capitalism equally. Throughout his long career, which would take the Cleveland-born Jewish tax lawyer into the forefront of American and American Jewish philanthropy, Sugarman would maintain his commitment to using tax law to allow individuals and groups to be free and do good. He would appear in front of Congress multiple times, first as a federal employee and then, once he left Washington and the Internal Revenue Service (so renamed in 1953) for a large law firm in Cleveland, as an expert on charitable tax law and an advocate for his clients, including Cleveland's Jewish federation. Whether speaking to Congress, fellow lawyers, or philanthropic leaders, Sugarman always reiterated, in his characteristically understated yet precise manner, that without a broadly applied charitable tax exemption, the United States and its citizens would be worse off. Sugarman's most lasting contribution to charitable tax law, to American Jewish communal life, to American philanthropy, and to the political and economic structure of the

United States came in the form of his unwavering protection of tax exemption as an American creed.[2]

That day in November 1952, Sugarman attempted to dispel Congress's suspicion that tax exemption offered a front for "un-American and subversive activities." "I have no hesitancy in stating," he testified, "that it is the firm policy of the Revenue Service to deny exemption to any organization which evidence demonstrates is subversive." While the term "un-American activity" did not appear as a disqualifier in the exemption regulations, Sugarman assured the committee that in practice such activity would never qualify as grounds for tax exemption, and, surely, Congress should not walk back the tax exemption based on fear of its use for subversive ends.[3]

From his platform before political leaders, first in the fall of 1952 and then again in the summer of 1954, when he offered a second round of testimony, Sugarman sought to redirect the congressional committee's attention away from its preoccupation with un-American forces masquerading as tax-exempt entities and instead toward how it might better define philanthropy and thereby apply its regulatory power more sensibly. Sugarman argued that the paragraph of Internal Revenue Code that identified "corporations, and any community chest, fund, or foundation, organized and operated exclusively for religious, charitable, scientific, literary, or educational purposes, or for the prevention of cruelty to children or animals" as eligible for exemption was hampered by its imprecision. The statute neither defined "foundation" nor "distinguish[ed] between so-called foundations and other organizations for purposes of the exemption." In an effort to direct Congress's work, he suggested that, rather than investigating tax exemption generally and casting a pall of suspicion over it, Congress would do better to offer clear definitions of charitable entities and institute regulations accordingly.[4]

Charitable tax law, as it developed throughout the 1950s and 1960s, reflected the complications of bringing legal exactitude to a set of practices that combined public intent with private means. Even if tax law was guided by policymakers' commitment to fair and even treatment, as Sugarman asserted it was, charitable tax law had to stretch and strain to be uniformly applicable across the craggy landscape of philanthropic organizations. As Congress collected testimony about philanthropy and tax exemption, and gradually drafted legislative proposals to offer just the sort of definitional precision Sugarman had requested, it also broadly reassessed how private interests could serve the public good.

Although for most Americans, whose charitable donations came in sums commensurate with their modest earning power, charitable tax law may have seemed far from their daily concerns, it in fact ultimately touched every American. This is because it affected how power operated in the United States. Mid-century liberal policy fed the expansion of state infrastructure with new and increased tax revenue, while also setting in place regulatory and subsidiarist structures that would empower private capital and actors more than ever before to act in the name of the public.[5]

Norman Sugarman was an underappreciated actor in the dramatic changes that occurred in American life from the 1950s through the 1970s. His work transformed the Jewish organizations he represented and those he did not, including American and non-Jewish philanthropy, the American public, and even American interactions with the rest of the world. Through his indefatigable efforts to craft, interpret, and apply tax law, he joined midcentury American policymakers in establishing a new balance between democracy and capitalism, where certain forms of philanthropically designated private capital would be given more freedom than ever to accumulate in the name of the American people and enriched by public tax subsidies.

Furthermore, Sugarman was one among thousands of American Jews who filled the ranks of the legal profession in the decades after World War II and played an underexamined role in crafting interpretations that governed the intersection of state and private power, especially through tax law. Even in the face of discrimination that kept them out of white-shoe law firms and motivated them to create their own, Jewish lawyers tended to exhibit an incredible faith in the law as a tool for this-worldly justice, in part because they believed it could embed Jews in state structures that guaranteed them equal protections and benefits. Those Jews—almost all men—who gained the privileges of legal training were able to occupy the role of the expert, interpreting dense legal codes and gaining a hearing in front of governmental officials.[6]

Testifying before the Senate Finance Committee in 1978, Sugarman, by then one of the country's foremost experts on charitable law and an old hand at offering statements to Congress, explained, "The Congressional encouragement of publicly supported charities evidences one of the proudest attributes of the American people: The impulse toward voluntary association to meet human needs. People are better people if they give." Speaking that day on behalf of Jewish federations across the country and using terminology that he had popularized over the prior three decades through a frenzy of speeches and articles that justified the expansion of philanthropic power, Sugarman glossed over his own tremendous efforts to present what amounted to a truly new balance between public good and private interests as a timeless emanation of

FIGURE 4.1. Norman Sugarman, December 1974, Folder 316, Box 4, Cleveland Federation
Papers, MS 4835. Courtesy of the Western Reserve Historical Society, Cleveland, Ohio.

the American character. Yet the historical contingencies, the legislative victo-
ries, and the emotional pleas, especially to Jewish organizations resistant to
his vision, that attended Sugarman's career in tax law reveal a world in which
it was neither natural nor historically certain how American policy, Jewish
institutions, and private capital could "meet human needs."[7]

In 1954, shortly after his second appearance before the congressional committee investigating tax-exempt organizations, Norman Sugarman left the
Internal Revenue Service and returned to his hometown of Cleveland to join
a large law firm. Cleveland was a better perch than most from which to help
foster philanthropic growth and experimentation. From the early decades
of the twentieth century, the city had developed a reputation as a philanthropic leader, and as Sugarman built his charitable law practice, he relied on
the city's philanthropic reputation and institutions to help him gain national
prominence.

Philanthropic innovation seemed built into the midwestern city. A port
city, Cleveland had become an important stop along the Erie Canal in the
mid-nineteenth century, supplying goods and materials to booming East
Coast cities and welcoming newcomers to serve as part of its expanding industrial labor force. Industrial capitalists and the professional class of lawyers
and financiers who serviced them prospered as the city grew, often reaping
substantial rewards from investments in infrastructure and real estate. The
city's significant capital concentration combined with its location outside of
the orbit of the East Coast establishment may have stirred among its residents
a thirst for social and economic experimentation.[8]

Cleveland was home to one of the earliest Jewish federations, the Federation of the Jewish Charities of Cleveland, established in 1904. As Sugarman
developed his practice, he fostered strong relationships with the leaders of the
Cleveland federation, eventually becoming the organization's primary attorney and also devoting considerable volunteer energy and personal income to
its pursuits. Sugarman used his city's federation as a test case for a new model of
philanthropic strength that would harness state benefits to reorient the federation's practices from capital circulation toward capital accumulation.

City leaders had already begun experimenting with new philanthropic
models in 1914 when they established the Cleveland Foundation, which wed
foundation-like financial practices to the collectivist ethos of distribution-
based charities. Staking out new philanthropic ground, the Cleveland Foundation held multiple donors' charitable dollars in a trust fund that grew through
both new donations and investment returns. Donors could make suggestions
about when, where, and how much to give away, but in placing their money in
trust of the foundation, they ultimately gave the foundation's distribution
committee final authority over the disbursement of funds. Eventually, this

model would become the basis for so-called community foundations, but when it started, the Cleveland Foundation was both unique and phenomenally successful as judged through capital held, increasing its trust fund from just a couple of hundred thousand dollars in the mid-1920s to $30 million by the mid-1950s.[9]

Jewish leaders in the city observed and, in some instances, participated in the remarkable growth of the Cleveland Foundation. In 1954, leaders of the city's Jewish federation authorized the creation of an Endowment Fund Committee and set a target to increase the federation's endowment, which stood at a modest $1 million, by six times. Advocates of endowment did not imagine it would replace the annual campaign, and they took pains to assure themselves and their donors that the campaign remained the centerpiece of their philanthropic model; however, they also sought to establish endowment-building as an equally legitimate method—and in some cases, a better method—for harnessing private wealth to communal and public interests.[10]

Although the staff and voluntary leadership of the Cleveland federation developed a sense of themselves as innovators, forging the path of federation-based endowment growth, they also sought validation from other federations. In 1954, one of the first acts of the newly formed endowment committee was to gather data on endowment growth in the largest federations across the country. The data showed that its peer federations were also in the throes of nascent efforts to establish endowments and convinced Cleveland leaders that if they worked quickly, they truly could lead the field.

A second study, conducted by the federation's long-serving executive director, Henry Zucker, and his assistant Rudi Walter in 1958 and published the next year, discovered that almost every large city federation had "intensified" its endowment-building efforts over the previous four years and reported a total of $46.5 million in federation endowment accounts across the country. This figure, arrived at by canvassing the thirteen federations classified as representing large cities for total assets held outside of their operating funds, revealed an increase of almost $15 million since 1954, and the study's authors speculated that total endowment assets had more than doubled since 1948. But the aggregate figures actually understated the exceptional endowment growth that certain individual federations' endowments had experienced, and here Cleveland was unparalleled. Its federation reported a more than 300% increase in endowment assets over the last decade, a percentage rivaled but unmatched by a few other federations, all, it so happened, located in the Midwest and similarly removed from the orthodoxies of the East Coast federations.[11]

FIGURE 4.2. Executive Director Henry Zucker (left) with his assistant Rudi Walter, at Walter's retirement celebration, March 1975, Folder 318, Box 4, Cleveland Federation Papers, MS 4835. Courtesy of the Western Reserve Historical Society, Cleveland, Ohio.

Federation endowments could experience such astronomical growth in part because, until only very recently, their development had been neglected or, as in the case of New York's endowment and several others, severely constrained. The growth in endowment funds was so new that, according to the 1959 report, everything from leaders' attitudes toward them to the investment policies governing them lagged well behind their size. Across the thirteen cities surveyed, more than half of the endowment assets were held in low-risk and relatively low-growth preferred stocks and bonds, with only about a quarter invested in common stocks. Zucker and Walter indicated that these "conservative percentages" revealed the limits of federation leaders' understanding of the assets they now controlled. Not only were some unaware of the gains in their own endowment funds, but even those attuned to the growth were slow to institute necessary policy changes to account for and foster it. The report identified the very beginnings of "liberalizing provisions" that would give investment committees more license to invest in riskier securities.[12]

Cleveland sought to lead the way, and in 1958, its Finance and Investment Committee successfully changed the federation's bylaws to increase the cap imposed in 1955 on funds that could be held in common stock from 50% to 60%. Although an incremental shift, it nonetheless reflected a new body of knowledge about endowment growth. Noting its endowment's threefold growth in just three years, the investment group argued that, for however much new donations enriched the corpus, investment returns were the steady engine of endowment growth. Risk-averse investment policies would thus run counter to the very purpose of an endowment, which was to serve as a long-term and sustainable source of capital growth.[13]

The 1959 report offered some observations, which themselves served as justifications, although far thinner than its financial data, about why federations were entering the business of endowment after generally eschewing it for many decades. At the top of the list was the fact that every federation the report surveyed discussed endowments in the context of future emergencies. The predictability of the unpredictable offered federations the clearest way of justifying their decision to divert funds from immediate distribution. For example, in its most recent rationale for endowment-building, Cleveland's federation had explained that the primary purpose of its endowment was "to help insure that our agencies will have sufficient funds to meet unusual emergencies and to weather really disastrous economic storms."[14]

While the most ubiquitous explanation for building endowment funds was the expectation of future crisis, Zucker and Walter also identified a second explanation that appeared wholly new in the 1950s: endowment growth to fund long-term projects beyond the typical support federations provided to its agencies. A case in point was Cleveland's endowment literature from 1958, which had set the goal for its endowment to "help Federation and its agencies to undertake important constructive work which cannot for practical reasons be financed from Federation's regular sources of income." In making the leap between capital accumulation as a hedge against emergencies and capital accumulation as a constructive strategy, the report suggested that the value of endowment exceeded its ability to address crises. Rather, endowment could usefully supplement crisis-based fund-raising by offering opportunities for leaders and funders to craft a deliberate vision for the future.[15]

In the 1950s, the constructive functions of endowments remained aspirational and vague, and Zucker and Walter noted that this justification was not uniformly endorsed by all of the federations they studied. Nevertheless, Jewish leaders' articulation of the purposes their charitable organizations could serve beyond fulfilling immediate needs—purposes that would require novel financial strategies—indicated the stirrings of a fundamental shift in the form and function of Jewish philanthropy. Already the practice of holding back resources, even if for some imagined future crisis, may have helped Jewish leaders see their own historical moment in a new perspective: the future could be worse and more urgent than the present. But when Cleveland's Jewish leaders articulated endowment as a way to free themselves from the cycle of collection and distribution for immediate needs by channeling capital into "special studies and research programs . . . and educational and cultural activities of high quality," they pivoted away from seeing the central purpose of endowment as the remedy for a future downturn or crisis.[16]

More than anything else, the 1959 report on federation endowments was itself a constructive document, using data to advocate a new path whereby American Jews could think differently about capitalizing their communal endeavors. "Throughout the years," its Cleveland-based authors observed, "the preoccupation of Jewish federations with raising money for current needs has left little time for consideration of the long-term financial needs of our federations. Members of the community have been well trained to give generously for Jewish philanthropic purposes on a current basis. They have not been trained to think in terms of future needs." Noting that 1948 had represented a highwater mark for annual campaign giving to Jewish federations, and assuming that no future crisis would parallel the Holocaust and no achievement the establishment of Israel, Zucker and Walter instead advocated a different logic (sustainable growth) and a different instrument (endowment) around which to orient Jewish philanthropy.[17]

In the final sections of their report, the authors described the flurry of activities that federations across the country were engaged in "to call attention to their endowment funds" and, especially, to train a professional class of advisors in the practices of endowment. Here, too, Cleveland was the trendsetter. Beginning in 1955, its federation hosted periodic tax seminars. Norman Sugarman, recently returned to Cleveland from the IRS and already a member of the federation's endowment committee, presented on "New Methods of Giving Through Personal and Business Foundations" at the first tax seminar in 1955. Attendees ranged from accountants to attorneys and estate planners to professionals from nearby universities, hospitals, and charitable organizations who sought knowledge about how to build their organizations' endowments.

Seminars such as this one provided a platform for Cleveland leaders to develop the culture of endowment-building, by rehearsing its logic and discourse and cultivating professional experts to replicate and normalize it. Lawyers, accountants, and investment managers with ties to the federation were often tapped to join advisory committees and conduct seminars, in addition to leading by example and donating some of their own personal wealth to endowment funds. In the late 1950s, to extend the scope of its training and educational apparatus, the Cleveland federation put Sugarman in charge of an editorial committee assigned the task of publishing a "Handbook for Attorneys" about endowments to serve as "a useful and handy reference" for those seeking guidance on endowment-building.[18]

Taken together, the 1959 report, the handbook that Sugarman edited, and the series of tax seminars all provided federation leaders with the sense that endowment-building was simply in the air, and that, in effect, everyone was doing it. This was by design. In the final pages of their 1959 report, the Cleveland authors recommended a "national publicity program" to raise the profile of endowment programs. Federations were not alone in their effort to draw attention to endowment-building as a strategy that could be broadened to suit a wider variety of philanthropic entities than ever before. As Zucker and Walter themselves noted, whatever publicity efforts federations pursued to popularize endowment would be echoed in "the rapid growth of the community trust, the expansion of the private and corporate foundation movement, and the success of educational institutions, church groups, and selected health and welfare agencies." At a national conference of federation leaders in 1961, the president of Cleveland's federation observed similarly that educational and religious institutions were all turning more attention than ever to "building up endowment monies," and that American Jews also had to be "willing to finance philanthropies in this way."[19]

Even as Jewish leaders would step onto the national stage more than ever in the 1960s and beyond to craft new methods for expanding the forms and power of charitable endowments, many other American Jews raised significant concerns over doing so, both because communal charitable practices had for so many decades eschewed endowment and because they supported the expansion of state responsibility over public welfare. Their faith in the American state to provide for the common good had increased during the 1930s and 1940s, clearly measured by American Jews' near-unanimous support for FDR when he ran for his third and fourth terms. Could one believe in a robust social welfare state, a state that intervened in countless facets of private life—from housing to nutrition to healthcare to education—while also advocating the expansion of state-enriched private capital accumulation in the name of the public good? The Jewish leaders who answered in the affirmative worked through technocratic channels, defined by tax law and finance, in order to normalize a new balance between capitalism and democracy that tilted away from state control and toward the expansion of private entities as custodians of the public good.[20]

———

Even as Norman Sugarman joined efforts to help acclimate American Jews to the practices of endowment-building, he focused the bulk of his energies on commanding the logic and language of charitable tax law so that more than simply applying law, he could help create the legal scaffolding that would unfetter certain types of private capital and interests from regulatory constraints. In 1961, he wrote a detailed article in the journal *Taxes* entitled, "Charitable Giving Developments in Tax Planning and Policy." Laying the foundations for a case he would develop over the next decade, he argued that the "philosophical base for tax exemptions" took on heightened importance as the field of philanthropic organizations expanded. He suggested that the IRS was searching for a clear philosophical premise that it could apply uniformly "as cases arise which have the potential of permitting dollars to escape taxation."[21]

Since the passage of the income tax in 1913, Congress had made only a few statutory changes to its charitable giving laws, allowing most deliberations about how to apply the tax to proceed through IRS rulings or the courts. Yet the charitable landscape had changed considerably thanks to the expansion of the income tax, the growth of the welfare state, and renewed suspicion about nonstate entities holding too much power. Sugarman surmised that Congress would enact legislative reform before too long and, with a deft hand, sought to guide that reform.

Sugarman felt certain that the only way Congress could avoid regulatory overreach, which he believed threatened private freedoms, was by codifying different categories of philanthropic entities. Dismissing the motive of the giver as a feasible source of differentiation—divining individual motive, he explained, "opens a Pandora's box"—Sugarman instead advocated a distinction between more public-minded and more private-minded philanthropic bodies. The Department of Treasury had already begun to distinguish between family-based, private capital foundations and other exempt charitable entities by placing a greater burden of proof on foundations to demonstrate their public-minded intentions. Should Congress follow Treasury's lead, he suggested to his tax-trained readers, it would be reasonable to expect private family foundations to draw greater regulatory attention than other, more ostensibly public-minded charities. While Congress deliberated over whether and how to formalize this distinction, Sugarman recommended that practice precede law: he advised tax attorneys to act as if the legal distinction already existed by treating their private foundation clients with special caution. In this way, they might demonstrate to lawmakers the feasibility of holding only certain philanthropic bodies—and not the entire sector—accountable to new regulations.[22]

Sugarman offered a constructive case for legislative reform, but between the lines, he was also building a defense of philanthropy, which he rightly presumed would face intense congressional scrutiny throughout the 1960s. In the spring of 1961, Representative Wright Patman, a Democrat from Texas, delivered a floor speech alleging charitable abuses tolerated by existing tax law and announced his intention to investigate tens of thousands of charitable entities. His populist concern that the wealthy were using philanthropy as a means of tax avoidance put the entire charitable sector on alert. Sugarman was part of a new class of philanthropic experts, shaped by its sense of the sector's embattlement, that tried to wrest the discussion away from political speechifying and instead provide Congress with technocratic solutions that would protect philanthropy—and, more generally, the private freedom to do public good—from Patman's regulatory zeal.[23]

Patman's investigation spurred philanthropic professionals—including the attorneys who served charities and foundations and high-level staff members of these same philanthropic organizations—to feel connected by a common cause. Increasingly, they directed their energies toward mounting a united defense of their work, a pursuit assisted by new institutions, such as the Council on Foundations and the Foundation Library Center, both relatively new ventures, to collect and share materials about charitable foundations. In 1965, Sugarman spoke alongside the chief of staff of Congress's Joint Committee on Internal Revenue Taxation on a panel at the annual Council on Foundations conference, where philanthropic professionals met. The chief of staff all but guaranteed that Congress, now in possession of a set of Treasury recommendations for better charitable oversight, including reporting and spend-out requirements, excise taxes on investment earnings, limits on individual deductions, and more enforceable measures against self-dealing (or gaining personal reward through charitable behavior), was poised to expand its regulatory power over private foundations. The only outstanding question was just how broadly it would apply the private foundation classification.[24]

Sugarman, who had fashioned himself an expert on the technical and philosophical aspects of charitable law, reiterated in his 1965 presentation that core American values would be compromised if Congress engaged in regulatory creep over philanthropy. "The basic problem I see," Sugarman explained, "is that Treasury, on the one hand, is saying that the value to society of foundations is their flexibility, their initiative, their experimentation. But, on the other hand, it is proposing to impose limitations" that would compromise just those qualities. Any new regulations, he suggested, should meet the test of doing more public good than harm; thus, those regulations that limited the possibilities for private abuse and were precisely applied to a subset of charitable entities most in danger of engaging in those abuses could stand, but anything beyond this would challenge the very political philosophy underlying freedom of association and the use of private means to do public good.[25]

As Sugarman explained, Treasury guidelines, even without congressional actions, had already created a de facto separation among philanthropic entities, based upon their assumption that certain institutions were by nature more charitably intentioned than others. In its new section 501(c)(3), the Revenue Act of 1954 repurposed statutory language from 1913 to define four criteria that qualified a body for tax exemption: drawing substantial support from the public; serving as a religious body; acting as an educational organization; or testing for public safety. Absent from the section was an explicit discussion of private foundations that did not fit neatly into any of those categories but nonetheless drew the benefits of exemption. Urging Congress to err on the side of philanthropic freedom, Sugarman advocated a precise definition of private foundations. He amplified his argument against broad regulation two years later at a meeting of the American Bar Association, where he averred, "The tax exemption is . . . for the purpose of permitting [philanthropic] organizations to operate outside of government controls so that they are free to operate with flexibility and vitality to perform valuable public service in the private sector."[26]

As he spoke to other lawyers, philanthropic professionals, policymakers, and lawmakers, Sugarman refined what he had called, in his 1961 article, the "philosophical base for tax exemptions": tax exemption must balance the weight of the state against the freedom of nonstate entities to do good. His philosophy came to guide the shaping of charitable tax law, even as it met

significant challenges from government officials, especially those working in
the Department of the Treasury, who maintained that tax exemption was a
state-granted privilege that empowered the government to extract demands
in the form of tight regulation. Sugarman was willing to allow that private
foundations required special regulations, but he made certain at every turn to
emphasize that Congress should define private foundations narrowly while
boldly freeing public charities from regulation, thus making the latter the more
attractive and, even, natural vehicles for philanthropy.[27]

Well before others understood the logic of a law yet to be passed, Sugarman
helped his clients appreciate that as long as they acted as if the public charitable
standard already existed and fit themselves into it, they could expect a wide
latitude of freedom over their charitable capital, so much so that they might
accumulate and grow it in ways that, in fact, resembled private foundations.

———

In the years that Congress deliberated over charitable tax reform, the leaders
of Cleveland's Jewish federation were engaged in a similar process of redefin-
ing philanthropic categories. Driven to expand their endowment to reach $6
million, a figure the endowment committee had set as a target in 1954, federation leaders had discovered that the more capacious their definition of endowment, the more success they would have meeting their goal and normalizing
endowment among donors and national federation leaders. A very straightforward understanding of endowment might have one believe that only capital
released entirely from individual control and put in the hands of a charitable
organization to invest and expend the income as it saw fit could be calculated
as part of that organization's endowment. But the will to grow endowment
funds produced new techniques to account for them. Cleveland leaders realized that their federation could achieve marked endowment growth by reporting philanthropic capital that was substantially controlled by individuals as,
nonetheless, part of the institution's endowment total.

By 1961, the Endowment Fund Committee celebrated an endowment that
had surpassed the $6 million mark and appeared to be growing at a rate of $1
million annually, due almost entirely to the creation of "a pioneering enterprise" of trust funds that they referred to as philanthropic funds. Each fund,
the committee explained, was "in effect a private foundation established
through contract within the Federation." The contract, a two-page form that
had gained approval from the IRS, stipulated that the federation would

administer the funds, but the fund holder could determine the grantees, as long as they qualified as charitable institutions. Most significant, the contract established that any "contributions which follow this form are presumed to be charitable contributions," meaning the capital gained the status and privileges of a completed charitable gift from the moment it was placed in the trust, earmarked for charitable circulation though not yet disbursed.[28]

Clearly reiterating the logic Cleveland federation leaders had already been presenting to potential donors, the Endowment Fund Committee reported that donors received myriad advantages from establishing federation-held trust funds, as opposed to private foundations. It noted that donors could retain the privilege of calling the fund by their own name, as they would any private foundation they might create, but they would avoid the burdens of managing the money and waiting the year (or more) it generally took private foundations to receive Treasury recognition and tax benefits. On the federation side, the gains were also substantial. A federation could count the capital held in these funds as part of its endowment, thus allowing it to showcase a growing endowment to other potential donors, since, according to the report, "One trust fund begets another." Beyond this, the federation expected eventual control over a portion of the funds. Many of the funds were designated as bequests to the federation after the death of the donor, and even before that, the federation made it common practice to include in each contract a stipulation for some percentage of each fund's income to go to the federation, whether as part of the donor's annual pledge or to support a special project.[29]

More than a simple update to apprise the endowment committee of recent activity, the 1961 report explicitly prioritized efforts to ensure "that the idea will spread" so that more donors would create trust funds in Cleveland and so that other federations would follow the Cleveland model. Serving as a trend-setter had great practical value. By stimulating the replication of the trust fund model, Cleveland leaders hoped to establish the practice as the norm, not the outlier, and to overcome the misgivings that many within the Jewish and broader American philanthropic worlds had about building endowments. Ex-uding confidence that Cleveland had arrived at a winning formula, the report concluded, "We may be proud of the fact that through this new approach, we have enlarged the resources of the Federation and at the same time provided an important service to contributors."[30]

In a speech delivered in 1963 at a conference of Jewish communal professions, Henry Zucker, the executive director of Cleveland's federation, noted that interest in endowment "is beginning to snowball" and asserted that although Jews had been reluctant to make any changes to their mass-giving charitable practices, as Americans they were coming to appreciate the value of endowment. In selling the idea, he pivoted between assuring his audience that endowment was nothing new and impressing them with the innovative vehicle for endowment that he and his colleagues had "pioneered." Invoking a populist spirit to describe something that was difficult to square with populist goals, Zucker described the trust fund model as a "poor man's foundation." Most people would have thought that trust funds and private foundations were the tools of only the very wealthy—and those paying attention to Congress might have known that public officials worried that these charitable vehicles allowed for the anti-democratic consolidation of power—but Zucker argued otherwise. Even a modest fund could help the federation build its endowment heft and would give those outside of ultra-wealthy circles access to some of the privileges of controlling a private foundation. In 1967, Zucker reported at a national meeting of federation professionals that more than half a million dollars from federation trust funds had been distributed to 287 agencies and organizations, emphasizing both the growth of the trust fund program and its integration with existing federation priorities.[31]

Throughout the 1960s, Cleveland staff tracked their federation's own endowment and kept tabs on federation endowments across the country. The simple fact of endowment growth would prove its value to the Jewish philanthropic project. Well before the matter was settled, a federation leader from Baltimore announced to his colleagues at a national convening in 1967, "We are past the point of having to project a rationale for development of endowment funds." Although a premature assertion, the statement fairly captured the concerted efforts to normalize endowment growth.[32]

Alongside their efforts to popularize their endowment model nationally, Cleveland leaders continued to work to win over wealthy donors to the wisdom of endowment gifts. In early 1967, they instituted a Foundation Advisory Council, which they described as "a service which Federation proposes to offer to donors and managers of independent charitable foundations." Positioning itself as a service provider—much as it was for internally held trust funds—the federation would make itself useful to foundations and, in turn, gain a seat at the table when it came to decision making, including succession plans for assets.[33]

In the quest to gain, calculate, and report ever-higher sums of endowment capital held, itself a justification for endowment, federation leaders became increasingly tied to the logic of private capital growth and accumulation. In

1967, Sugarman chaired a seminar for stockbrokers, now significant players in the model of capital growth and expansion that he was helping to construct. Robert L. Merritt, a partner at a local law firm, addressed "How to Obtain Maximum Tax Advantages by Using Stock and Other Securities to Fulfill Charitable Commitments." The instructions were relatively clear once stockbrokers and their clients understood that a stock donated to charity was not subject to any tax on appreciation and still could be deducted at its full appreciated value. In the hypothetical he offered, Merritt portrayed a donor who wanted to give a $5,000 gift to a charity. The donor could give that amount outright, but if donated as stock and calculated properly, the donor could effectively save $3,500 through tax benefits, while still completing a $5,000 gift. Even better, the lawyer suggested, a donation to Cleveland's trust fund program could earn the donor the same tax benefits, while also allowing the gift—now the principal of an interest-bearing account—to generate new untaxed charitable income and providing the donor control over when and how to distribute the income. Describing this program as a "private family foundation with maximum tax benefits, and with no administrative burden," Merritt emphasized that the IRS had given a "blanket blessing" to this financial arrangement, and he provided stockbrokers with templates for the legal paperwork to transfer their clients' shares to federation-held trust funds.[34]

Sugarman was nearly peerless in his commitment to opening new channels for private capital to flow toward philanthropic ends. By the late 1960s, he started to crisscross the country in a flurry of speaking engagements addressed to Jewish and non-Jewish philanthropic entities, lawyers, policymakers, and legislators to make the case against imposing regulations on the accumulation of philanthropic capital. He was an ideal expert, who spoke with the assuredness of his grasp on tax law, all undergirded by the "philosophical base for tax exemptions" he was helping to construct, normalize, and legalize. At its heart, his philosophy pivoted on the belief that government should not stand in the way of private capital intended to benefit the public. Before he convinced naysayers, he sought to gain the support of those within the philanthropic sector, in part by helping them see the untapped resources they could access by embracing strategies such as endowment-building. Sugarman worked with remarkable speed and vigor because he suspected that, before the end of the decade, Congress would act to clarify the division between private power and public good, and he tried to stay one step ahead of its policy deliberations, crafting models for legal reform by enacting them preemptively.

Fearful that Representative Patman's investigations throughout the 1960s had whipped Congress into a whirl of suspicion about philanthropy, Sugarman hoped that the law it eventually passed would show restraint and not use regulation as a knife to cut away at private freedom to serve the public good. He intended to do whatever he could to free philanthropic power from government regulation in the broadest way possible, including making political calculations to endorse the distinction between private and public charity. As he put it, charitable tax law had become "a political football," and even as he bemoaned that state of affairs, few were as deep in the game as he.[35]

———

If only at times a political football, philanthropy was always political. Philanthropic entities had long been embedded in the political economy of the American state. They participated in its most fundamental contest about the extents and limits of democracy and capitalism. Their tax attorneys, especially ones as skilled as Sugarman, used the political power of technical expertise and bureaucratic savvy in order to encourage the state to empower private means to act in the name of the public good. Modern American philanthropy emerged from state-based associationalism, and it extended the possibility of suturing private property to the public interest. Although congressional investigations in the 1960s momentarily channeled political energy to loosen these stitches or even snip them entirely, especially when politicians worried that private entities had agglomerated excessive power over the public, the more significant political momentum moved in the direction of routinizing the fact of a public and a private conjoined through their mutual reliance on capital growth.

The American Jewish philanthropic complex would emerge only when Congress and other bodies of the American state, including the Department of Treasury, authorized philanthropic entities to serve as sites of political consolidation and capital growth and accumulation, justified not by electoral ambitions or the profit motive but by the intent to benefit the public. Able to parse tax law expertly, Sugarman helped American Jewish leaders imagine shifting their communal financial model away from rapid distribution and toward accumulation and growth. He believed government had the dual-pronged obligation to free and support philanthropic capital. Thus, he fought mightily to ensure that philanthropy received the benefits of government incentives with as few of the costs of regulation as possible, arguing that government's job was to encourage, not hinder, private freedom to do public good. His certainty of the rights of philanthropic capital was so firm that he, the consummate technocrat, dove into political life. He testified in front of Congress and eventually drafted legislation and pieces of tax code, and enlisted his clients and friends, many of them important Jewish leaders, to use whatever resources they had to tip the political balance to allow philanthropic capital to operate free of government interference or regulation.

Along the way, as American Jewish leaders spoke in front of state bodies and lobbied Congress to protect their philanthropic endeavors, they honed a new form of politics, specifically a "depoliticized" politics, marked by an effort to strip behaviors or policies of their political nature. Once again, Jewish philanthropic leaders and institutions moved in concert with state transformations. State policies sanctioned a notably restrictive definition of politics, leaving an opening for charitable entities and their leaders to engage in a wide range of political activities that, nonetheless, would not be marked as political. This was the nature of depoliticized politics.

With growing fervor, Jewish leaders invoked a Jewish consensus or, sometimes, nonpartisanship to justify plunging into deeply political waters—for example, related to American diplomacy in Israel or tax policy—and engaging in unmistakably political behavior, such as lobbying for legislation or supporting electoral campaigns. The phenomenon of depoliticized politics, similar to the public empowerment of private finance that Sugarman helped achieve through tax policy, fortified philanthropic associations in unprecedented ways, laying the foundations for the emergence of the American Jewish philanthropic complex.

5

Politics

IN LATE 1969, Max Fisher wrote to the presidents, executive directors, and board members of the almost two hundred Jewish federations in the United States, urging them to lobby Congress as if their very future depended on it. New to the role of president of the Council of Jewish Federations and Welfare Funds (CJFWF), the national body that had coordinated Jewish federations since its establishment in 1932, but hardly new to the business of politics, Fisher realized that more than a decade of congressional hearings about philanthropy were about to culminate in significant legal reform. Now, as the legislative session was ending, federation leaders had to use any pull they had to lobby for reform that worked in their institutions' favor.[1]

By the late 1960s, Fisher was the most prominent leader in American Jewish communal life and a rising star in Republican political circles. An oil magnate who invested remuneratively in real estate, he had proven to be a master fundraiser, first in Detroit's Jewish community, then for the Michigan Republican party, and eventually, for the national Republican party. In 1969, when Richard Nixon took the White House, Fisher's record of support earned him the new president's admiration and a quasi-official appointment, described in memos and correspondence as "liaison for the Jewish community."[2]

At the time he issued his call to federation leaders, Fisher sat close to state power. While Norman Sugarman did not occupy a position nearly as proximate to political leadership as Fisher, he also had notable access to it. The lawyer had successfully parlayed his nearly unrivaled expertise in tax law into political influence, gaining hearings with members of Congress, drafting tax code proposals, and building alliances with powerful philanthropic entities. Both men used their political capital to influence state policy and to gain standing with state officials to speak on behalf of Jewish interests consolidated by and rendered through philanthropic institutions.

Yet, these two figures so central to the political standing of organized American Jewish life in the middle decades of the twentieth century consistently positioned themselves and their Jewish interests as removed from politics. Certainly, Fisher was transparent about his Republican loyalties, but he depicted himself as primarily an advocate for unified Jewish interests that rose above partisan or political commitments. Sugarman, who offered no evidence in the historical record about his party loyalties, likewise perceived his work as advancing Jewish (and broader charitable) interests and, thus, as separate from the business of politics. He was not running for office; he was reading tax code for the sake of his clients and his Jewish community. Both assumed a posture of representing a Jewish consensus and using their knowledge, networks, and proximity to American state officials and offices to advance the very interests they worked to consolidate into that consensus. A disavowal of being political was core to their brand of consensus-based political influence—what I characterize as depoliticized politics.

Far from aberrations, Fisher and Sugarman embodied the depoliticized norms of American civic life. Already in debates about associationalism in the nineteenth century, political thinkers had worried that if associations became too strong, as if political entities unto themselves, they would rival the government. As the state developed its particular pattern of incentives for and regulation over associational life, it imposed discipline on the way associations accessed state benefits. The formation of charitable tax law reflected the give-and-get pattern, demanding that associations surrender some of their autonomy in return for state benefits, and by the 1930s, the state's effort to legislate the political limits of associational life through the convenient vehicle of tax law served to reinforce that pattern. Yet the state defined political behavior in narrowly specific terms, which gave philanthropic associations and their leaders permission to act in extraordinarily political ways while still formally complying with the rules of American democracy.[3]

State policies that governed the exercise of political power in associational life shaped the development of American Jewish institutions, especially as they grew over the second half of the twentieth century. Although one can surely find historical traditions of Jewish leaders in different times and places exercising quiet political influence and claiming to speak on behalf of all Jews to state officials, the specific mode of depoliticized politics must be understood in the context of mid-twentieth-century American statecraft. The possibility of exercising political influence within a state-based legal framework that designated them as nonpolitical actors provided American Jewish institutions and their leaders with vast opportunities to participate in high-level American statecraft. This same framework also allowed them to control public presentations of Jewish interests as driven not by a desire to influence the state's political process but rather by avowed consensus about what was good and necessary for American Jewish collective life. As a consequence, the political capital consolidated within Jewish philanthropic organizations not only functioned to present a unified face to state officials, whether about Israel or tax policy, but also exercised control over Jewish communal life, delimiting an American Jewish consensus (the so-called public good that these organizations aspired to serve), regardless of whether one, indeed, existed.[4]

The effort to circumscribe political behavior through charitable tax law gained new momentum beginning in 1930. That year, the United States Commissioner of Internal Revenue faced a lawsuit for denying a deduction to an individual taxpayer. The petitioner had made a series of donations to the American Birth Control League, deducted them from his income, and then received notice from the IRS that his deduction was impermissible due to a single word in the tax code: "exclusively." In its allowance of individual charitable deductions, a measure enacted in 1917, Congress mandated that deductible contributions were those made to "corporations or associations organized and operated exclusively for religious, charitable, scientific, or educational purposes."[5]

Treasury did not dispute the American Birth Control League's charitable purpose, only that this was its exclusive purpose. According to its charter, the American Birth Control League sought the repeal of anti-birth control laws. In the eyes of the Commissioner of Internal Revenue, this disqualified an individual from deducting gifts to it, and, upon review, the courts agreed with that judgment. However, in rendering its decision, the Second Circuit noted that the legal question was not entirely settled, since "many charitable, literary, and scientific ventures" may "require changes in the law" for their success and, thus, engage in "ancillary" political activity in order to fulfill their primary charitable purposes. Throwing the matter back to Congress, the court demanded clarification of permissible political activity for tax-exempt organizations.[6]

Hoping to settle the question, Congress added a new clause in 1934 to its statutory definition of qualifying exempt organizations that mandated "no substantial part of the activities" of such organizations could be directed toward the "carrying on of propaganda, or otherwise attempting to influence legislation." Now, not only did exempt organizations have to meet the positive test of exclusive purpose, they also would have to meet a negative test barring "substantial" legislative activity.[7]

Twenty years later, in the summer of 1954, when Norman Sugarman testified before Congress as the Assistant Commissioner of Internal Revenue, he confronted a Congress concerned about subversive political activity among tax-exempt organizations. Responding to a request that he discuss "political propaganda" in the framework of tax exemption law, he reminded the body, "The phrase 'political propaganda' as such does not appear in the tax code or regulations. Nor are the terms 'propaganda' and 'political' defined in the tax statutes or the regulations." His response suggested that, even among members of Congress, it was commonly believed that the tax code actually barred charitable organizations from engaging in "political propaganda." Schooling Congress, he instructed that only "propaganda which is to influence legislation" appeared in the tax code as a prohibited activity and then only if it met the threshold of comprising a "substantial part" of an organization's activities. He concluded, "Thus, with such terms as 'educational,' 'exclusively,' 'substantial' and 'propaganda' in the statute, there has been a long history of varying interpretations and difficulty in establishing readily definable lines as to exemption . . . and the effect of 'political' activity in determining exemption." Given these amorphous legislative guidelines, Sugarman explained, "resort to the courts is a natural result."[8]

Prior to 1934, under the "exclusively" charitable standard, the courts maintained considerable leeway to determine if activities were political and, thus, disqualifying of an organization's exempt status. However, since the 1934 amendment, Congress had tied the courts' hands, in Sugarman's view, by "circumscrib[ing] the exemption with a restriction against substantial activities to influence legislation," though it had refrained from passing proposed language to extend the prohibition to "participation in partisan politics." As would be his wont for years to come, Sugarman took it upon himself to tell Congress what its spare legislative language meant in practice: "We must conclude that it is now reasonably established under the law that an organization may have as its ultimate objective the creation of a public sentiment favorable to one side of a controversial issue and still secure exempt status." That is, an organization could be political by most reasonable standards without jeopardizing its exempt status.[9]

For Congress, in the throes of anti-communist hearings and plagued by concerns that subversion could be happening under its nose, the indeterminacy of the tax code may have felt unsatisfying and, even, dangerous. Just a month after Sugarman gave his June 1954 testimony before the House committee, Senator Lyndon B. Johnson introduced an amendment on the Senate floor to broaden the definition of prohibited activities to include participation in elec- toral campaigns. With no debate, the amendment—often referred to as the Johnson Amendment—became law. Historians generally explain this change in tax policy as Johnson's attempt to extract payback for a rancorous senatorial primary, when certain charitable organizations backed his opponent. While that may have been the immediate context for the amendment, the better one can be found in the longer history of Congress's concern with granting tax exemptions to organizations that might, in return, use their resources to inter- fere with the American political process.[10]

By narrowing political behavior to campaigning for a political candidate or engaging in substantial legislative lobbying, Congress created a philanthropic world it could manage. In his 1954 testimony, Sugarman had suggested that Congress could either issue a blanket ban on all political activities, a move that would give the courts interpretive authority and allow them to set precedents establishing what was or was not political, or it could be more specific in its statutory language. While seemingly choosing the latter path, Congress's nar- row ban, over time, became the totality of what it meant for philanthropic enti- ties and their leaders to act politically. Everything else gained the cover of not being political.

———

As Congress legislated a narrow standard for what political activities disquali- fied an organization from charitable status, American Jews were channeling an unprecedented amount of money through their charitable organizations to support a new political entity: the State of Israel. Even before the nation's establishment, American Jews had actively contributed money to support state-building efforts through several Zionist and foreign aid Jewish organ- izations. Starting in 1939, the vast majority of American Jewish dollars to sup- port foreign Jewish communities, whether in Palestine or elsewhere, flowed through the United Jewish Appeal, created that year to merge the fund-raising activities of the American Jewish Joint Distribution Committee and the United Palestine Appeal. The United Jewish Appeal steadily supplied philan- thropic capital to Jewish settlements in Palestine, with its efforts surging in 1948, when it sent $85 million to the newly established state, exceeding its earlier allocations many times over. The figure would only grow, reflecting rising American Jewish wealth, the vast needs of the new country, and the growing claims from Jewish leaders and philanthropic organizations that the State of Israel, no matter how controversial and divisive pre-state Zionism had been among American Jews, deserved their unequivocal support.[11]

Within the American tax system, funds channeled through tax-exempt organizations to foreign powers received a subsidy from the American state. By exempting charitable dollars for overseas causes from taxation, the American state seemingly released its sovereign claims on its tax revenue, yet from another vantage point, the American state also scattered its power far and wide. Particularly during moments of vulnerability or diplomatic tension, the state might call in or gather that power. The delicate nature of Cold War diplomacy in the 1950s put immense pressure on the American state to define and defend the nature of its power, as evident in McCarthyite concerns among American state leaders that one part of the state might be working at odds with another.[12]

In 1956, President Eisenhower found himself ensnared in a web of Cold War politics that required a balancing act to avoid full-scale military escalation in the Middle East. The Suez Crisis, precipitated by Egypt's decision to nationalize the Suez Canal and potentially choke off a crucial highway for international trade, put Eisenhower in the position of trying to talk down French, British, and Israeli aggression while ultimately hoping to thwart Soviet access to greater swaths of the Arab world. As a result of the president's maneuvers, and facing resistance from Congress, the Eisenhower administration crafted a UN resolution that mandated the suspension of military aid to any party, including Israel, in the region until it withdrew its forces from Egypt.[13]

By the time of the Suez Crisis, American Jewish leaders maintained that fund-raising for Israel operated in concert—and certainly not at odds—with American Cold War policy to contain the spread of Soviet communism. Not only did United Jewish Appeal fund-raising efforts direct American Jews toward this understanding, high-ranking American officials also expounded it, praising Jewish philanthropic support of Israel as good for American democracy. As Jewish fund-raising goals appeared to align well with American foreign policy goals, the United Jewish Appeal broadened its base of Jewish donors and channeled more and more money to Israel. But in the fall of 1956, Eisenhower's diplomacy suddenly pitted the interests of the American state against those of Israel, and American Jewish donations to the young country, once praised as patriotic, now threatened American sovereign power.[14]

If the United States truly wanted to leverage the full extent of its economic power to compel Israel to withdraw its troops from Egypt, it would have to stanch the flow of American dollars, which moved not only through state-based foreign aid programs but also through philanthropic channels. By the 1950s, one of the most common ways that American Jews supported Israel was by purchasing Israeli government bonds, a program that Prime Minister David Ben-Gurion had initiated as he reconciled himself to the fact that American Jews might not move to Israel but they could still invest in it. In the 1950s, Americans bought between 40 and 60 million dollars' worth of Israel bonds annually. Although a bond purchase would not receive a tax deduction, bond-holders could donate them to charitable organizations, such as the United Jewish Appeal, and then receive a deduction based on the value of the contribution.[15]

As Eisenhower struggled to enact his sanctions, he worried that private donations to Israel, which soared as American Jews feared that a new conflict in the Middle East could jeopardize the state's existence, diminished his dip-lomatic power. His sense of vulnerability at the hands of private money that might contravene his power led him to consider proposing a UN resolution to extend the foreign aid sanctions to private donations, in addition to govern-mental ones. When word of Eisenhower's plan spread to Jewish leaders, they mobilized, using the organizational strength of their philanthropic enterprises to launch a full-scale campaign against the president's efforts to stop American aid, through governmental and private channels, to Israel.

The chair of the Israel Bond Executive Committee was on high alert throughout the early months of 1957, working to coordinate Jews across the country to oppose Eisenhower's sanctions. In April of that year, he celebrated the decision by Congress to weaken the magnitude of Eisenhower's pressure against Israel, but he also took that success as a sign to build an organized American Jewish political apparatus to respond to future crises. "No matter how much money we raise for the United Jewish Appeal and Israel Bonds," he wrote in a letter to Max Fisher, then a rising star fund-raiser from Detroit, "ISRAEL will still be faced with desperate political problems. . . . There is nothing more important to ISRAEL today than to re-establish and maintain firm bonds of friendship with our Government." American Jews' support for Israel could not stop at their checkbooks; rather, they had to use the full extent of their political influence so that the checks they wrote would be assured state enrichment, in the form of tax exemptions and, even more so, in the form of American policy and aid.[16]

For American Jewish leaders in the 1950s, the chance to access the power of the American state, not only through exemptions or deductions but also through policy channels, emerged as a critical—perhaps the most critical—dimension of their philanthropy. The same men who led federation campaigns, who themselves donated significant property to Jewish philanthropic organizations and convinced their friends to do the same, became vested in structures of American power that could protect their property and through which they could work to consolidate Jewish interests in ways that validated their claims on the American state and its resources. The link between Jewish philanthropy and American politics, in other words, did not have to be made as much as it had to be made manifest, and the post–World War II efforts to draw a division between politics and philanthropy ironically did just that.

———

In 1950, the Jewish intellectual journal *Commentary* ran side-by-side articles by Dorothy Thompson and Oscar Handlin under the headline, "Israeli Ties and U.S. Citizenship." A famed American journalist who had been expelled by the Nazis while reporting from Germany in 1934, Thompson took the position that American Jews must demonstrate singular loyalty to the United States and instead of searching for redemption elsewhere, they should feel that "this country is their Zion, their home, and the representative of their democratic faith." In his rebuttal, Handlin, the Jewish Brooklyn-born Harvard historian, issued a defense of the "hyphenated American" as the true American. He explained that American Jews could maintain an interest-based politics, oriented around a basic consensus of support for Israel, without compromising their ability to fit into the American state. This was a "product of the freedom of many diverse groups to organize their cultural life with very few restraints"; that is, associationalism made room for the hyphenated American. He concluded his case with a declaration that American Jews' support for Israel would always be predicated upon their commitment to the same values—"the spread of democracy through the world, the self-determination of nations, international action for peace, the desirability of aiding small peoples against great oppressors"—that animated all Americans.[17]

In the early 1950s, precipitated by Israeli statehood and its precarity, as well as American Jews' uncertainty about how consistent their country's support for Israel would be, American Jewish leaders sought to construct a unified set of Jewish interests visible to the American state. At the same time, they felt

hemmed in by the rising Cold War mandate for shows of patriotism and loyalty. Philip Klutznick, a Missouri-born Jewish lawyer who had moved to Washington, DC, to serve as the commissioner of the Federal Public Housing Authority under President Franklin Delano Roosevelt and later was elected
president of B'nai B'rith and served briefly as a UN delegate in 1957, recalled
the Eisenhower administration requesting that American Jews present a unified voice on Israel and other issues. According to Klutznick's recollection,
Eisenhower's secretary of state, John Foster Dulles, had griped that too many
different Jewish leaders were seeking his time on matters related to Israel and
suggested that it would save him trouble if just one spokesperson would provide the Jewish view. In his account, Klutznick credited Dulles's grievance for
serving as the impetus for the creation of a united Jewish advisory body to
presidential administrations, eventually named the Conference of Presidents
of Major Jewish Organizations.[18]

Dulles's aggravation, however, was hardly the sole impetus for Jewish leaders'
efforts to coordinate a set of Jewish interests, represent them to state powers, and
gain approbation for them. Throughout the early 1950s, Klutznick, Zionist
leader Nahum Goldman, and Maurice Eisendrath, the head of the Reform
movement in American Judaism, worked to convince the presidents of Jewish
organizations that for whatever differences their groups may have had, they
would benefit from consolidating their commitments and presenting them for
state recognition as consensus Jewish interests deserving of a fair hearing. Before too long, they had secured sixteen participants from across the spectrum
of Jewish religious movements, Zionist organizations, and communal
groups.[19]

Even as Klutznick championed the Conference of Presidents throughout
the 1950s and 1960s, the group gained little standing among state officials. During the Suez Crisis, for example, Klutznick met with Dulles, but noted that none
of the other members of the recently formed Conference of Presidents were in
the room. Sensitive to the political demands of his times, Klutznick was well
aware of the significant pitfalls involved in trying to coordinate Jewish interests
and create a conduit to Washington leaders. The more that Jews appeared as a
singular political entity, the more likely they could be perceived as clannish, un-
assimilable, and, thus, incapable of fulfilling the duties of national citizenship. In
the late 1950s, when a group of senators demanded a Treasury investigation of
the United Jewish Appeal's tax status, concerned that the fund-raising organization was directly supporting a foreign government and, potentially, engaging
in substantial legislative propaganda, the Conference of Presidents again had

little sway. Under pressure of possible investigation, the United Jewish Appeal instead restructured itself in the early 1960s to designate an American corporation to collect and disburse funds to a nonstate agency in Israel.[20]

Klutznick worked steadfastly to clarify exactly how the Conference of Presidents could secure—and not endanger—Jewish and American interests. In her 1951 book on totalitarianism, German-born Jewish philosopher Hannah Arendt had suggested that the closer Jews moved toward the center of state power, the more likely they were to be targeted when popular energy surged against the state: "each class of society which came into a conflict with the state as such became anti-Semitic because the only social group which seemed to represent the state were the Jews." To the contrary, Klutznick insisted that American associational structures provided Jews with a way to attach their interests to the state without becoming overly identified with it and without entirely squelching their own internal diversity. Calling upon his experience as a delegate to the United Nations, he explained that even sovereign states realized the benefits of surrendering some portion of their autonomy and self-determination to the cause of international human rights. Likewise, Jewish organizations, certainly not "more sovereign than either the United States or the Soviet Union," could coordinate for particular strategic purposes under the umbrella of the Conference of Presidents without breaching their individual interests or appearing to put their collective loyalties above their American ones.[21]

Klutznick's standing by the early 1960s as an affluent lawyer with a profit-making real estate portfolio, the leader of a major Jewish organization, and a Washington insider recognized for his commitment to the Democratic party, may have been one of the strongest arguments for what he hoped to create on a larger scale: an institutionalized Jewish seat at the table of American political power. To a group of Jewish leaders, he intoned, "Voluntary association is the very bulwark of a democratic society." The ability to fit into the generic structure of a voluntary association would help Jewish philanthropic institutions avoid the taint of illegitimacy, whether from appearing too different from or too cozy with the American state. Even when these institutions were representing interests that may have appeared contrary to those of the American state, they drew power from the ability to express them through a sanctioned and legible structure and to speak with the authority of consensus.[22]

After President Kennedy's election, Klutznick received a certificate of "commendation," signed by the new president to honor "the effort you have expended during the 1960 campaign on my behalf." Beyond the paper

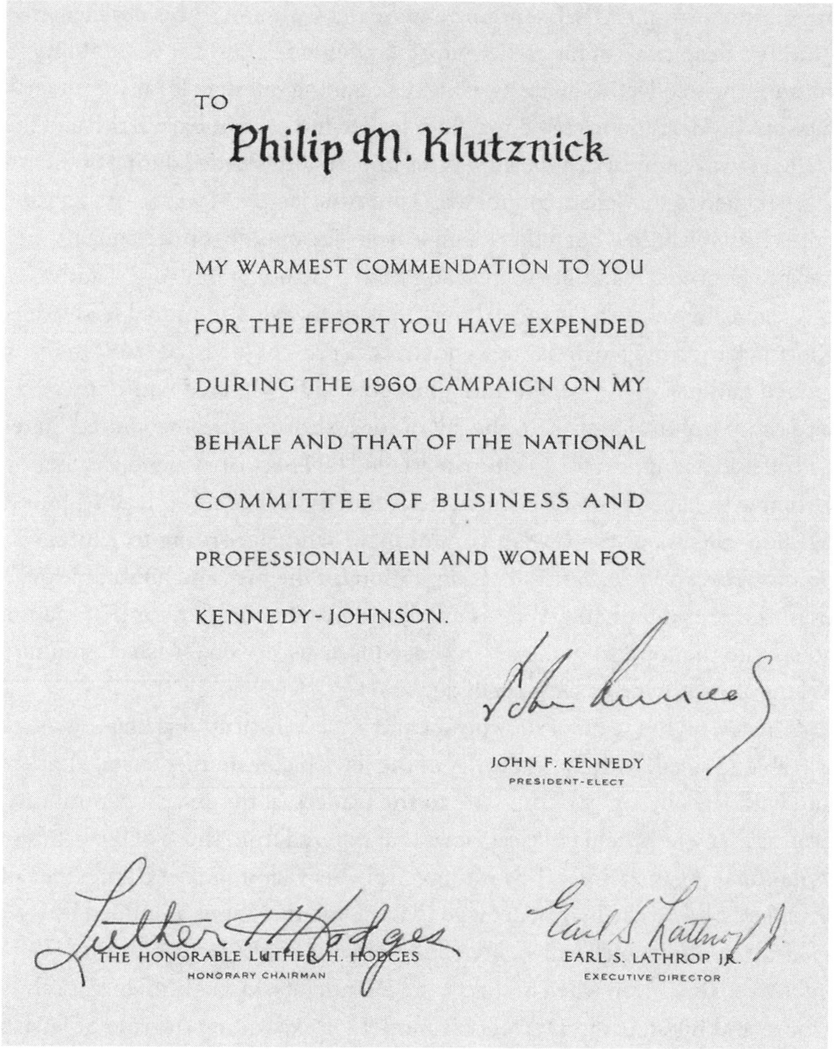

TO

Philip M. Klutznick

MY WARMEST COMMENDATION TO YOU

FOR THE EFFORT YOU HAVE EXPENDED

DURING THE 1960 CAMPAIGN ON MY

BEHALF AND THAT OF THE NATIONAL

COMMITTEE OF BUSINESS AND

PROFESSIONAL MEN AND WOMEN FOR

KENNEDY-JOHNSON.

JOHN F. KENNEDY
PRESIDENT-ELECT

THE HONORABLE LUTHER H. HODGES
HONORARY CHAIRMAN

EARL S. LATHROP JR.
EXECUTIVE DIRECTOR

FIGURE 5.1. Letter of commendation from John F. Kennedy to Philip Klutznick, n.d. [1960], Folder 96, Box 8, Philip Klutznick Papers. Courtesy of the Special Collections Research Center, University of Chicago Library, Chicago, Illinois.

appreciation, Klutznick also gained a toehold in the new administration. In his memoir, Klutznick described receiving a phone call from Sargent Shriver, the president's brother-in-law and one of his advisors, who wanted Klutznick's advice about potential appointees and, then, as the conversation wrapped up, asked directly, "What do *you* want?" The answer came in Klutznick's appointment to the UN Economic and Social Council. At his confirmation hearings, despite all of his earlier efforts to defend American Jews' ability to advance their collective interests while maintaining full state loyalty, Klutznick held out his decision to step down from leadership roles at B'nai B'rith and the United Jewish Appeal as indication of his impartiality. Pushed during questioning, he stated to the Senate committee, "I hope the fact that I was born a Jew, and not a chauvinistic Jew, but rather a simple believing one, does not disqualify me," and he reaffirmed his ability to treat all nations, including Arab ones, fairly.[23]

Even as he vacated his formal positions of Jewish communal leadership, Klutznick used his proximity to Kennedy to represent Jewish interests as both unified and narrowly specific and, thus, able to be satisfied without wading into other political arenas. In the fall of 1963, shortly after the United States had offered its support for an ultimately failed UN Security Council resolution favorable to Israel, Klutznick contacted Kennedy on behalf of "leading public opinion makers of the Jewish community" who, according to Klutznick, "without exception . . . are full of admiration for the firm and honorable position" the president had taken. Kennedy, or any state leader, for that matter, could gain the support of the organized, consensus-driven Jewish community as long as he satisfied a clear set of demands.[24]

Situated on the seam of state power and Jewish institutional life, Klutznick was able to speak with the authority of the Jewish community to state leaders and with the authority of the state to the leaders of the Jewish community, even as many Jews held political views that differed from those of the heads of communal organizations. This was precisely his vision for the Conference of Presidents, which he had analogized to the United Nations as guided by a set of ideals around which a diversity of participants could concur for the sake of influence. Thus, even when his party, the Democrats, lost control of the White House and his status in DC fell, his model for expanding the role of Jewish philanthropic organizations to serve as consolidators of Jewish interests and as conduits for state recognition and influence endured, embodied most clearly by Max Fisher, the Detroit oil and real estate tycoon.

———

In October 1968, Fisher wrote Teddy Kollek, the mayor of Jerusalem, explaining he would be unable to attend an upcoming mission to Israel because "I have become a politician." Well before he sent this missive, Fisher had been politically active. Over the last decade, he had raised significant sums of money for Israel, traveled there to meet with prominent political figures, and become intimate with them (he addressed the mayor "Dear Teddy"). Likewise, he had fund-raised for and befriended high-level American political leaders. To read what he wrote to Kollek, then, one might have guessed he was now running for office, perhaps the one thing he could have done that was more political than what he had already been doing. He was not. He was simply intensifying his political commitments, which now placed him within striking distance—as close as the upcoming election of his candidate, Richard Nixon—of the center of American state power.[25]

Much like Klutznick, Fisher considered himself someone who could consolidate Jewish interests into a unified form, legible and rewarding to American political leaders and expedient for the status of Jewish philanthropic organizations and their leaders. Fisher happened to work through the Republican party, but he rarely drew attention to political ideology. Having served as the president of the United Jewish Appeal and then of the CJFWF, Fisher knew how to raise money and operate across the political spectrum. As he moved into political fund-raising, first as a supporter of George Romney's gubernatorial campaign in Michigan in the early 1960s and then for Nixon, he drew upon his Jewish networks and his particular success supporting partisan ends while avoiding partisanship.

Crucial to Fisher's political success was his ability to maintain the trust of wealthy and communally powerful American Jews from across the country and, primarily, from the opposing side of the political aisle. These Jews knew Fisher less as a Republican and more as a rallying Jewish leader with excellent fund-raising skills. Later he would tell a journalist that it was "obvious" that Jewish political donors would come from the same ranks as those who gave significantly to their Jewish federations and the United Jewish Appeal. Throughout the 1960s, Fisher only reinforced his commitment to controlling the process of consolidating Jewish interests through his leadership of the Conference of Presidents. He did not hide the fact that he raised money and support for the Republican party, but he complemented this work with clear dedication to bolstering a structure that would present a consensus view of Jewish interests to gain influence no matter which party held sway.[26]

In the months before the November 1968 presidential election, the Conference of Presidents arranged meetings with Nixon and his challenger Hubert Humphrey to brief each on matters of Jewish concern, especially related to US-Israel relations. The chairman at the time, Rabbi Herschel Schacter, an Orthodox rabbi, emphasized that member organizations should not seek private audiences with either candidate, implying that Jewish interests would be best served by postures of partisan neutrality and consensus.[27]

Balancing two political mandates, Fisher simultaneously attended Conference of Presidents convenings and tapped his powerful Jewish friends, many of whom led organizations represented in the Conference, to back Nixon. Fisher's public fealty to Nixon and the Republican party, although clearly out of step with the overwhelming majority of American Jews who supported the Democratic party, seemed to have no bearing on his authority within Jewish communal circles. In those places, he was generally appreciated first and foremost for his efforts to advance the interests of American Jews, both through fund-raising and lobbying. At least to Jewish audiences, he always invoked Jewish interests as rising above any particular political loyalty and, as Nixon's Jewish community liaison, he continued to cultivate that image.[28]

In the fall of his first term, Nixon hosted a state dinner for Golda Meir, the new prime minister of Israel. For Fisher, the dinner presented a prime opportunity to improve American Jews' perception of Nixon, and Nixon's perception of American Jews. Despite the president's pragmatism when it came to the Middle East, Fisher attempted to showcase Nixon's affective connection to Israel, believing this would resonate among American Jews and, in turn, help project American Jewish confidence in Nixon back to the president.

Using contact lists from his communal roles, Fisher blasted out thousands of copies of the toast Nixon had delivered at the dinner and suggested that the rabbis and Jewish leaders who received it pass it along to their local Jewish newspapers. He hoped that American Jews far and wide would read the president's welcoming, though ceremonial, words to Meir. Working both ends, Fisher also relayed summaries of Jewish encouragement back to the president, in the process instructing Nixon on how to gain and maintain the support of American Jews. In one memo, Fisher explained to the president that the dinner and toast "had a tremendous impact on the Jewish community," and, in another, wrote that the "warmness" of the evening had left many presidents of Jewish organizations "ecstatic." Finally, as he orchestrated the symbolic significance of this dinner, for American Jews and for the president, Fisher made certain to highlight the value of his own role. Tellingly, in one of his memos to the president, he interjected the first person, explaining he had shared the toast with "a very select group [of Jews] that I have throughout the country." In like fashion, Jewish leaders copied Fisher on their letters of praise to the president, rightly suspecting that Fisher's cognizance of this correspondence was as important as the correspondence itself.[29]

To Max Fisher
With deep appreciation for his loyal support
over the years from his friend,

Richard Nixon

FIGURE 5.2. President Richard Nixon and Max Fisher, 1969, Box 309, Max M. Fisher Papers. Courtesy of the Walter P. Reuther Library, Archives of Labor and Urban Affairs, Wayne State University, Detroit, Michigan.

Fisher threw himself into the task of creating a perception of affection between the president and the Israeli prime minister, and between the president
and American Jews in part because that sense of connection was hardly self-
evident to the president or Jews. At the end of 1969 and beginning of 1970,
Fisher was flooded with letters from Jewish friends, acquaintances, and strang-
ers across the country who were upset that the president appeared to be courting Arab interests. One note, from a rabbi in Connecticut, began bluntly:
"Dear Mr. Fisher, Where are you?" Another, handwritten by a man from a
Detroit suburb, admonished Fisher that as "a highly respected and influential
personality in our community and with pride I might ad [sic] a national figure . . . [you have] the duty to contact our president Mr. Nixon and convince
him how badly Israel needs the friendship of our U.S.A." Some letter writers
strategically divulged that they were just beginning to warm to the Republican
party, even though they had not cast their vote for Nixon in the last election,
but they would surely pull their nascent support if Fisher could not deliver
Nixon's support for Israel.[30]

Certain that his assurance would make a difference, Fisher studiously responded to each letter and enclosed a copy of a statement written in Nixon's
name that emphasized his administration's support for Israel. To the most
prominent letter writers, Fisher added personal notes. For example, in response to a successful businessman and Jewish leader in St. Louis, who had
contributed $25,000 to Nixon's campaign and was now distraught, Fisher re-
sponded, "Ben, the President is a good friend. I can honestly say this to you. I
hope to have the opportunity to visit with you and talk with you 'off the record'
in order to give you a little more background on the relationship between Israel and our country. I am sure you will feel much better after we discuss the
matter."

Fisher fashioned his responses, even when not promising such intimate
knowledge of the White House, to make American Jews feel as if they had
an inside track in Washington and could rest easy knowing that, even when
the news seemed to the contrary, the president's conduit to the Jewish community would safeguard their interests—interests that Fisher had helped
shape to be visible to the American state as consensus Jewish interests. Indeed, Fisher consistently put his standing as a representative of Jewish interests and of the American state on display through the letters he wrote and,
also, his willingness to make invitations to the president to appear at Jewish
communal events (although in most cases, Nixon sent greetings but did not
appear in person).[31]

In early 1970, in response to growing skepticism among American Jewish leaders that the Nixon administration was adequately supportive of Israeli interests, Fisher arranged a meeting between Nixon's secretary of state, William Rogers, and more than forty Jewish men, including leaders of the American Jewish Committee, the United Jewish Appeal, and the Anti-Defamation League, as well as prominent businessmen and lawyers. Press coverage of the closed meeting noted that among the attendees were Democrats and Republicans, but that party affiliation appeared to be checked at the door. One attendee, the former Hollywood studio head and playwright Dore Schary, then acting chairperson of the Anti-Defamation League, described in his *Washington Post* obituary as a "lifelong liberal," observed, "We weren't satisfied with all of [Secretary Rogers's] answers, but we know the administration is conscious of its responsibility." Likewise, another participant, simply described as a Republican, noted that Rogers "put his honor on the line" to promise the group that Nixon's negotiations would never include questioning Israel's sovereignty.[32]

In his account of the meeting to the press, Fisher used the term "grass roots" to characterize the group he gathered, an assertion that strained even the credulity of a reporter who instead described the group as a "blue ribbon" one, comprised of Jewish powerbrokers with access to significant communal and capital resources. Indeed, Fisher's strategy was exactly this: to coordinate the interests of powerful—almost exclusively male—Jews, depict their views as the consensus or "grass roots" concerns of American Jews, and, then, find ways to make them coincident to the interests of the American state. A Kansas City businessman reflected that the private meeting had given him the chance to offer his viewpoint to the secretary of state and left him with the hope that "our expressions of concern will have a positive effect." Others shared his assessment and described themselves as "reassured" by the "civilized meeting."[33]

Watching from the sidelines and across the political aisle, Klutznick wrote an encouraging note to Fisher after learning of the meeting: "I am happy that you are making it possible for some of our people to understand that foreign policy is not made by protest meeting and mimeographed sheets . . . I wish we could train our Jewish leadership to understand the importance of being a bit more sophisticated during this critical, difficult and potential [sic] tragic moment." While Klutznick was no Nixon supporter, he endorsed Fisher's mode of coordinating Jewish interests and asserting influence, a method he had helped shape. So clear was Fisher's position as a molder and representative of putatively consensus Jewish interests that a *New York Times* article from the spring of 1970 noted that, before Nixon made decisions that affected Israel (in this case, a decision to deny Israel's request for more jet fighters), Fisher received word so he could "explain to Jewish leaders around the country" the policy and head off criticism. The reporter observed that the Nixon administration was learning from earlier missteps to keep Fisher in the know: "The gray-haired millionaire [Fisher], who gave more than $107,000 to Republican candidates in 1968, does not have the best credentials with the predominantly Democratic Jewish community. But the response to the jet-sale rejection was muted, in marked contrast to the strongly critical statements that had followed previous Nixon Administration moves."[34]

Although no one could dispute Fisher's partisan loyalties, he gained consistent attention and accolades for his efforts to depict Jewish interests as above politics. In 1970, a few months after organizing the convening with the secretary of state, he coordinated a much more intimate meeting between just a few Jewish leaders and the Nixon administration—and this time, the president himself attended—to discuss the treatment of Jews in the Soviet Union. Lasting about forty-five minutes and hardly a substantive policy discussion, the meeting provided the president with an opportunity to attest to caring about the interests of Jews, and it displayed Jewish interests as sufficiently unified and specific to present in a clear fashion to the president. Press coverage identified Fisher as representing the CJFWF and noted that he attended the meeting alongside Rabbi Herschel Schacter and Dr. William Wexler, both leaders of the Conference of Presidents. Schacter and Wexler were long-time Democrats, but by the time of the 1972 election each would shift his party loyalty to galvanize Jewish support for Nixon's reelection.[35]

Oval office meetings, off-the-record reassurances, greetings conveyed from the president to large Jewish gatherings: these all highlighted to American Jews the value of representing their interests as united and narrowly consolidated in the face of the American state. Fisher carefully curated how Jewish leaders expressed their views and spoke on behalf of American Jews with an eye toward diminishing the perception of politicking and instead highlighting that of collective consensus on particular matters. This approach allowed him to position himself as a fair and politically neutral representative of Jewish interests. Yet, Fisher realized that Nixon's trust in him, while it might have compromised his posture of neutrality, gave him commanding authority among Jewish leaders who relied on him no matter their political affiliations.

Throughout 1972, Fisher worked tirelessly to convert the access to official state power he had offered to Jewish leaders—who attended meetings,

FIGURE 5.3. White House meeting to discuss Soviet Jews, December 1970. From left to right John Ehrlichman, William Rogers, Max Fisher, Rabbi Herschel Schacter, President Richard Nixon, William Wexler, and unidentified participant. Box 306, Max M. Fisher Papers. Courtesy of the Walter P. Reuther Library, Archives of Labor and Urban Affairs, Wayne State University, Detroit, Michigan.

received immediate updates about the president's positions on Jewish interests, and had a channel to voice their concerns—into votes and dollars to
support Nixon's reelection. That spring, he arranged a lunch (with kosher
food) for Nixon to meet the publishers of Jewish newspapers. Even as the
publishers well understood the political gambit as, according to one, "a bold
bid for the Jewish vote," they showed up, and in the months prior to the election, reporters observed a sea change among American Jews, who some ana-
lysts believed just might deliver Nixon double the votes they had given him in
1968. At Fisher's encouragement, a group of prominent Jews, among them
many former Democrats, had thrown themselves into the campaign through
the creation of "Concerned Citizens for the Reelection of the President" and
would continue to drive Jewish support to Nixon. Fisher boasted that his
"work had never been easier" and that he had outraised Jewish contributions
to Nixon's 1968 campaign by more than three times.[36]

Just months before the election, Fisher organized a meeting between the
president and thirty-one Jewish leaders, who Fisher described as half Democrats or Independents, in New York City. Putting his shoulder to the wheel and
using every skill he had honed over his decades of political and communal
organizing, Fisher sought to convince these well-positioned Jewish leaders
that their Jewish interests demanded they rise above their traditional political
loyalties. At the same time, he sought to prove to Nixon that American Jews
would lend him support in return for his good-faith commitment to a small
set of issues. In the briefing he delivered to Nixon and Attorney General John
Mitchell prior to the meeting, Fisher explained he "felt confident" he could
deliver one-third of the Jewish vote and noted that he had already raised $5
million from Jews, even as the American Jewish community "was wrestling
with its own conscience" about leaving the party of FDR. He instructed the
president to address three issues: Soviet Jewry, quotas, and the Middle East.
Finally, he suggested that "if the Jewish community were given greater opportunity to fill jobs in the Administration, it would tie the community in to the
Republican Party on a long-range basis." Pleased, Nixon told Fisher he knew
he had "worked his butt off" and said "there was absolutely no question" that
Fisher would maintain his White House access should he win a second term.[37]

Later in the day, when he met with the group of Jewish leaders, businessmen, and rabbis, Nixon dutifully repeated Fisher's talking points. Hoping to
remind the group of how impressed Jewish leaders had been with the warmth
he showed Golda Meir when he hosted her at a state dinner early in his

administration, the president told the group he wished "to talk to you like I speak to the Prime Minister," and noted, "I have always felt an admiration for the people of Israel." Quickly abandoning the language of emotion for pragmatism, the president then explained to the assembled group "that the interests of the United States foreign policy are served by aiding Israel," and likewise, "If Israel is to survive it is because of the commitment of the United States to it." In similar terms, Nixon also explained he was "totally sympathetic" to the plight of Soviet Jews and asked the leaders to "trust me" to do the right thing. And, finally, when it came to quotas, he listed the individual Jews in his administration as evidence that while he disagreed with the premise of quotas, American Jews as a whole had access to his White House, and then quipped, "If we had a quota for Jews . . . I would be entitled only to ¼ of a Henry Kissinger."[38]

With Fisher's counsel fresh in his mind, Nixon had offered Jewish leaders a clear rationale to support his reelection on the basis of the interests that Fisher had represented to him as matters of consensus, apart from party politics, among American Jews. Measured by the letters of gratitude that streamed into the White House from attendees and others who had read about the meeting in press reports (it was notably well-covered in the Jewish press), Fisher's advice proved sound. The Republican received approximately one-third of the Jewish vote, depending on the source consulted. This was a healthy gain from 1968, much remarked in the press.[39]

A month after the election, Fisher called in the president's debt to him for more political appointments for Jews. In his letter to Nixon's special assistant, Fisher maintained that these appointments would be as beneficial to American Jews as they were to the future of the Republican party. He wrote, "[M]y principle [sic] concern is to tie in to the Administration on a permanent basis the large vote we generated in the Jewish community during the campaign. I indicated to them at that time that they would have a place for input." Hardly masking the quid pro quo, Fisher concluded by affirming his intention to remain in place as a liaison to the Jewish community and then presented a list of twenty-three names, divided into first and second priorities. Each of the men (not one woman appeared) had been active in supporting Nixon's reelection, and many had attended meetings with him. True to form, Fisher listed each man's qualifications and his prominence in the Jewish community, and then made special note of those who had been Democrats, including Dr. William Wexler and Rabbi Herschel Schacter, the men who had attended an intimate meeting with the president in 1970.[40]

To Max Fisher

Jimmy Carter

FIGURE 5.4. Cabinet Room meeting between President Jimmy Carter and Jewish leaders, with Max Fisher seated on the far left, fourth from the front, July 6, 1977, Box 309, Max M. Fisher Papers. Courtesy of the Walter P. Reuther Library, Archives of Labor and Urban Affairs, Wayne State University, Detroit, Michigan.

Shortly after Nixon's reelection, however, Fisher's loyalty to the president would jeopardize his strategy of presenting a political face to the president but a far more consensus-driven and depoliticized one to Jewish philanthropic leaders. During the Watergate scandal, and even after Nixon's resignation, Fisher offered dogged support for the man, so much so that when audio evidence of Nixon's use of antisemitic slurs came to light, Fisher blasted, "I did not think there was anything wrong with it even if Mr. Nixon did use those slang terms. Hell, we all do the same thing once in awhile." In a memo marked "Eyes Only" penned well after he had resigned from office, Nixon noted that chief among Fisher's strengths—which included knowing "Israel government leaders intimately" and his "enormous contributions on the fundraising front"—was the basic fact that "he is one of those rare individuals supporting Israel's position who can always be counted upon for total, loyal support for whatever decision is made by the Administration."[41]

As much as Fisher may have proved Nixon a good judge of character, his unswerving loyalty to Nixon was ultimately less significant than his effort to construct a Jewish consensus around a clear set of issues that he sought to portray as beyond politics. To be certain, his aim was to drive the consensus in the direction of the Republican party, and he made no effort to hide this. However, for all of his dedication to the Republican party, Fisher envisioned a future in which the exponents of a Jewish consensus could gain a hearing no matter which party controlled the White House, just as long as they could make the case that they were representing Jewish interests. He invested in structures, such as the Conference of Presidents, that would outlast any particular presidential administration, and he built the precedent for a class of Jews to expect that they could translate some element of their standing in the Jewish community as philanthropic leaders into stature and influence in the eyes of the state. Even in the early 1980s, when Fisher would play an instrumental role in creating the Republican Jewish Coalition, he continued to believe that core Jewish interests, in Israel and in the survival of the Jewish people, rose above politics but also depended upon the ability to influence them. This was the strange logic of mid- to late-twentieth-century depoliticized politics that demanded collectives disavow politics at the very same time that it embedded them deeply within a political structure of power.

———

A month after Nixon's reelection, Fisher received a note from Philip Bernstein, the executive vice president of the CJFWF, asking for his assistance blocking pending tax legislation that once again appeared to target charitable benefits. Fisher had no particular expertise in these matters, but the play was an obvious one: Fisher had received significant assistance from prominent Jews with ties to federations, so here was a federation leader asking for his due. The executive concluded his plea, "Your own help on this will be uniquely valuable." Fisher was no Norman Sugarman, but what he could not offer in expertise, he could provide through connections to state political leaders. Bernstein included briefs on several bills introduced in Congress that would limit or abolish the charitable deduction and posed a threat to the federation. Central to the federation's defense was its assertion that "charity is not a loophole," and, thus, that any tax bills concerned with foreclosing abuses of the tax system were looking in the wrong place if they focused on charity.[42]

Whether a loophole or not, as soon as charitable donations and institutions received special tax treatment, charity became an instrument of the American state and, thus, fundamentally political. Much as Fisher hoped to designate consensus Jewish interests as removed from the American political process, all the while pressing for their consideration in state affairs, the contradictory impulses to name philanthropy as removed from politics while simultaneously demanding its special treatment under tax law revealed the logic of depoliticized politics. Jewish philanthropic leaders knew that in order to sustain their efforts, they could not focus on donations alone. Rather, they had to cultivate policies, laws, and practices to prove that philanthropic growth was necessary to the American political and economic order. In other words, they had to continue to work to find those points of intersection, where state power and what Jewish leaders and their institutions tried to define as consensus Jewish interests could overlap in mutually reinforcing ways, just as Fisher had hoped to do through the Nixon administration.

The Jewish leaders who Fisher brought into the room with Nixon and, more generally, offered a seat at the American political table were all tied to American Jewish philanthropy and its transforming logic in the 1960s and early 1970s. Many of them were presidents of large Jewish institutions that participated in the Conference of Presidents, and almost all of them, like Fisher, had learned how to access state power through their communal organizations. Reflecting Congress's efforts to classify only a narrow band of associational activity as political, these leaders operated within a political economy that confined politics in such a way as to make it feasible and desirable to consolidate Jewish interests into the shape of a consensus, putatively nonideological and nonpolitical.

Depoliticized politics operated in tandem with a new set of financial strategies that over the coming decades would similarly enable philanthropic entities to consolidate and accumulate capital strength, while maintaining a guise of operating outside of the world of profit and finance. On both counts, political and economic, philanthropic organizations in the United States were able to exercise influence without having to reckon with how much their strength relied upon the particular organization of American state power that flowed toward their benefit and, notably, less and less toward the benefit of other sectors of the American public that were not organized into well-capitalized state-related associations. By the late 1960s and, then, increasingly throughout the 1970s and 1980s, the American regulatory state favored private capital growth through new policies. Economists note that in these same decades, the inequality index—the size of the gap between the wealthiest and the rest—turned upward, reflecting the financial and political policies that invested public trust in private entities to accumulate power.[43]

The political consolidation of Jewish communal life that Fisher helped achieve would fall far short of Klutznick's vision to unify Jewish concerns under the umbrella of presidents of Jewish organizations, but it would gain sustenance from state policies that encouraged financial and political consolidation. The forms of Jewish political life appeared tangled and diverse throughout the late 1960s and 1970s, especially as Jews learned the language and politics of identity. Yet the financial and political organization of Jewish communal life tended toward consolidation, an order—and an emergent complex— limned by state regulations that set and reinforced these patterns.

6

Finance and Identity

IN NOVEMBER 1969, a band of young Jewish activists staged a protest at that year's General Assembly, a national convening of federation professionals and leaders hosted by the CJFWF. While their strategy of choice was a sign of their countercultural times, their core demands betrayed their reverence for the culture of philanthropic capital and their belief in its unrivaled power to set the Jewish community's agenda.

When Gordon Zacks, a wealthy businessman and federation leader from Columbus, Ohio, learned of the students' plans, he agitated to give them an official slot on the conference agenda. Recalling "a tremendous sense of uptightness" among the two thousand Jewish philanthropic professionals and lay leaders who had gathered for the General Assembly, Zacks understood that walling out the students would only cause tensions to mount and would fuel the students' grievances. Also, by some accounts, he harbored his own disgruntlement with national federation leaders, so may have relished the chance to see some of them squirm.[1]

As busloads of students, armed with leaflets and signs that read "Don't Let Us Perish" and "Support for Jewish Education Is Support for Israel," appeared outside of the Boston Sheraton, one of their leaders left the fray to take the stage inside. Hillel Levine, an ordained rabbi and a graduate student at Harvard, began his remarks with a placating tone: "We see ourselves as your children, the children of Jews who with great dedication concern themselves with the needs of the community, the children of Jews who bring comfort to the afflicted, give aid to the poor, who have built mammoth philanthropic organizations . . . who give more per capita to charity than any other group in America."[2]

But who better to see their parents' flaws than children? Just as Levine appeared to humble himself before his elders, who perhaps would have exhaled and basked in the praise, he flipped the script, trading admiration for indignant rebuke. "We want to participate with you in the building of a vision of a great Jewish community. It is when we think of this that we become dismayed with the reality of Jewish life," a reality he described as full of "crass materialism" paraded in the "multi-million-dollar Jewish presence" in American suburbs. Jewish federations across the country raised almost $300 million collectively, with tens of millions more enriching new endowments: everywhere they looked, the young protestors saw Jewish money, but they accused its stewards of using it in all the wrong places. Funds were sent off to agencies "deficient in Jewish education" and to programs bereft of Jewish "identity," a word that would come to define the future of Jewish philanthropic practice.[3]

With the air of an expert and the sharp tongue of a critic, Levine pro-nounced, "[I]dentities are based on ideologies and experiences and neither can be offered by Jewish swimming pools and game rooms." He may have been shocked to hear the raucous applause that followed his speech. But hardly missing a beat, Zacks, the Ohio man who had given Levine his platform, pro-posed setting aside $100 million in an endowment for a new "national founda-tion for developing Jewish identity."[4]

For however much Levine and his comrades had thumbed their noses at the elders' materialism, they endorsed the capitalist logic of American Jewish phi-lanthropy and, in fact, helped craft the case for a new mode of Jewish philan-thropic practice, where capital would accumulate and grow for the sake of an always moving future of enriched Jewish identity. As an observer of the student activists noted, the protestors "dwell in the America of capitalism, the Constitu-tion, Coca-Cola and flush toilets. They must deal with material richness and a paucity of spiritual leadership in the larger Jewish and surrounding communi-ties. They need new liturgies and income-tax exemptions. . . . They are, after all, thoroughly Americanized." Thus, they wagered on Jewish philanthropy as, ac-cording to that same observer, the "political process that is prerequisite to ob-taining allocations." Their bet was validated by the applause Levine received, Zacks's pie-in-the-sky resolution, and, in the long term, the emergence of future-looking, identity-building projects as the anchor of Jewish philanthropy.[5]

The new financial logic of Jewish philanthropy came to take as one of its core rationales the mandate to capitalize identity for the future by pulling back from rapid distribution and, instead, moving toward accumulation and growth. But this logic would have faltered absent changes in American political economy and absent American Jewish leaders' investment in lobbying for those changes through channels they had established to consolidate Jewish political influence and insulate it from appearing tendentiously political. At the same 1969 General Assembly, the convened body passed a resolution to redouble its tax lobbying efforts. Its statement read, "Our Jewish Federations and Welfare Funds, and the millions of dependent people assisted by our organizations along with many organizations and individuals have a profound stake in tax laws affecting philanthropic gifts." The resolution set out the five "principles" of effective charitable tax legislation, including maintaining and extending "tax incentives to greater charitable giving" and considering charitable deductions as "separate from all other provisions affecting tax deductions, with which they have nothing in common."[6]

Throughout the 1960s and 1970s, the interweaving of two emerging trends—the rise of identity politics and the emboldened financialized logic of American statecraft—transformed the nature of American Jewish philanthropy. During those decades, the American state continued to pursue a course set in the New Deal and immediate post–World War II period of liberal expansion, but did so increasingly through outsourcing its power to private entities, through public-private partnerships, and through policies of financial deregulation and so-called market freedom. The project of funding Jewish identity was rooted in this political economy.[7]

In order to understand the interlacing of finance and Jewish identity within philanthropy, one must be precise. At issue is not simply money and Jewishness, but rather the practices, as shaped by historical contingencies, that Jewish leaders, Jewish communal entities, and state bodies developed to manage finance and identity. This is very different from saying that the way any individual might identify as Jewish is an outgrowth of finance—or, conversely, that finance is an outgrowth of how an individual might identify as Jewish. Either of these formulations is historically and interpretively vacuous, at best. Instead, here I show how the practices that Jewish philanthropic professionals and their funders developed in the 1960s and 1970s to fund something called identity stitched together financial strategies, political influence, and the concept of Jewish identity in a mutually constitutive fashion limned by state structures and policies. In motion, we can witness the emergence of the American Jewish philanthropic complex.

————

The students in Boston had a tangible result in mind for their 1969 activism: to capture new streams of funding for Jewish identity projects. But contrary to the portrait of neglect they painted, well before the protestors descended upon the General Assembly, federations had started to direct notable sums to fund what leaders variously termed "Jewish culture" and "Jewish identification." Although any number of activities, from sports teams to discussion groups to dance classes, could fit under those rubrics, the percentage of total federation allocations earmarked for "cultural recreational activities" increased from 9.6% in 1935 to 17% in 1945. This trend only accelerated in the 1960s and 1970s, according to studies that drilled down into spending patterns and focused on educational initiatives in particular. A 1968 survey reported that the fifteen largest federations had designated more than one-quarter of their allocations in 1968 to Jewish education. The next year (six months before the 1969 General Assembly), in a discussion of future funding priorities, a New York federation board member called for even more of an "intensification" of Jewish educational programs. Noting that "Blacks, Spanish-Americans, and other ethnic and cultural minorities" were exploring their own cultures, he argued, "Such education will be a unifying force in furnishing our future generations with their necessary identity as Jews notwithstanding [the] diversity of their beliefs and practices."[8]

Jewish identity may have been a problem that philanthropists hoped to solve—how to make Jews act and feel more Jewish—but it also offered a solution to a different puzzle about the purpose of Jewish philanthropy in an era of abundance. As more Jews had access to wealth, their demands on Jewish social welfare agencies decreased. Furthermore, the sorts of agencies that Jews had long funded, from hospitals to vocational training programs to poverty relief services for families and children to refugee resettlement organizations, were newly eligible for government grants. These grants enriched agencies' access to capital without depleting Jewish philanthropic dollars, but also tended to come with requirements to serve populations beyond the Jewish community. In short, Jewish philanthropic entities stood to have more access to Jewish donor dollars just as they seemed to need them the least. And, over the long term, Jewish communal leaders feared that this fact would only exacerbate the conclusions of a slew of sociological surveys in the 1950s and 1960s that Jewish assimilation—which, among other indicators, would be marked by the dissolution of Jewish communal agencies—would be an inevitable outgrowth of socioeconomic comfort in the United States.[9]

Identity provided an elegant solution to the puzzle of Jewish philanthropic purpose in a time of plenty. A nebulous concept, rooted in midcentury psychological and sociological theory, identity was capacious, yet measurable through specific markers, and its philanthropic demands could be similarly broad, with long time horizons, while still calculable. Best of all, when wedded together, one could fuel the other. In the 1950s, adopting language from developmental psychologists such as Jewish-born Erik Erikson, Jewish social workers wrote about philanthropy as fostering "positive Jewish identification" through "an indigenous American-Jewish cultural heritage," and noted the importance of supporting a "group identity–group survival model" that, as one federation professional in Chicago explained in 1956, would "become constructively concerned with the cultural and educational wellbeing of the normal Jewish population." Similarly, as a professor of social work and a federation staff member observed in 1959, Jewish fund-raising, beyond generating money for important causes, also carried "functional significance" as "the means by which millions of Americans visibly identify themselves as Jewish, as belonging to an entity known as the 'Jewish community.'" No matter what the dollars ended up doing—supporting agencies that served broad non-Jewish populations, funding programs thousands of miles away in Israel, or capitalizing endowments established for perpetuity—the very act of raising them served identity-building purposes.[10]

An early indication of Jewish philanthropic bodies' shift toward identity work, and the ways in which financial practices guided and reflected that shift, can be found in the inception of the National Foundation for Jewish Culture. In its establishment, the National Foundation for Jewish Culture conceived of culture as an identity instrument dependent upon long-term investments, even as some of its founders also appreciated culture for its non-instrumental purposes.

In 1959, the General Assembly of the CJFWF voted to create the National Foundation for Jewish Culture in the wake of a year-long "National Cultural Study." The report, produced under the direction of federation leaders from almost every large and midsize Jewish city, with technical advice from scholars and rabbis and staff support from the federation's national office, described traditional Jewish philanthropy as oriented around "humanitarian needs, material and spiritual, at home and abroad," and averred that "national cultural efforts" were glaringly absent from this kind of philanthropy. The authors argued that the time had come for American Jews, well accustomed to contributing to "overpowering needs dramatically presented," to turn their largesse to funding the less urgent but equally important project of Jewish culture.[11]

In the words of the study, the rise of Jewish culture in the United States would serve as proof of the movement of American Jewish life beyond its first "frontier" stage of material need and crisis. The authors wrote, "As in all frontier societies, fundamental services had to be created first—care for the aged, the orphaned and the sick. . . . Central communal structures to collect and disperse funds and to plan for communal needs soon followed. All these institutions are of course 'cultural' in the broad meaning of that term and undoubtedly they form the necessary foundation on which cultural institutions in the more specific meaning can be built." But despite the authors' acknowledgment of blurred categories, they embraced a civilizing model: "We have now reached the stage in Jewish life when our religious and communal organizations and our health and welfare institutions have been so developed that the American Jewish community is in a position to extend its interests in a comparably serious manner to the cultural field."[12]

Looming over the report, however, was a different rationale, tied to exigencies of the recent past more than civilizing projects, for supporting Jewish cultural creation in the United States. No matter how "reluctant American Jewry" may be or how it may feel "it is being forced into cultural maturity almost against its will," the authors insisted that there was no longer any other Jewish community in the world more able to cultivate Jewish culture than the American one. Some of the authors may have hoped that the new Jewish state would start to produce Jewish culture, but few believed it had the stability or riches to step into the immense void left by the destruction of European Jewish life. In clear terms, they pressed their case, noting that the "survival" of the Jewish people depended upon this initiative and without it, Jewish life would meet a certain fate of "impoverish[ment]," of an existential if not material variety. Averting cultural deprivation would demand a different set of philanthropic tools than confronting material poverty had, but the authors explained that the need was no less grave. Jewish culture required a new "face" and "address" that reflected American Jews' "genius for organization" and their material abundance.[13]

During its first years, which were almost exclusively devoted to fostering Jewish scholarship and research, more than fifty different federations contributed to the National Foundation for Jewish Culture, earmarking funds as they did for any other federation-supported agencies. But before too long, its board realized that in order to succeed, the organization had to break the mold of typical federation funding. The president, a Philadelphian named Edwin Wolf, who was active in the city's federation and instrumental in rebuilding the Library Company of Philadelphia, chided the board in 1961 for "sitting around talking about the Foundation as though it were another philanthropic agency like those we've been dealing with for a long time." To fund Jewish culture, Wolf argued, the group had to act like a real foundation. (Despite its name, it technically was not one.) He explained, first and foremost, "A Foundation has an awful lot of money," not to spend immediately but to use as a source of autonomy and long-term sustainability. What he called the "chicken feed" method of asking for small allocations from federations and donors would never allow the organization to build the corpus it needed in order to free Jewish culture from fickle funding cycles and from the narrow range of activities currently pursued.[14]

Wolf's call for the National Foundation for Jewish Culture to behave like a foundation was a significant statement about the changing nature of philanthropic finance. From his position as president of Philadelphia's federation, Wolf knew well that even federations were gradually ceding their old model of philanthropic finance, with its money-in and money-out logic, and instead embracing endowment-building and other practices to ensure long-term capital accumulation and growth. In other words, he knew that federations were gradually coming to resemble private foundations. He envisioned the National Foundation for Jewish Culture as leading this charge, unimpeded by the weight of tradition under which federations struggled. More substantively, he also maintained that cultural funding was different from material-needs funding. Cultural projects demanded abiding investment and freedom to develop over time, without the pressure of donor validation at every turn and without the expectation that funds would be spent immediately or evenly.[15]

With aspirations of eventually raising their own endowment, the leaders of the National Foundation for Jewish Culture assiduously tracked endowment growth among the federations in large cities and sent targeted letters to those federations, hoping they would agree to designate a portion of their endowments to create a sustainable funding base—a corpus—for the new organization. Detroit and Cleveland quickly volunteered to provide short-term support from their endowments but would not agree to any perpetual arrangements unless they were joined by other federations. This proved to be impossible. The executive director of the federation in Los Angeles, for example, explained that his community was "preoccupied with building our own unrestricted Endowment Fund," so would be unable to deplete that fund through a grant to the National Foundation. He noted that should he run across endowment donors "who are especially interested in Jewish Education and Jewish Culture," he would mention the possibility of creating a "direct bequest or a bequest to our own Jewish Community Foundation which can make some provision for the National Foundation for Jewish Culture," but he could not commit to anything beyond this.[16]

By the late 1960s, the board of the National Foundation for Jewish Culture intensified its effort to raise endowment funds but abandoned its hope of capturing those funds from federations, instead shifting its sights to private family foundations with track records of supporting arts and culture initiatives. Yet if potential donors thought the National Foundation was simply an arm of the federation, they would likely be confused by separate solicitations, a concern that led the board to differentiate the organization from federations, in part by expanding its cultural purview beyond research and scholarship and toward the arts more broadly.

Extending the civilizing language from the initial report that had established the National Foundation, a new proposal penned in the mid-1970s suggested that since the Six-Day War in 1967, the communal Jewish "body" had developed "more sophisticated needs" than either material or research ones and was now "ready to be served by art of Jewish force and focus." "Painters, sculptors, musicians, poets, dancers, choreographers, composers," and other artists could help American Jews attain this next level of development, but only if the Jewish "body" also matured beyond the collectivist approach to its material resources, characterized by federations that raised capital exclusively to serve broad Jewish needs. "For its own well-being the Jewish community—made somewhat lopsided by its very mandatory success as an organization capable of tapping and channeling its collective financial resources—requires the leaven and the liberty of private Jewish voices." In other words, unleashing the individual to create Jewish art also required untethering the individual from the communal capital process. Identity, like finance, could not grow in a purely collectivist system.[17]

In braiding together finance and identity, through the rubric of cultural production, the National Foundation for Jewish Culture redirected Jewish philanthropy away from present wealth distribution and toward capital accumulation. However, its efforts made sense only within the context of broad shifts in the American political economy that validated the organization's claims of the deficiencies of collective economic modes and of the efficiencies of liberating individuals to use their citizenship, their creativity, and their capital in the name of collective benefit.

Identity discourse, as it developed in the 1960s through the framework of culture and individualism, corresponded with a liberal understanding of the sovereign self, able to move through the world and make choices absent coercion, whether from the state or other powerful forces. Parlayed into institutional contexts, such as a National Foundation for Jewish Culture, the claims of identity merged with the logic of midcentury capitalism, both of which idealized the capacity of private entities to do the most good when set free.[18]

———

In 1969, as Congress deliberated over a sweeping set of tax reforms, Jewish philanthropic leaders jumped into the political fray as never before, motivated by a commitment to protecting philanthropic capital. They lobbied Congress, wrote drafts of legislative proposals, petitioned the IRS for rulings, formed coalitions with non-Jewish charitable organizations, and built new charitable structures. Unsurprisingly, the former IRS staff attorney Norman Sugarman stood at the helm of these efforts. He used his well-regarded expertise in charitable tax law, his connections in the Department of the Treasury, and his professional and voluntary role as counsel for Cleveland's Jewish federation and the national CJFWF to create a movement to broaden state benefits for publicly minded private endeavors and capital, a movement that resembled the National Foundation for Jewish Culture's call to support "the liberty of private Jewish voices."

Sugarman, similar to many other midcentury policymakers, maintained that the private sector's freedom was so valuable that the public sector should invest in it. The ironies of setting free private enterprises by subsidizing them with public dollars had already been visible in the framework of state-based associationalism but only became etched more deeply into American statecraft in the twentieth century, as the American state simultaneously gained and outsourced power. Like many of his contemporaries addressing private industry, Sugarman found himself in the position of advising governmental restraint when it came to private regulation, but activism when it came to private subsidy. In February 1969, for example, appearing before the House Ways and Means Committee as he had several times already over the decade, Sugarman professed, "I believe that a sound principle is that legislative solutions which restrict the private sector of our economy should be imposed only with respect to problems requiring resolution and should go no further than the specific bounds of those problems."[19]

A few days after Sugarman's 1969 appearance before Congress, the president of the CJFWF testified, repeating many of Sugarman's specific talking points about the problems with regulating philanthropy, but concluding with a far more transparent statement of what he, in fact, wanted from government: "We would strongly urge that no deterrents be placed in the way of existing tax incentives to giving and that such incentives be extended to encourage even more generous contributions." In a clear bid to shift the balance of congressional energy toward private incentive and away from public regulation, the president asked for the carrots without the sticks.[20]

Yet from the moment Congress passed the first federal income tax in 1913, politicians had issued perennial calls to tighten regulations on philanthropy, often as a way to position themselves as populists, against governmental pork and patronage. More posture than policy, these calls resulted only in narrow legislative tweaks (such as the new rules limiting political engagement), but by 1969, the desire for philanthropic reform appeared as fierce as it had ever been. Alongside new growth in the philanthropic sector, the fact that more and more Americans had become subject to the income tax alerted a broad portion of the American population to the potential inequities—what President Truman had called "loopholes" in his 1950 address to Congress—in systems of economic distribution. Directly focusing Congress's attention on philanthropy were a series of legislative proposals the Treasury Department released in 1965 to address what it deemed were the worst philanthropic abuses, from self-dealing (receiving private benefit from philanthropic gifts) to the excessive accumulation of charitable capital to charities' involvements in business interests "unrelated" to their charitable purposes.[21]

Congress's concern for philanthropic abuses appeared primarily limited to private foundations, but because existing legislation did not include clear statutory definition of private foundations, all philanthropic entities were on high alert as the House set to work on tax reform in 1969. In their efforts to defend the freedoms and privileges of philanthropy, American Jewish leaders collaborated with other charitable entities, helping to nurture a self-conscious and unified American philanthropic sector. In the winter of 1969, the CJFWF announced its intention to form a partnership "with other major welfare and health organizations . . . with educational, cultural and church bodies which would be affected by any changes in tax provisions." As the group formed, it issued a joint statement that maintained, "It is not the intent of the Federal government in 1969 to impair the strength of our charitable agencies, our private hospitals, private universities, museums, symphony orchestras or our religious institutions. It is these very institutions, painstakingly and devotedly built up through the years, that help keep our country strong and add to our democratic way of life."[22]

On the local level, comparable partnerships across philanthropic entities emerged. For example, Cleveland federation staff joined forces with the United Appeal of Greater Cleveland, Case Western University, John Carroll University, Catholic Charities, and the Cleveland Foundation to lobby Congress along similar lines, with the intent to persuade legislators that their efforts to regulate philanthropy were misguided and against the interests of the public good.[23]

Jewish federation leaders across the country increasingly depended on Sugarman to guide them in the art of political lobbying and coalition-building. They relied on his connections, often through his client base, to non-Jewish philanthropic organizations and also to key political operatives. "As you know," a staff member in Cleveland wrote to a lawyer and lay leader in the community in the summer of 1969, "Norm Sugarman keeps in close touch with the tax reform developments in Washington." Cleveland's federation served as a conduit between Sugarman and national federation headquarters, a role that allowed Cleveland to solidify its own position of national leadership when it came to philanthropic policy and strategy. Correspondence between the national office and Cleveland flew back and forth almost daily throughout 1969 as the two worked in tandem to share information and develop strategies. Sugarman had little doubt that Congress would pass new regulations, but he also believed that with proper pressure and legislative savvy, those regulations could be limited in scope and open to credible interpretations that just might open new avenues for philanthropic creativity.[24]

Throughout the spring and summer of 1969, most concerning to Sugarman were House proposals to reform tax rules for gifts on appreciated property that he believed would have a chilling effect on endowment-building. According to statistics compiled by the CJFWF, gifts of appreciated property, ranging from stock to real estate to art, accounted for up to one-quarter of local federations' income and supported many of their endowment efforts. For many years, the tax treatment of these gifts had reflected a hybrid form of valuation that allowed donors to declare the property's initial value for the purposes of capital gains assessment (meaning there would be no gains to report or pay taxes on), but to use its final value, which included whatever appreciation had occurred, to claim a tax deduction. From drafts of new legislation, Sugarman knew that Congress was targeting just these sorts of tax preferences, and he was certain that if Congress reversed its hybrid treatment of gifts of appreciated property, the philanthropic world would suffer losses. He had already thrown his weight behind endowment as the wave of the philanthropic future, a calculation largely based upon his assessment that donors to endowments could gain substantial benefits from placing large noncash gifts in endowments. Absent this incentive, he knew his case in favor of endowment would fall flat.[25]

Following Sugarman's advice, on the eve of the House vote in early June 1969, the executive vice president of Cleveland's federation sent a telegram to Congressman Charles Vanik, a Democrat who represented many of the Jewish neighborhoods in Cleveland and with whom federation leaders had established close lines of communication: "Present proposals on tax treatment of charitable gifts of appreciated property would have catastrophic effect on [the] ability of this Federation and comparable organizations to meet human needs." At the national level, Louis J. Fox, the president of the CJFWF (Max Fisher would assume the office later that year), similarly instructed the leaders of every local federation to lobby their elected officials. He supplied scripts for them to use in phone calls and letters that highlighted the detrimental effects of "proposals to tax appreciated securities," and he instructed them to focus special attention on members of key House and Senate committees. Almost certainly referring to Sugarman, he emphasized, "We are told by our friends in Washington that the people who will make and influence the decision there have not been hearing from their constituents around the country."[26]

As Sugarman helped coordinate a broad-based but focused lobbying campaign, he also fixed his attention on two preemptive efforts to neutralize the most damaging effects that legislative reform might have on his clients. First, he told federation leaders to prepare for the worst that the new legislation could bring. A lawyer who worked alongside Sugarman and often provided advice to Cleveland's federation wrote to the staff, "Under these circumstances, this might represent the last opportunity for a taxpayer to avail himself of the right to dispose of appreciated property, deduct the full value thereof without taking into income any portion of the appreciated value of the property." Therefore, the lawyer suggested federation staff might use the threat of legislative reform to nudge on-the-fence donors to make significant gifts of appreciated property while the favorable tax treatment lasted.[27]

Sugarman's second move was to enter the process of lawmaking himself. He started to feed Congress language that intentionally created an opening for a new legal strategy he was devising to protect philanthropic capital, including gifts of appreciated property, from extractive regulations and other disincentives. He had glimpsed the availability of this strategy in Congress's clumsy attempts to differentiate among types of charitable entities. In its hearings on philanthropy over prior decades, Congress had almost exclusively focused on private foundations, and, likewise, Treasury's 1965 report had limited almost all of its recommendations to private foundations. But even as it leaned on the distinction between private foundations and other kinds of charities, Congress still had never defined the line with statutory precision. As Sugarman closely monitored Congress's actions throughout the winter and spring of 1969, he realized just how much hinged upon that distinction. A tax attorney like Sugarman could foresee the necessity of legislating around it and could help guide Congress's hand to offer the broadest possible privileges to those charitable entities, termed "public charities," that fell outside the classification of private foundations.[28]

———

By the fall of 1969, with a tax reform bill out of the House and into the Senate, observers could feel confident that as much as the Senate might refine elements of its approach to philanthropy, the division between private foundations and public charities would serve as its architecture. All philanthropic entities would be sorted between the two categories, with those that met the criteria for public charities receiving more favorable treatment and being subject to fewer regulations. Until the final legislation passed, no one could be certain what benefits public charities would receive, but those who paid attention realized that falling on the public side of the divide would bring notable privileges.

On the face of it, Jewish charitable organizations, from federations to defense organizations to international aid institutions to social welfare agencies, all seemed to meet the threshold for classification as public charities. According to precedent, these sorts of organizations had already qualified for favorable treatment, such as allowing donors to deduct a higher percentage of their adjusted gross income for gifts made to them. By category (for example, hospitals, churches, or schools) and by operation, many Jewish charitable organizations had simply assumed the benefits of public status. Yet, as the new law appeared intent on divvying the charitable world into public charities and private foundations and apportioning treatment accordingly, it drew scrutiny to the dividing line and, especially, to those activities that might compromise a public charity's status.[29]

Here, in Congress's promise to pay greater attention to charitable classification, Sugarman's commitment to endowment-building, especially through creative and donor-directed approaches, appeared on a collision course with the new tax law. Already the House bill revealed the intent of Congress to keep philanthropic accumulation in check by requiring private foundations— defined by their inability to qualify for public charitable status—to spend a certain percentage of their assets each year, to pay an excise tax on investment income, and to adhere to caps on tax-deductible gifts of appreciated property. Where would this leave public charities' endowments, particularly restricted funds such as the philanthropic funds that Cleveland's federation had so enthusiastically marketed to its donors as providing them with a measure of autonomy—like a private foundation held—over their funds and with advantageous tax benefits, especially when it came to donations of appreciated property?[30]

Worried that the growing sum of assets their federation now held in philanthropic funds might put its tax treatment in jeopardy, Cleveland's staff and leadership sought legal opinions and received dispiriting advice throughout the summer and early fall of 1969. A local lawyer who worked closely with Sugarman and was a federation donor speculated, "In my opinion, the private trusts established with the Federation as trustee come within the definition of private foundations as contained in the Bill." Grimly, he outlined exactly how these philanthropic funds, if treated as private foundations, would lose their favorable tax treatment and flexibility. The benefits that had so easily sold Cleveland leaders on the philanthropic fund and that had been touted at national meetings to other federation leaders would wither under the new tax regime.[31]

Unsurprisingly, Cleveland's concerns filtered up to national leadership at the CJFWF. Over the last decade and often in communication with Cleveland, its leaders had also gradually embraced endowment, forming new committees to survey endowment growth and recommend investment policies, organizing sessions at national conferences to share models for raising endowments, and publishing materials devoted to helping federation offices establish a variety of endowment funds. If the new tax law required federations to partition certain endowment accounts, especially the increasingly popular philanthropic funds, from their other assets and treat them as if they were private foundations, then donors and federations would likely balk, and a decade's worth of work—and capital—would be seriously compromised. The only person federation leaders trusted to remedy the situation was the same person who had helped lead them into it: Sugarman.

In close communication with Philip Bernstein, the executive vice president of the CJFWF who had begun his federation career in Cleveland, Sugarman spent the fall of 1969 redrafting sections of the House bill with an eye toward ensuring that federations could retain their full public charitable status while continuing to hold philanthropic funds. Relying on information from a handful of senators with whom the national federation office had strong relationships, Bernstein learned that with some delicate editing work to the bill, the Senate might be amenable to giving public charities significantly more latitude to hold gifts of appreciated property and other capital in endowment without breaching their public classification. Writing to the Cleveland office, Bernstein emphasized his hope that "Norm could suggest specific language which would accomplish what the senators want."[32]

By the time President Nixon signed the Tax Reform Act into law at the end of 1969, Sugarman's modifications had made their way into it. As his clients would come to see, his language made it reasonable to interpret the legislation as approving public charities' ability to absorb gifts of appreciated property, including private foundations, without compromising the favorable tax treatment they received, even if they designated these gifts as part of restricted endowment funds named for individual donors. This was in distinction to private foundations, which under the new law became subject to regulations aimed to thwart their excessive accumulation of capital through annual spend-out requirements and excise taxes on investment earnings, and a considered, though not ultimately legislated, measure to limit their lifespan. With a sense of satisfaction, the Budget Research Department of the CJFWF concluded, "The relative harshness of the House of Representatives' bill was ameliorated," and "the final bill represents a major accomplishment in preserving tax incentives for contributions."[33]

Over the year-long battle that federations had waged to protect philanthropy with the full privileges of state-based incentives and from the drain of government regulations, Jewish philanthropic leaders sharpened their vision of philanthropy. The IRS's recognition of Jewish institutions as public charities, embodying the highest level of publicly minded but privately controlled philanthropic behavior, would enable those institutions to access state benefits and carry within them the trust of the American public.

———

Across their lobbying efforts, federation spokespeople championed "tax equity," employing that exact phrase in a resolution passed at the November 1969 General Assembly. The resolution supported almost every dimension of tax reform that sought to distribute the tax burden in a progressive fashion so top earners paid their proportionally fair share. When it came to charitable tax benefits, however, they were certain that philanthropy already did the work of economic redistribution, so taxation on it would act as a hindrance to the common purpose of the income tax and philanthropy. But the 1969 Tax Reform Act laid the groundwork for both philanthropy and the US tax system to back away from a commitment to progressive and state-mandated economic redistribution and, instead, to entrust private entities to hold public goods.[34]

As the Tax Reform Act of 1969 went into effect, Norman Sugarman knew its intricacies and openings as they affected charitable tax law better than almost anyone else. Far from resting easy after the passage of the legislation, his most intense labor began as he worked to move the new law from theory into practice. Addressing the General Assembly of the CJFWF in 1970, Sugarman explained that the "considerable gloom" with which some leaders of American philanthropy regarded the new law was misplaced, and that "with some imagination and use of initiative . . . we can find some real hope, and by directing our attention to new programs I think we can find an even greater opportunity, for continuing efforts to build charitable funds." Although he served multiple clients, including the National Council of Community Foundations, the New York Community Trust, and Cleveland's United Way, Sugarman maintained a personal affinity for Jewish federations. In his same 1970 address to the CJFWF, he pronounced a special position for them in the new era of philanthropy: "Jewish community federations can provide leadership in such efforts in the interest of protecting valuable community resources and making them more effective under the new law."[35]

Above all else, Sugarman's first instruction to his clients was to petition for public charitable status from the IRS. Having worked on parsing the disparate treatment for public charities and private foundations, he knew just how valuable that formal designation would be to his clients, so much so that he and his law firm supplied the language for Treasury's "Temporary Regulations" for charitable organizations seeking classification as public charities. Most important, these regulations mandated that every charitable organization, no matter how self-evident its public status, had to file notice and receive approval in order to occupy that tax category. In Sugarman's view, far from a formality or, even, a hurdle, this step conferred the appropriate value to the public status. In the new law, the government took the public designation so seriously that once it gave its approbation to an organization's public status, it would trust that organization to act in the interest of the public with very little oversight. Thus, the bureaucratic procedure was no less than a performance of trust.[36]

The bond of trust between the state and public charities was essential to Sugarman's vision of the creative opportunities afforded by the new law. Despite the fact that lawyers had suggested to Cleveland's federation that they prepare for their philanthropic funds to be classified as private foundations at a significant loss of benefits, now with Sugarman's astute and ongoing legal interventions, the law was not nearly as clear on the matter as these lawyers had assumed it would be. Throughout the 1970s, in a series of memos to the Treasury Department, Sugarman built a tight case for its regulations to adopt the most interpretively capacious definition of a public charity possible. Doing so, he argued, would uphold the spirit of Congress's decision to give preferential treatment to public charities and achieve its implied policy goal of encouraging as many charitable dollars as possible to be placed in public charities.

In an April 1970 memo proposing a procedure to Treasury for the transfer of private foundations to public charities, Sugarman reasoned, "The new provision reflects a policy of the Congress which should be augmented by the regulations, pointing the way by which private foundations may make their assets more useful in interests of public charities." Sugarman pressed for Treasury to draw a "safe haven line" around private donors that would protect them from the new burdens foisted upon private foundations and gifts of appreciated property so long as they channeled their capital into public charities. That safe haven, he maintained, could also allow private donors who gave formal control over their funds to a public charity still to retain authority over the name of the fund as well as its allocations. In this way, philanthropic funds would not compromise the status of public charities, and they could also become newly attractive to donors who might have otherwise thought to create private foundations.[37]

Philanthropic funds represented the center of Sugarman's vision for how the 1969 legislation, once perceived as a threat to philanthropy, could, in fact, reinvigorate it. His case for transferring private foundations and private donations into philanthropic funds was only as good as Treasury's acceptance of his reasoning, so in addition to firing off memos to his contacts there, he also created test cases using Cleveland's federation to force the IRS to render a judgment about the status of private foundation transfers and philanthropic funds. In May 1970, he personally delivered documentation of each case to the IRS and requested rulings.

The next fall Sugarman received the private-letter ruling—that is, the IRS's direct response to a petitioner's request that cannot necessarily serve as precedent—he had been after: "You will establish a fund which shall be known as the [a family's name] Philanthropic Fund.... [The fund holders] may submit to you names of organizations to which they recommend distributions be made. Such recommendations shall be solely advisory, and you may accept or reject them, applying reasonable standards and guidelines."[38] As long as the philanthropic fund's allocations went exclusively to organizations that met the standards of section 501(c)(3) of the Internal Revenue Code, then the IRS agreed that philanthropic funds carrying the name and advisory privileges of an individual account holder could receive the full benefits of a public charity. This meant that assets contributed to them would be immediately tax-deductible, and donations of appreciated securities would gain "double tax saving," in the words of a Cleveland federation staff person, since they would provide an income tax deduction while avoiding capital gains tax on appreciation. In the case of the transfer of private foundations into philanthropic funds, the IRS similarly agreed to grant them public charitable status and waive any tax penalties for the dissolution of a private foundation. Later, as Congress and Treasury ironed out transfer rules, Sugarman provided the sole testimony upon which new regulations were based.[39]

Unable to draw precedent from the IRS ruling, Sugarman shared it widely with his clients and with federation leaders across the country, encouraging them to construct similar test cases so they, too, could receive IRS approval for this flexible use of public charities. Despite warnings from Treasury that it would be vigilant against private foundations that repurposed themselves as public charities "in name only" for tax benefits, the IRS did not object to the cases Sugarman shepherded and his efforts to bolster the use of philanthropic funds.[40]

Sugarman's enthusiasm for philanthropic funds practically overflowed from the usually measured man. To a group of Jewish leaders in St. Louis, he extolled the funds for allowing "individuals, who would like to create a fund as a memorial, a monument, or for current charitable purposes, to have the advantage of current income tax deductions in building such a fund, as well as the benefit of creating a permanent fund as part of their long-range program." In a meeting with Cleveland Jewish leaders, he similarly enthused, "What we're really talking about [is] providing an endowment for the community.... [And] it can have the maximum flexibility." He added that he expected these funds would become the "backbone" of federations' endowments and outlined how federation executives could make the strongest case—based on tax advantages, individual control, and high-quality investment services—to persuade private family foundations to transfer their assets to philanthropic funds held in federations. By the early 1970s, newly appointed as chair of CJFWF's National Endowment Fund Development Committee, Sugarman had yet another perch from which to press the case for growing charitable capital through tax-based financial vehicles. Furthermore, he reached beyond the Jewish world to preach the benefits of his new model. Throughout the 1970s, he traversed the country speaking to United Way chapters, tax professionals, attorneys, and national philanthropy conferences, and he published articles in popular and professional outlets where he tirelessly outlined the tax and other advantages that individuals and philanthropic institutions would receive upon creating philanthropic funds.[41]

The more public charities received IRS approval to hold philanthropic funds and absorb transfers of private foundations, the more normalized the practice would become. In Sugarman's estimation, this would serve as a fulfillment of the very purpose of Congress's new philanthropic regulations by putting more charitable capital into the hands of public charities. However, the opposite seemed at least as likely to occur: that public charities could become colonized by private capital so thoroughly that one would have to ask whether all of this new capital truly served their missions. To be certain, Sugarman's model appeared to promise capital-rich futures for public charities, but it also threatened to strip them of everything but the most legally narrow control of funds and to press them into acting more and more as financial service entities for donors.

———

With little hesitation, Sugarman embarked on a mission to expand public charities. Not only did he want to see existing public charities grow through new contributions of dissolved private foundations and philanthropic funds, but he also hoped to encourage the growth of a whole new class of charitable vehicles—so-called community foundations—within the Jewish community and beyond to serve the purpose of holding individual philanthropic funds, providing services to invest and grow these funds, and adhering to donors' allocation recommendations. Prior to 1969, community foundations, such as the Cleveland Foundation, the first of its kind established in 1914, or the New

York Community Trust, founded in 1924, held donors' gifts (often bequests) in trust and empowered a distribution committee to allocate the investment earnings from the funds to charities. Community foundation boards, historically comprised of wealthy community leaders, protected individual donors' charitable interests and gave individuals informal, if not formal, methods of accounting for how their money was spent. Starting in the 1950s, as Congress slowly puzzled over how to distinguish between different kinds of philanthropic capital, community foundations did not receive specific consideration as public charities, and when it came to the 1969 Tax Reform Act, Congress appeared not to know how to treat community foundations, so it remained silent about them.[42]

Just as Sugarman had kept his eye on expanding the qualifying practices of public charities, he likewise believed he could solve what he called the "limbo" status of community foundations by filling the legislative lacunae with his interpretive acumen. As part of a private commission to inform philanthropic policy initiated in 1973 at the behest of John D. Rockefeller III, and with the support of several members of Congress and the Secretary of Treasury, Sugarman wrote what became a definitive brief on community foundations and their deservedly public charitable status. In it, he exported the same logic he had used in seeking public charity status for philanthropic foundations and private foundation transfers to justify designating community foundations as public charities. Drawing particular attention to philanthropic funds, which he called for the first time "donor advisory funds," a slight variation from the name that would eventually stick (donor-advised funds), Sugarman explained these were untapped resources that if not captured by community foundation endowments might slip away from the philanthropic process entirely. He believed that community foundations could coax capital out of individuals' pockets and into philanthropic coffers by promising favorable tax treatment.

Sugarman maintained, however, that more than convenient vehicles for individual donors, community foundations embodied the very spirit of trusting private entities to provision for the public good and, thus, fit squarely within the public charitable category. As he wrote, "Community foundations should be encouraged to be a model for involvement of the private sector in the community as an alternate and supplement to governmental programs." With their status clarified, the number of community foundations grew significantly throughout the 1970s.[43]

Although community foundations tended to be location-, not identity-based, Sugarman saw little reason to limit their reaches. In 1970, he and the executive director of the Cleveland Federation had traveled to New York City to meet with a group of Jewish leaders, connected to New York's federation, who wanted to expand Jewish endowment resources in their community. The New York leaders noted that Sugarman "has had considerable dealings with the Internal Revenue Service . . . and succeeded in establishing what may well be the model Jewish Community Foundation in this country." What they characterized as Cleveland's "Jewish Community Foundation" were simply the philanthropic funds and other endowment accounts housed within the federation, though it is noteworthy that the New York leaders perceived these financial vehicles as so distinct from the federation's typical activities that they assumed they were separate from it and used the appellation of a community foundation to describe them.[44]

Even more resolute in their desire to create a new structure for endowment dollars after their meeting with Sugarman, the New York group reported to the board of the federation, "Since the new [1969 tax] law, the effectiveness of the Communal Fund, as an instrument for long-range funding, has taken on an extraordinary development and promises to be a significant factor in the financing of philanthropic endeavors." From their efforts, the Jewish Communal Fund emerged in 1972 and would serve as a model for several other similar entities that arose in the coming years.[45]

New York's Jewish Communal Fund, from its inception, stood in distinction from the federation. Although its founders relied on New York's federation as the legal basis for the fund—according to the new tax law, a charitable entity could not receive the benefits of the public charity classification unless it had been in existence for five years—they guarded its separate status from the federation through a legal design that would set it "loose on an independent course" once it received standing. The chair of the founding committee, a lawyer named Herbert Singer, envisioned the Jewish Communal Fund as a "philanthropic bank" that would not compete with annual fund-raising drives, but would complement the federation's time-bound and distribution-based mechanisms with its focus on perpetuity through capital growth. For donors who wanted to give appreciated securities and gain the fullest possible tax advantages; who sought "to accumulate a philanthropic fund, with distribution deferred to some future date"; and who saw the advantages of rolling their private foundations into a public charity, a Jewish community foundation would be attractive in a way that a donation to a federation's annual campaign would not.[46]

Of course, many federations, such as Cleveland's, were trying to be both—a revolving door funder and a philanthropic bank—all at once within one institution. But the process of establishing New York's Jewish Communal Fund exemplified the sharp distinction between the two models, even as Sugarman and other philanthropic leaders attempted to use the public charity status to paper over the differences. So widely had they succeeded in applying this status, however, that some of the very basic questions that had driven congressional action in the first place seemed to reappear as soon as the law was enacted: Should capital, designated to act in the interest of the public good and subsidized with the full extent of public benefits, be allowed to accumulate in perpetuity? And to what extent should individuals be able to designate the direction in which public charitable dollars moved when they placed their wealth in funds that offered them immediate tax deductions (sometimes doubly so if they donated appreciated property), and that grew from untaxed investment income?

———

In 1972, just as the Jewish Communal Fund filed its incorporation papers, a proposal for yet another philanthropic endowment emerged on the American Jewish scene. The student activists who had demonstrated at the General Assembly in Boston in 1969 had demanded the reallocation of Jewish communal resources to support education and identity projects. While Gordon Zacks's cry to commit $100 million, only slightly less than the total assets held in all federation endowments across the country, to the cause went unanswered, the students' pleas would not fall on deaf ears. Almost immediately, the CJFWF established a task force to explore the matter, and then three years later, in 1972, it agreed to pledge a far more modest $250,000 annually for a period of three years to create the Institute for Jewish Life.[47]

From even before its inception, the Institute for Jewish Life was plagued by instability, extending from its mission to its finances. Some detractors worried that local federations would bristle at being asked to channel their funds to a national initiative that might seem distant from their own concerns, while others thought the new project would compete with existing institutions. Harry Barron, the executive director of the National Foundation for Jewish Culture, registered his dismay that a task force charged with exploring the "cultural, educational, and religious" dimensions of Jewish life "in the face of attenuating identification" did not call upon his organization.[48]

Despite an illustrious board, whose membership included figures like Max Fisher, Elie Wiesel, and Abraham Joshua Heschel, the Institute for Jewish Life ended its first year with an $81,000 deficit. As some opponents of the plan had predicted, many local federations failed to contribute their assigned share, and because the national federation office had no authority beyond persuasion, it could do little to compel them. The director of the Institute for Jewish Life, Leon Jick, a rabbi and historian of American Jewry, later complained of local federations' "shtetlism" that kept them from seeing beyond their own immediate interests. Others, however, worried that federations were being asked to trade their local and traditional work for newfangled national initiatives. Reporting at the 1972 General Assembly, the president of the board of New York's federation noted that the CJFWF "has recently funded a large scale project, called the Institute of [sic] Jewish Life; this has been followed by a very substantial interest in projects relating to Jewish identity and the continuity of Jewish life in other Federations, even to the point of beginning to cut back substantially on health services and child and family care agencies in order to provide funds for Jewish education and Jewish identity projects."[49]

The zero-sum calculation—that to expend more for identity programs would necessarily involve cutting funds from material-need programs—might have seemed mathematically accurate, except that it occluded a very different calculation of federations' long-term prospects for Jewish support and relevance. That calculation accounted for the growth in federal funding for social welfare programs, including grant dollars channeled through Jewish agencies; the rising wealth of American Jewry; and the growing power of identity language to address what many commentators were calling a survival crisis in Jewish life, precipitated not by deprivation or violence but by opportunity and abundance. A longtime federation director, who had served in both Detroit and Los Angeles, told federation leaders in 1971, "We have, in short, at least on the domestic scene, begun talking less and less about personal, physical, creature survival and more and more about identity and group survival." He observed a new "thesis that the Federation idea is a strong instrument for reinforcing positive Jewish identity," mentioning the National Foundation for Jewish Culture as one such example and, surely, had it been formed, he would have also noted the Institute for Jewish Life.[50]

In the first three decades of its existence, New York's federation expended roughly 40% of its total allocations to its various agencies, most of which focused on health and human services. Starting in the 1950s, that percentage started to fall, totaling 30% in 1951, 17% in 1961, and a mere 5% in 1971. The student activists who protested at the Boston General Assembly in 1969 and, then, the following year, a group of one hundred activists who occupied New

York's federation offices demanding "the appointment of a 'citizens' committee' . . . to conduct public hearings on whether Federation was sufficiently democratic and reflective of community interests" held a misperception about federations' financial structures. The young activists saw federation-supported agencies providing services for non-Jews and seemingly choosing to serve a broad American community at the expense of the Jewish community. They accused Jewish leaders of allowing their assimilationist attitudes to guide financial decisions that led Jewish communal dollars far astray from true Jewish needs.[51]

What Jewish student activists did not realize was just how few Jewish-generated philanthropic dollars by the late 1960s made their way to the agencies that they believed manifested their elders' lack of concern for Jewish vitality. But this fact was clear to those working within the Jewish philanthropic system, so much so that in 1972 the executive director of Cleveland's federation complained, "Preserving the integrity of our Jewish purpose discourages indiscriminate lusting after the federal dollar, as some of our agencies have done, to the point where they have traded away their sectarian commitment." When they drew from the well of governmental funding, Jewish organizations had to prove they could deliver services in a nonsectarian manner, but as the executive director well understood, these grants allowed agencies to operate with far less funding from the Jewish community than in the past, freeing up Jewish philanthropic capital to move toward "undernourished Jewish culture and Jewish education" projects.[52]

A misperception of federation finances may have fueled student protests, but the actual state of Jewish philanthropy made it far easier for leaders to fulfill the students' requests than it would have been had thousands of agencies been wholly reliant on Jewish funds. In 1970, a mere few months after the group of students occupied the offices of New York's federation, the federation allocated funds to create a Jewish Association of College Youth and increased its support for Jewish education. These allocation decisions mirrored those of other federations that were channeling new funds to Jewish education and identity programs and also ran parallel to the centralized effort, through the National Foundation for Jewish Culture and the Jewish Institute for Jewish Life, to commit the national federation system to identity work.[53]

Despite the lackluster performance of the Institute for Jewish Life, officially terminated in 1976, it and the myriad other Jewish identity endeavors funded in the same years represented a new calculus of Jewish philanthropy. The same year the Institute for Jewish Life folded, the theme of the federation's General Assembly was "Continuity," itself a word that had entered the lexicon of Jewish philanthropy that decade to describe the goal of funding—and, truly, endowing—Jewish identity. The link between Jewish continuity and a financial model of perpetuity, achieved by allowing more capital accumulation and growth than capital distribution, has been overlooked in the ample literature documenting the rise of Jewish identity concerns in the 1970s and beyond.

The impulse to capitalize Jewish identity aligned with a new political economy woven through tax legislation, philanthropic efforts to expand endowment practices, and the consolidation of political influence coordinated through philanthropic institutions. In seeking capital returns on identity, Jewish philanthropy moved in step with broad American trends that steadily empowered the rule of capitalism and its putatively free and private market over the public good.[54]

7

The Market

THANKS IN NO SMALL PART to Norman Sugarman's legal interpretation, a tax law meant to favor those charities that drew broad public support instead fostered the expansion of private philanthropic influence. On Columbus Day, 1975, he told a group of St. Louis federation leaders that the day called for celebration and not only because "government offices are closed!" Rather, six years ago to the day, "The Senate Finance Committee completed its work on certain phases of the 1969 Act," making the date, according to Sugarman, "almost as famous as July 4," at least "in the tax field."[1]

Judged in full, the Tax Reform Act of 1969 appeared to reaffirm the post–World War II commitment to progressive taxation, with its treatment of charitable taxation a seemingly minor exception to the legislation's broader spirit of expanding public revenue generation. But the better interpretation is that the Tax Reform Act's charitable provisions anticipated what was to come. These provisions replaced regulatory measures and direct taxation with a system of "tax expenditures." Writing in the *Harvard Law Review* in 1970, Stanley Surrey, who had been the Assistant Secretary of the Treasury for Tax Policy from 1961 to 1969, defined tax expenditures as "special provisions of the federal income tax system which represent government expenditures made through that system to achieve various social and economic objectives." He concluded that tax expenditures "have decidedly adverse effects on equity" because they "make high-income individuals still better off and result in the paradox that we achieve our social goals by increasing the number of tax millionaires." Contrary to the logic of a progressive tax system, a tax expenditure was regressive, rewarding the wealthiest with more capital power and placing public control in the hands of private entities.[2]

Tax expenditures made good sense if one maintained that the state's primary responsibility was to strengthen private actors, interests, and markets.

Before the passage of the 1969 legislation, Sugarman had obliquely made this case to Congress, but he spoke more plainly and frequently about it throughout the 1970s, when philanthropic associations and Jewish federations across the country invited him to conduct tax and endowment seminars. To several audiences, he asserted, "Our tax system . . . helps to finance the role of the private sector."[3]

A pro-market philosophy of taxation held sway over a growing number of policymakers in the 1970s and would guide future decades of tax reform. Steadily, progressive policies intended to spread out wealth concentration through downwardly redistributive mechanisms were replaced by supply-side and trickle-down policies that valued concentrations of capital and threw the weight of the American state behind them. Whatever economic equity might be achieved would be channeled through more, not less, private power. Under Nixon's watch, the government's reliance on private capital and entities to do public work grew stronger than ever, sidelining more centralized and state-controlled mechanisms of resource distribution. In step, libertarian economic ideas, once relegated to small think tanks or journals with modest readerships, slowly made their way closer to the center of American economic policy, thanks to some tenacious and well-heeled supporters. In addition to advocating the privatization of formerly state services, libertarian exponents also encouraged massive tax cuts and retrenchment on social welfare spending.[4]

The Reagan administration embraced the ideals of market and individual freedom through privatization and slashed the highest marginal tax rate from 50% to 28% in 1986. Not only did these cuts make it seem impossible for the government to fund social welfare, despite the fact that government spending, particularly for defense and at the growth of a deficit, actually increased under Reagan, but they also fueled a shift in public perception about the relationship between government and citizens. While socially liberal ideals about protected classes of people gained traction in law, legal protections tended to favor negative rights (the right to do what one wanted) as opposed to positive rights (designed to use government power to provide access and equality). Good government under Reagan was envisioned as small and unobtrusive because in any grander form it would constrain its citizens' ability to flourish freely in the market economy. In countless realms by the 1980s, private freedom prevailed over public rule. With the state and the market pulling in much the same direction, philanthropic institutions no longer felt the same countervailing pressures that had once allowed and, even, mandated them to balance, no matter how imperfectly, between the requirements of democracy and the rule of capitalism. As the American state embraced market practices as its governing strategy, all sectors—from the public to the private to whatever existed between—seemed to point toward capitalism.[5]

In the 1970s and 1980s, public charities, such as federations, intensified their efforts to accumulate capital by offering their donors a broad range of financial services. Proving to their donors that they could manage and grow their philanthropic property became a central task for federation leaders. As philanthropic practice increasingly aligned with models of private finance and market services, philanthropic entities joined a surge of political will to invest in the ideals of market freedom through a mix of deregulation and state assistance. Already in their advocacy efforts to shape the 1969 tax reform legislation, philanthropic leaders had developed language to talk about why government should not interfere with the business of charity and, conversely, why government should subsidize philanthropic activities; all support and less discipline would make philanthropy stronger.

By the 1980s, Jewish philanthropic leaders exercised measurable political influence, evidenced as much by their ongoing efforts to lobby for favorable philanthropic tax policy as by their ever more vocal campaigns to win political support for Israel. Nonetheless, even when Jewish philanthropic leaders engaged in openly political and, even, partisan activities, they still operated under the rules of depoliticized politics. Accordingly, they stepped into deeply political roles and often brought their communal institutions' infrastructure with them, but also disavowed these institutions as nodes of political and economic influence. As long as they could present themselves as working on behalf of the American Jewish community and its consensus interests, they seemed comfortable with their newfound political activism, perceiving it as the advancement of their public's good. This was how depoliticized politics worked and contributed to the market logic of the emergent American Jewish philanthropic complex.

———

Throughout the 1970s, federations across the country expanded their endowments, with an unprecedented total of sixty federations reporting significant endowment-building activity. In just two years, from 1975 to 1977, the sum holdings across all federations' endowments increased by almost $100 million, reaching $276 million. Yet despite these gains, reports from the late 1970s

FIGURE 7.1. Family at Temple Beth El, Cedarhurst, Long Island, June 8, 1977, Subgroup III: United Jewish Appeal-Federation Joint Campaign, Public Relations Series, Photographs Subseries, Box 714110. Courtesy of the American Jewish Historical Society at the Center for Jewish History, New York, NY.

betray the impatience that federation endowment boosters felt. Writing to
Sugarman in 1977, the executive director of Cleveland's federation speculated
that if only other cities would follow its embrace of endowment and stop cling-
ing to the old revolving door, money-in and money-out model, then "the national total [of Jewish endowment dollars] would already be about $1 billion."
Compounding leaders' frustration over not adequately capturing Jewish philanthropic capital was fear that other entities, whether private foundations,
other Jewish or non-Jewish charitable institutions, or for-profit institutions,
would compete for that wealth.[6]

As early as the 1960s, federation leaders had worked to build relationships
with Jewish philanthropists who had gravitated toward more individualized
methods of charitable giving. Unsurprisingly, Cleveland took the lead on this
front. In the mid-1960s, its staff members began to meet with Jewish families
who held funds at the Cleveland Foundation, the community trust established
at the beginning of the century, and they volunteered to serve as consultants
to help those families explore Jewish giving possibilities. Hoping to exercise
some sway over philanthropic capital not directly under their control, Cleveland federation leaders created the Foundation Advisory Council "to influence
the use of foundation funds for the benefit of the Jewish and the general community" and to help with the "housekeeping services" with which small private foundations often struggled.[7]

These attempts to serve Jewish philanthropists whose capital resided outside of the orbit of Jewish communal philanthropy were early indications of
what would become a new and central role for federations: financial services.
Whether as consultants to private Jewish families—what we might today call
wealth managers—or managers of their own growing funds and portfolios,
federations not only used the tools of finance but also began to court donors
by offering financial services to them and their handlers.

With Sugarman at its helm, a committee of Cleveland lawyers (all men)
produced a "Handbook for Charitable Giving" in 1972. Its preface stated, "This
Handbook is intended as a helpful guide for persons interested in philanthropy, particularly highlighting developments as a result of the Tax Reform
Act of 1969. It brings together in one place information, forms and tables."
More than ninety pages long, the handbook surveyed everything from the new
law to the tax treatment of different forms of charitable property, and included
a lengthy appendix that reprinted IRS rulings, forms for gift transfers, and tax
rate tables. A full section on "philanthropic funds" provided clear instructions
on how to craft IRS-compliant funds, including transfers from private

FIGURE 7.2. Handbook for Charitable Giving, published by the Jewish Community Federation of Cleveland, 1972, Articles and Addresses, Vol. 6, 1971–1974, Box 3, Norman Sugarman Papers, P-633. Courtesy of the American Jewish Historical Society at the Center for Jewish History, New York, NY.

foundations, within a public charity and referenced rulings and forms provided in the appendix.[8]

The handbook revealed the growing universe of expertise that Jewish philanthropic leaders believed necessary to command in order to thrive in the new legislative climate. Lawyers, already a strong presence in Jewish federations, gained even more authority as they produced documents, conducted seminars, and advised federations on almost every facet of philanthropic practice. However, their authority was increasingly matched by that of men who worked in the financial industry, overseeing investments, trading stock, and offering expert advice to federations. Financial service professionals both guided the changes afoot in federations and also increasingly contributed the funds that made those changes tangible, replacing the business owners of the past who had been the most substantial givers.

Already in the 1940s, when New York's federation cautiously started to expand its endowment, it had sought lay leaders to help create investment policies with an eye toward modest growth, but the need to manage investments well became all the more urgent as federations' endowments expanded. The rapidity of endowment expansion, fueled in part by the rising popularity of philanthropic funds, caught federations unprepared to manage their new capital. For example, even as its endowment nearly doubled from 1971 to 1979, New York's federation had only a single staff person assigned to oversee its endowment across a variety of stock, bond, real estate, and mortgage options. Reliant on the voluntary labor of a committee and responsible for an ever-growing portfolio, that person was ill-equipped to make quick decisions that might have resulted in higher returns.[9]

In 1979, pressed to make the difficult choice to invade its endowment to offset a deficit, the chair of New York's volunteer investment committee noted, "Federation's financial needs . . . put great pressure on our investment assets to produce the maximum amount of income," yet this goal was hardly feasible given the current staffing. The next year, the board decided to hire "professional investment advisory managers" to ensure its endowment was achieving the highest returns possible. Clearly, the board believed the service fees for hiring outside investment specialists would be more than recouped by the returns those specialists could generate.[10]

By the late 1970s, although many federations began to retain outside individuals and firms to service their ballooning endowments, they also recognized that they could offer their expertise to entice donors to invest in their endowment vehicles. They could position themselves as experts who knew how to operate in the increasingly complex financial world of philanthropic options and tax policy, and they could sell this service to prospective donors. In a note to Sugarman, Cleveland's executive director proposed renaming the federation's endowment program "the endowment fund-foundation idea." He continued, "If you agree with this thinking, is it not logical to suggest that the CJF [the national Council of Jewish Federations, until 1979 known as the Council of Jewish Federations and Welfare Funds] endowment office reorient itself to the foundation idea and assist the local Federations to improve their relationships with foundations?" Even if deeper ties to private foundations, in addition to community foundations, did not immediately put funds into federations' endowments, these ties could generate good will and also perhaps gifts to federation endowments down the line.[11]

In the fall of 1981, the board of trustees of the New York federation considered a proposal to establish an in-house consulting service for private foundations. Offsetting the cost, estimated at $110,000 annually, the proponents of the proposal saw a plethora of potential gains. Most basically, centralizing the administrative expenses of running a private foundation would put more dollars into philanthropic play. As an efficiency proposition, the federation's foundation services could thus conserve community resources. Moreover, advocates of the proposal explained that the federation would have a shot at accessing that conserved capital, both through fees for service it could take and by developing strong relationships with foundation leaders and their custodians, who would come to "see Federation in a favorable light."[12]

Greater efficiency and the opportunity to gain favor in the eyes of donors were the steps along the way toward the proposal's ultimate goal: to exert influence over the wealthiest members of the Jewish community. Here, however, New York federation leaders tread carefully. The proposal promised to give foundations majority representation on an oversight committee it would establish to coordinate its consulting services, and its crafters emphasized the desirability of "setting up a mechanism whereby Federation could service private foundations, bringing them into the building without controlling them." And yet the proposal was attractive only insofar as it held out the promise for the federation to exercise some control over private donors.[13]

In advocating for the proposal, Sanford Solender, a trained social worker and the executive vice president of the New York federation, offered the example of a Jewish donor who creates a private family foundation with the intent of using it to support the Jewish community, but as time passes, the donor's descendants "may drift away from the Jewish community." By embedding the foundation in the federation's service apparatus, that drift could be minimized: "The connection would inevitably influence what they do over the years, even though there is no requirement that they contribute to the Jewish community." A lay leader who helped solicit funds for the federation's annual campaign concurred that "ongoing meaningful contact with such foundations through provision of valuable services to them, even without written contracts or understandings, would inevitably accrue to Federation's benefit." The board of New York's federation offered its unanimous endorsement of the proposal and charged the staff with creating an in-house consulting office, signifying a steady shift in Jewish communal philanthropy toward providing financial services for donors or potential donors.[14]

————

Across the country, Jewish federations busied themselves marketing new funds and programs for donors to use the federation as a service-providing philanthropic entity and pass-through. Philanthropic funds were the centerpieces of these efforts. New York's Jewish Communal Fund, legally independent of the federation but with a board comprised of many federation leaders, held $20 million in philanthropic funds as of 1978, but more common were efforts to keep these funds under the institutional auspices of federations. With the highest ratio of philanthropic fund assets to endowment assets of any federation, Cleveland served as the model for philanthropic fund expansion. By the late 1970s, it reported holding more than half of its $22.5 million endowment in such funds.[15]

The infrastructure to capture philanthropic funds—first, to receive IRS approval for them and then to sell them to donors—had occupied so much of federation leaders' attention that the process for using the funds lagged behind, even in Cleveland, where they had become a cornerstone of philanthropic practice. Only in the late 1970s, as the lack of any process was threatening to overwhelm the federation's infrastructure, did Cleveland develop a set of guidelines for accounting for the funds and their disbursements. According to its newly minted rules, fund holders could not request allocations of less than $100 because scores of small payouts were over-burdening the staff at the federation, making the funds costly to maintain. More substantively, the new rules established a Philanthropic Fund Advisory Committee, with a mix of lay volunteers and staff people, to meet monthly and review disbursement requests. Women, notably absent from any leadership roles in endowment development across many decades, appeared on this committee. For example, Barbara Mandel, who with her husband, Morton Mandel, was among the wealthiest Jewish families in Cleveland, served a year-long term on the committee.[16]

According to the procedures of the newly established Philanthropic Fund Advisory Committee, all allocation requests from philanthropic funds were now divided among four categories—federation; non-federation Jewish organizations; local organizations and educational institutions; and other—with the committee then approving, rejecting, or deferring requests. Most

important, to uphold legal mandate, the committee ensured that each designated grantee fit the requirements of a charitable organization as defined by
section 501(c)(3) of the Internal Revenue Code. The categories made the process easier, as the committee could focus its attention on those requests that
fell outside of the usual and familiar suspects. The primary reasons, as recorded
in their notes, that the committee denied a request were either because the
allocation amount fell below $100 or because the committee had been unable
to verify the tax status of the grantee. In a few cases, the committee appeared
to reject a request because it disapproved of the organization. For example, it
did not allow a $250 gift to be sent to the Chautauqua Institution, an educa-
tional center for Bible study summer courses in New York State founded by a
Methodist minister in the late nineteenth century that by the mid-twentieth
century also offered a broad array of cultural and educational programming,
and noted only that "information had been received by staff concerning the
organization." Another request for a donation to be sent to the American
Council for Judaism, an anti-Zionist organization established in 1942, received
a deferral but never reappeared on the committee's roster.[17]

Philanthropic funds in Cleveland by and large supported the federation and
Jewish organizations. Over the last six months of 1978, a full 81% of the $1.6
million requested for allocation fell into those two categories, although the
distribution of grantee organizations was spread much more evenly across the
four categories of giving, meaning that philanthropic fund holders gave much
larger gifts to Jewish organizations, even as they allocated more modest gifts
to a nearly equal number of non-Jewish organizations. The records are not
comprehensive enough to indicate the exact percentage of total assets from
the funds that were allocated, but assuming a relatively constant rate of disbursement over 1978, approximately 25% of the $12.5 million held in philan-
thropic funds was spent over the course of 1978. This was five times the mandated annual spend-out rate for private foundations but, of course, fell far short
of the annual campaign disbursement model. Still, assuming, as advocates of
philanthropic funds did, that this capital otherwise would not have entered
federations' asset streams, endowment spending from philanthropic funds was
a boon to federations and other Jewish organizations.[18]

A final component of Cleveland's new process for reviewing disbursements
from philanthropic funds focused on donors' rights. Above all else, committee
members were instructed, "Confidentiality of the donor is maintained." Donors
could choose when they wanted to be recognized for their charitable gifts and
when, instead, they wished to give anonymously—so that an organization's

records would reflect only receipt of a donation from the Cleveland federation and not from a specific fund holder. But anonymity was just one piece of the power that Cleveland was careful to spell out for its philanthropic fund donors. Indeed, the entire process indicated just how much freedom donors retained to recommend when, where, and what amount they gave. The federation would respect these recommendations, save extraordinary circumstances.[19]

By the early 1980s, federations were slowly transforming themselves into financial-service providers for privately controlled philanthropic capital. This transformation gave federations a new purpose and way to calculate their value, at a time when the real value of annual campaign donations was falling. While annual campaign trends may have indicated the diminishing relevance of communal giving to Jewish life, endowment fund growth appeared to prove just the opposite. Federation leaders found they could tell a more compelling narrative of continuity and survival through endowments and even through private foundations for whom they consulted than they could through diminishing annual campaign returns. In particular, they saw untapped growth potential in donor-directed philanthropic capital that could be accumulated within Jewish communal infrastructure. A confidential memo circulated to the leaders of the national federation office conjectured, "Untold millions have been lost because lawyers or accountants never heard of Philanthropic Funds—to the detriment of their clients and the Federations."[20]

———

Federations' turn toward the tools of finance is intelligible only in the framework of similar transformations in the American state that saw public interests increasingly beholden to market-driven models of growth and progress. Through tax reform, cuts to social welfare spending, and policies to deregulate and subsidize the financial industry, the American government steadily put the public good in the hands of private entities that controlled and benefited from the market economy. American Jewish leaders and their philanthropic institutions were hardly removed from these changes, and not only because they affected how Jewish organizations ran. Much as Max Fisher had done under Nixon, some of the most prominent leaders of American Jewish philanthropy found that their positions in Jewish philanthropic circles provided a conduit toward state recognition and a platform from which to represent a set of consolidated Jewish interests as, at the least, recognizable and nonthreatening to state interests, if not coincident with them.

In 1982, Jonathan Woocher, a professor and researcher of American Jewish philanthropy at Brandeis University, diagnosed Jewish communal life as afflicted by the "politics of scarcity." He used the word politics in its most formal sense, resting the problem of scarcity squarely on "the Reagan budget cuts." Barely masking his own dismay with the Republican administration, Woocher explained, "[T]he government's new 'safety net' will bounce many more Jews into the arms of our social service agencies at the very time that government funds to support these agencies' programs are being cut back." Despite Woocher's despair about the deleterious effects that depleted federal and state funds would have on Jewish agencies and his anticipation of a spike in needy populations, more American Jews than at any other time in the century had cast their vote for the Republican president. As reported in the *American Jewish Year Book*, the 39% of Jews who voted for Reagan represented the highest percentage of American Jews who backed a Republican presidential candidate since Abraham Lincoln's election.[21]

Whether longtime Republicans or so-called Reagan Democrats, a substantial percentage of American Jews, through their electoral behavior, endorsed a vision of economic privatization and market-directed government that by the following decade would transcend party lines and appear as integral to Democrat Bill Clinton's platform in 1992 as to any Republican contenders' platforms. In the shifting political economy of American life, philanthropy came to occupy a new position, not only as a material resource to confront Woocher's "politics of scarcity," but also as an enabler of those politics. The promise of philanthropy—augmented through a rapidly expanding nonprofit sector—legitimated the state's contraction of its social welfare responsibilities. In its financial structure, underwritten by the state yet free to move through the market to accumulate and grow capital, philanthropy fell in line with Woocher's description of the new American political landscape, exemplifying the logic of meeting public scarcity with private enrichment.[22]

President Reagan's signature belief that freedom was the antithesis of government regulation appealed to many American Jews for the same reasons it did to a majority of Americans. On the heels of a deep economic crisis, Reagan proved that the New Deal model for social welfare and state intervention was easy to abandon in favor of trickle-down progress. The twin ideals of freedom and progress that suffused Reagan's speeches, according to historian Daniel Rodgers, offered a "privatized and personalized" vision, enacted as much through policies such as tax cuts and the shrinkage of social welfare programs as through the rhetoric of individualism and self-actualization. Instead of fueling philanthropy with direct government grants to provision social welfare, as had been the practice for many decades, Reagan's ideal state would use philanthropy just as it used the market: as a symbol of freedom, of the superiority of individualism over collectivism, and of the best fruits of democracy. And just as Reagan's market remained propped up by indirect and out-of-sight government subsidy, especially through tax expenditures, philanthropy would likewise be given the same treatment.[23]

While it would be an overstatement to say Jewish philanthropic leaders neatly aligned with the Reagan administration—the Republican party's simultaneous overtures to the Christian Right dissuaded even many right-leaning American Jews from feeling entirely at home in Reagan's party—the nature of American Jewish philanthropy became entangled with and dependent upon its political economy. Most concretely, prominent Jewish philanthropic leaders facilitated material and ideological links between Reagan's America and Jewish philanthropy. In the emergence of the Republican Jewish Coalition, formed in the early 1980s out of the success of mobilizing Jewish votes for Reagan, one can perceive how the deep interpenetration between Jewish philanthropy and American state politics fortified the development of market-based Jewish philanthropy and stitched Jewish philanthropy, the American state, and capitalism together into a mutually reinforcing complex. And yet, as tight as its weave was, the complex remained vulnerable to its own political nature and relied instead on the repetition of the article of faith that Jewish philanthropic interests floated above partisanship and politics.[24]

Max Fisher, who had served as the Jewish liaison in the Nixon administration, played a critical role in efforts to claim Reagan as a friend of American Jews and to designate Jews as key supporters of the new president. Calling upon many of the same strategies he had used to gain standing under Nixon, Fisher convened a group of communally powerful Jews to join him in the Coalition for Reagan-Bush, a group he cochaired with fellow Jewish philanthropic leader and Reagan's longtime friend Theodore Cummings. The coalition served as the focal point for Jewish efforts to build support for the Republican candidate. Members drew on their networks in the Jewish community and developed talking points to construct a specifically Jewish case for supporting the candidate.

As he had in the past, Fisher continued to believe that the more he could deliver visible Jewish support to his candidate's campaign, the more he could request tangible evidence of gratitude should that candidate prevail. Such a strategy hinged on Fisher's ability to represent Jewish interests as consolidated

To Max Fisher
With appreciation and best wishes,

Ronald Reagan

FIGURE 7.3. President Ronald Reagan and Max Fisher, with portrait of President Dwight Eisenhower in the background, August 1, 1981, Box 309, Max M. Fisher Papers. Courtesy of the Walter P. Reuther Library, Archives of Labor and Urban Affairs, Wayne State University, Detroit, Michigan.

and coordinated around a few key issues, most significantly support for Israel. As Reagan took the White House, with pollsters reporting record-high Jewish support for his election, and with the Coalition for Reagan-Bush offering clear Jewish support for the new president, Fisher's strategy landed well (and Cummings landed an appointment as the ambassador to Austria).[25]

Nonetheless, some prominent Jews who had supported the Reagan campaign were not entirely satisfied that they were receiving their due, and cracks began to appear in Fisher's strategy of influence. In early January 1981, Gordon Zacks, the Ohio businessman who had supported the student protestors at the 1969 General Assembly and had become an active member in the Coalition for Reagan-Bush, wrote a memo to Reagan's top advisor, Edwin Meese, proposing the creation of a "President's Advisory Commission on Jewish Affairs." Emulating Fisher's strategy under Nixon, Zacks hoped to convert the visibility of Jewish electoral support for Reagan into White House access, and he carefully explained in his proposal that at present, the administration was not giving Jews appropriate standing: "No Jews have been appointed to Senior Cabinet positions," he noted, and, "The Administration has few within it who have a real understanding of and sensitivity to the Jewish Community."[26]

Rather than designating a single liaison, Zacks recommended providing a small group of Jews who were "prominent national figures" with a clear channel of communication to the president, so they could advise him on Jewish interests. The group would function much like the Conference of Presidents and, in fact, its proposed membership had significant overlap with the Conference, but it would not be hamstrung by the appearance of nonpartisanship. In return, these Jewish leaders would work to strengthen the Jewish community's support for Reagan and his policies. Expressing far more self-consciousness than Fisher ever had, Zacks acknowledged that his plan was not perfect. Inevitably, some Jewish leaders would feel excluded, and even more significantly, "If not properly understood, the organized Jewish community could view this operation as a threat," presumably because it would feel shut out from the process. On balance however, Zacks believed Reagan would be more responsive to a group of Jewish leaders who were open in their support for the Republican party than a group, such as the Conference, that claimed to be nonpartisan.[27]

Following up on Zacks's proposal, Reagan invited a small group of Jewish leaders, including Zacks and Fisher, to meet with him in March of 1981. Yet on the eve of that meeting, Reagan came under fire for his intention to sell American-made surveillance planes (called AWACS) and aircraft equipment to the Saudis, a plan that some members of Congress and many Jewish leaders perceived as presenting a threat to Israel. The cadre of leaders now had to decide whether to move forward with the meeting, risking censure from others in the Jewish community who would see them as backing the president's actions through blind partisanship, or to boycott it, jeopardizing their line of communication with the president by taking a public stand against his administration.[28]

Fisher's pragmatic understanding of how Jewish influence could work had always led him to believe that American Jews were best off maintaining their proximity to state power and gently exerting pressure from within, using their communal networks and financial resources to gain value in the eyes of state officials. A reader will recall that while this posture had earned him Nixon's praise for his loyalty, it had also hampered the kind of influence he could have over policy. Desirous of more specific sway over policy and not nearly as invested in displays of loyalty, younger members of the delegation invited to Reagan's White House were at odds with Fisher's strategy. According to a report in the Washington, DC, *Jewish Week*, division mired planning for the meeting and "clearly demonstrated that the two elder spokesmen of the Republican Jewish Leadership were out-of-step with their younger colleagues." A generational divide was evident, with Fisher and Cummings both in their early seventies and more than fifteen years older than the average age of the thirty or so attendees.[29]

Willing to be louder and more assertive in the face of state power than Fisher, the younger members of the delegation characterized silence on the president's actions as "acquiescence" and spoke of being "haunted" by their support for a president who would put Israel in danger. Flexing their muscles, they put in Fisher's hands a statement against the aircraft sale and demanded he—the ceremonial spokesperson of the group—deliver it to the president at the start of the meeting. According to reports, the septuagenarian read from the statement in a "barely audible" and "trembling voice," going off script just once to replace the word "deeply" with "a little bit" in describing how disturbed American Jews were by the president's behavior.[30]

Throughout the spring of 1981, in the wake of the strained meeting with Reagan, prominent Jewish leaders operated on two levels—one reflecting Fisher's strategy and the other the new generation's approach—to gain traction in Washington, DC. Consistent with the old model, Fisher continued to wield considerable authority, feeding Meese names of Jewish leaders who should be invited to meet with the president and pursuing his characteristically "quiet diplomacy." Yet, simultaneously, a group of Jewish leaders sought to build a bolder, more public, and more partisan Jewish organization than ever, through what they called in a late March proposal "A Republican Jewish Caucus." The proposal listed eight purposes for the new organization, starting with "To represent the interests of the 43% [4% higher than the figure cited in the *American Jewish Year Book*] of the Jewish electorate who voted Reagan/ Bush to the Administration," and including an effort to broaden the Jewish base, gain more Jewish influence within the Reagan administration and the Republican party, and "to assist the Administration in interpreting and developing grass roots support among the Jews for the Administration's priority agenda items."[31]

Different from granting a handful of Jewish leaders direct access to the president, the new Jewish caucus intended to expand the role of the Republican party in Jewish life and, likewise, expand the role of Jews in the party. By gathering approximately one hundred leaders who would represent cities with significant Jewish populations across the United States (roughly correlating with the locations of Jewish federations), the group could simultaneously call itself representative of American Jews and also make new inroads into Jewish communities to gain more Republican adherents. Yet despite its gesture toward a representative and "grass roots" model, membership was originally by invitation only and limited to registered Republicans who were "proven/ recognized by our leader[s] in local Jewish community," pledged $1,000 annually to the organization, and served on at least one committee. A spare organizational chart listed Max Fisher as the honorary chairman—a nod to his enduring stature—but the younger generation, many of whom had attended the March meeting with Reagan, dominated the list of potential chairmen.[32]

The nascent group of Republican Jewish leaders, a group with significant overlaps with the lay leaders of Jewish philanthropic organizations and the Conference of Presidents, sought formal recognition from the Republican National Committee. As a first step toward that goal, they contacted its director for outreach, a man named David Weinstein, to learn about other groups that had established caucuses within the party. Weinstein pointed them to the Heritage Groups Council, which began in the early 1970s "to approach ethnic Americans as a visible Republican organization that would prove that the G.O.P. welcomes ethnics and, is, in fact, the Party that represents best the ideals they cherish." Yet Weinstein offered a realistic assessment of the position of ethnic affiliates within the party and explained that Jewish leaders would have to push hard if they wanted true investment, including resources and institutional support, from the party. In the late spring of 1981, Weinstein stepped down from his position at the Republican National Committee to begin a new job at the national offices of the United Jewish Appeal.[33]

Israel occupied a central, though not entirely settled, position in the creation of a Jewish Republican caucus. The same group of Jewish leaders who had demanded Fisher rebuke the president for his plans to supply the Saudis with surveillance aircraft equipment constituted the core group of Republican

Jewish leadership. These men and the few women among them believed a strong presence in the Republican party and a foothold in Reagan's White House would enable them to lobby for Israel's interests in American policy. In clear terms, the proposal to create a Republican Jewish caucus specified that any invited members had to be "committed to Israel." Yet Republican Jewish leaders also wrestled over their loyalty to Reagan and the Republican party versus their single-issue and avowedly nonpartisan commitment to America's support for Israel. Continuing to focus attention on stopping the deal with Saudi Arabia, the group developed a strategy to lobby Congress by getting "the key group of influentials"—that is, Jews with political sway and, often, deep pockets to fund campaigns—to use their networks to determine which senators could be persuaded to oppose the deal. A strategy document noted the importance of media coverage to showcase "the appearance of strong bipartisan Congressional opposition" and called for "major community demonstrations" if the matter was not resolved in favor of Israel by the fall.[34]

Although Republican Jewish leaders positioned themselves as spearheading the lobbying strategy on behalf of Israel, they also believed that critical to their success was the ability to frame support for Israel as operating beyond partisan or political divides. In part, they pursued this goal by gaining the imprimatur of recognizably nonpartisan organs, such as the Conference of Presidents of Major Jewish Organizations, the American Israel Public Affairs Committee (AIPAC), an outgrowth of 1950s American Zionist organizing that gained notable lobbying power in the 1970s, and the National Community Relations Advisory Council (NCRAC), a Jewish defense and advocacy organization established by the federation's national body in 1944.

In the early 1970s, NCRAC had developed standards for political engagement that it promulgated to Jewish communal organizations. Notably, the standards did not simply reprint the IRS guidelines, although they mentioned that organizations were "barred by law" from certain political activities; rather, the standards dictated that organizations should avoid "the impression" that they were working on behalf of "a political party or candidate." The impression, as much as the law, justified the standards, an indication that NCRAC hoped to guide organizations to stay above the political fray and protect themselves from appearing as operatives of a particular party. However, the standards carved out one critical exception to their nonpartisanship: "Neither Jewish leaders nor Jewish organizations" were bound by the guidelines when it came to "speaking and acting on public issues of concern to the Jewish community, even when such conduct may be interpreted as approval or criticism of positions of candidates for political office." In other words, perceived partisanship and, even, American tax law could be sidestepped in the interest of advancing broad issues that philanthropic leaders had represented as the consensus interests of the Jewish community.[35]

To be certain, in the case of Jewish leaders' efforts to protest Reagan's eventually successfu deal with the Saudis, they were not jumping into electoral politics, but they were walking a thin line between organizing a group intended to be an arm of the Republican party and positioning themselves as the defenders of American Jewish interests in Israel. So evident were these overlapping agendas that one of the founding members of the Republican Jewish group, a man named Douglas Glant, who ran a large family business recycling scrap metal in Seattle and in the fall of Reagan's first year in office was appointed to his Export Council, wrote to Max Fisher expressing concern that the caucus would become solely a "modified version of AIPAC." He continued, "There are many issues that impact our people; e.g. the domestic economy, national security, education, crime, drugs, etc. and we do neither the Administration nor the Jewish people much good if we neglect these issues. We are Republican Jews and can provide a vital vehicle for expressing views to-and-from the White House, the RNC [Republican National Committee], and the Jewish community but we will have neither clout nor credibility if we become just another single-issue group." Repeating himself a year later, Glant wrote that the overwhelming focus on Israel would alienate potential recruits: "You should know that most of the young Jews I will be bringing to the Party are very pro-Israel but most of them consider themselves Americans first, and are concerned with such things as domestic national security, economic stability, fair taxes, crime, schools, etc. in addition to Israel."[36]

Announcing itself as the Republican Jewish Coalition in the summer of 1981, the newly visible organization relied on its Israel-related work to gain stature in and support from the Jewish communal world, while also making a point to align itself with a small set of other issues, especially economic ones, that extended beyond purportedly nonpartisan advocacy for Israel. For example, that summer, Max Fisher issued a public statement signed by the founders of the coalition announcing, "Jewish Republicans enthusiastically support the President's economic program of budget reductions and tax cuts," and encouraged those in agreement to lobby Congress for its passage. A signed letter from Reagan praised the Republican Jewish Coalition's support as a symbol of its "public-spirited concern for the welfare of all Americans and a sophisticated understanding of our efforts to restore prosperity to this nation."[37]

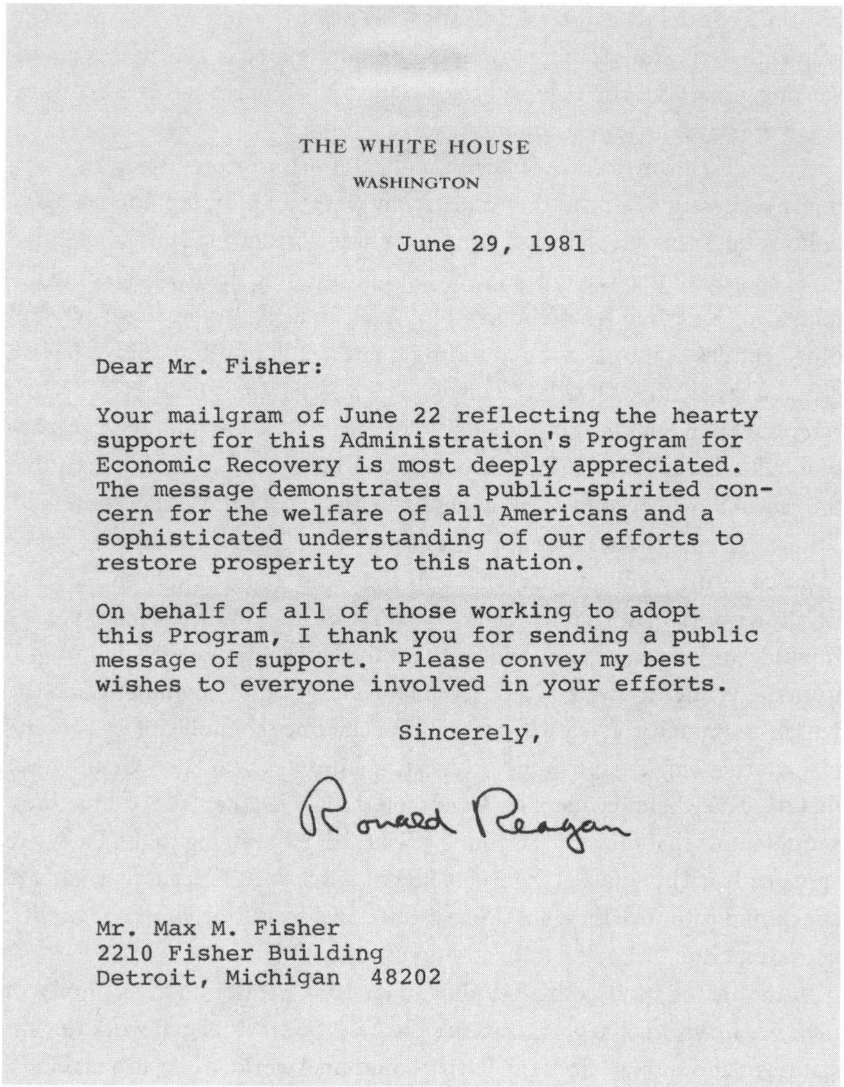

THE WHITE HOUSE

WASHINGTON

June 29, 1981

Dear Mr. Fisher:

Your mailgram of June 22 reflecting the hearty
support for this Administration's Program for
Economic Recovery is most deeply appreciated.
The message demonstrates a public-spirited concern for the welfare of all Americans and a
sophisticated understanding of our efforts to
restore prosperity to this nation.

On behalf of all of those working to adopt
this Program, I thank you for sending a public
message of support. Please convey my best
wishes to everyone involved in your efforts.

Sincerely,

Ronald Reagan

Mr. Max M. Fisher
2210 Fisher Building
Detroit, Michigan   48202

FIGURE 7.4. Letter from President Ronald Reagan to Max Fisher, June 29, 1981, Signed Letters, Reagan Folder, Box 2, Max M. Fisher Papers. Courtesy of the Walter P. Reuther Library, Archives of Labor and Urban Affairs, Wayne State University, Detroit, Michigan.

Republican leaders had come to believe that Jews, even if not dependable for their broad-based support of the party, brought significant resources to it. A memo marked confidential from the executive director of the Republican Jewish Coalition, himself a former federation executive from New Jersey, to the chairman of the Republican National Committee, appraised Fisher's donations directly to the party at $100,000, a significant sum. But more important if less calculable was Fisher's tremendous influence over other wealthy and communally prominent Jews: "Together with the Taubmans, Kravis, Miller-Ratner, Barnett money, etc. that Max brings in each year, the Republican Party cannot afford to lose this man or his 'followers.'" Noting the names of prominent Jewish families from Detroit, Tulsa, New York City, Cleveland, and Louisville, the executive director highlighted the current and potential value of nurturing Jewish Republican support.[38]

Republicans who sought to define themselves as specifically Jewish Republicans focused a great deal of attention on their advocacy for Israel and thus constantly melded their agenda with other Jewish communal organizations' missions, making the task of defining what was a strategy of Jewish Republicanism versus what was simply a strategy of pursuing issues of Jewish concern a difficult one. An internal memo from the chair of the Republican National Committee to the Republican Jewish Coalition encouraged it to solidify its position "as the Republican voice of the Jewish community and the Jewish voice of the Republican Party," and instructed its members specifically to "act as Republican liaisons to the major Jewish organizations." But his call overlooked the fact that the best weapon the Republican Jewish Coalition had in its arsenal was the ability to blur the lines between Jewish Republican interests and Jewish interests.[39]

———

Plenty of American Jewish leaders who were outspoken in their support for Israel were Democrats and gave money to the Democratic party. However, Jewish Democrats had not designated themselves institutionally or even rhetorically as specifically Jewish Democrats. A Democratic caucus to parallel the Republican Jewish Coalition emerged only in the early 1990s. To be certain, Jews were far more historically tied to and well-represented in the Democratic party than the Republican party, so the impetus to announce themselves as Jews and Democrats was not nearly so strong. The connection was often just obvious. Yet beginning in the early 1980s, some Jewish leaders and philanthropic institutions began to question the Democratic party's commitment to matters of Jewish communal concern—most pointedly, Israel and antisemitism. These leaders argued that defending Israel and opposing antisemitism were simply within the interests of American Jews, and if one party happened to fall short on these counts, then, in a show of depoliticized politics, it deserved the reprobation of American Jewry, partisanship aside.[40]

As Reagan prepared for his reelection bid, the Republican Jewish Coalition, in collaboration with a political consulting firm, developed a plan to capture new Jewish voters. Setting its sights on Jewish communal leaders and "rank and file Jewish voter[s]," it sought to persuade Jews that none of the likely Democratic contenders could "out Israel President Reagan." The strategy document recommended "He Stands by Us" to be the unique theme "for the Jewish campaign . . . evocative of positive feelings regarding Israel," and offered some sample copy, "If it wasn't for President Reagan we would still be on the outside looking in."[41]

When the Republican Jewish Coalition rolled out its reelection strategy in the summer of 1984, it replaced the word "Republican" with the word "National" in its name. A press release announced the National Jewish Coalition as a "Bi-Partisan Organization" that "will demonstrate to fellow Jews that genuine and immediate Jewish interests are at stake . . . and that these interests are best served—and best protected—by the re-election of the Reagan team." While noting Reagan's strong record on improving the American economy and providing leadership on social issues, including his opposition to quotas and affirmative action, the release particularly highlighted the aid he provided to Israel and its economy. As campaigning heated up in the fall of 1984, the head of the Illinois chapter of the National Jewish Coalition reported, "Our surrogate speakers have been making appearances at synagogues, Jewish organizations and campuses, highlighting the outstanding achievements of the Republican Administration."[42]

Carefully clipped and preserved in Max Fisher's papers is an almost full-page advertisement placed in the *New York Times* by a former supporter of the Democratic party, a wealthy New York Jewish businessman, who announced to the world—or, at least, the paper's readership—that he was voting Republican because the Democratic party "Is Afraid To Speak Out Against Anti-Semitism." He castigated Democrats for aligning themselves with Jesse Jackson, who was connected to the Reverend Louis Farrakhan, the African American leader of the Nation of Islam on record for making antisemitic remarks. After much "soul searching," the Jewish businessman had concluded that Reagan's policies on Israel along with the Democratic party's embrace of a politician who consorted with an antisemite pointed him in the direction of voting Republican.[43]

Primarily through the United Jewish Appeal, American Jews gave money to Israel, but they also learned that, through political influence and donations to candidates, they could offer broader benefits to Israel. A study of Jewish donations to political candidates found that from 1970 to 1982, those who were recognized as pro-Israel received as much as 15% of their total campaign donations from Jews. Leaders of the Republican Jewish Coalition helped nonpartisan Jewish communal bodies think of themselves as partners in this political strategy, while insulating them from appearing partisan. In a diary-like entry from the summer of 1982, Max Fisher recorded that the executive committee of the Republican Jewish Coalition had decided to put some distance between itself and the Conference of Presidents, an indication of just how blurred the boundary between the two had become and, also, of the enduring value, beyond the narrow matter of legal compliance, that Jewish leaders perceived in maintaining an appearance of Jewish interests that rose above partisanship.[44]

———

By the late twentieth century, the complicated and historically situated threads of American policies and Jewish institutions now wove into a new pattern: the American Jewish philanthropic complex. The newly spun fabric of the American Jewish philanthropic complex created an illusion of solidity, cloaking the history and constitutive pieces that had formed it. As the complex grew, the long history of American associationalism and transformations in political and economic policy was ever more difficult to discern. Likewise, the complex obscured the historical forces that had led American Jewish institutions to invest in the market of futures of capital and identity and to seek security in the depoliticized language of nonpartisanship. The more individuals and institutions invested in it, the more the complex appeared timeless and certain. It was just how things were.

In 1986, when Norman Sugarman died at the age of sixty-nine, his obituary in the *Washington Post* simply noted that he was the author of the standard reference work on charitable tax exemptions, not that he was the originator of the philanthropic fund, by then more commonly known as the donor-advised fund. Only five years after his death, Fidelity Investments would be the first commercial entity to create an inhouse donor-advised fund purveyor, Fidelity Charitable Gift Fund, and by 2016, it would top the list of largest charitable organizations in the United States. A 2013 study of Jewish federations' endowments revealed that one-third of the approximately $16 billion in total endowment assets was held in donor-advised funds. The Jewish Communal Fund, the New York organization founded in 1972 with Sugarman's counsel, reported $1.5 billion in charitable assets, almost all in donor-advised funds, under its

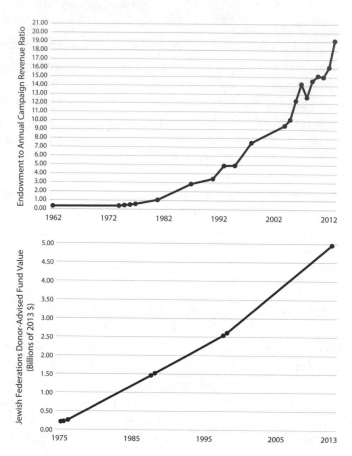

FIGURE 7.5. (*top*) Jewish Federations of North America, endowment to annual campaign revenue ratio, 1962–2013. Note: As the trajectory exceeds 1.00, the ratio shows that endowment dollars have outpaced annual campaign revenue. (*bottom*) Jewish federations donor-advised fund value (USD billions 2013). Graphs courtesy of Peter Ganong. Sources: 2013 Annual Survey of Planned Giving and Endowment Programs, Jewish Federations of North America, copy in author's possession; Status of Endowment Funds, 1976, 1977, and "CJF Endowment Development Program for 1979," December 28, 1978 (prepared by Louis Novins), Folder 1033, Box 43, Jewish Community Federation of Cleveland Records, Series II: Endowment Funds 1936–1990, Western Reserve Historical Society, Cleveland, Ohio; Gerald B. Bubis, "The Impact of Changing Issues on Federations and Their Structures," *Jewish Political Studies Review* 7, nos. 3–4 (Fall 1995): 89–112; Wayne L. Feinstein, "The Future of Philanthropy in the American Jewish Community," *Journal of Jewish Communal Service* 66, no. 2 (Winter 1989): 136–141; Stanley B. Horowitz, "Economic Concerns in Jewish Communal Service," *Journal of Jewish Communal Service* 55, no. 1 (Sept. 1978): 44–49; Donald Kent and Jack Wertheimer, "The Implications of New Funding Streams for the Federation System," *Journal of Jewish Communal Service* 76, no. 1 (Fall/Winter 1999): 69–79; Barry A. Kosmin, "New Directions in Contemporary Jewish Philanthropy: The Challenges of the 1990s," *New Directions for Philanthropic Fundraising*, no. 8 (Summer 1995): 41–51; Jack Wertheimer, "Current Trends in American Jewish Philanthropy," *American Jewish Year Book*, vol. 97 (Philadelphia: Jewish Publication Society, 1997), 3–92; and Henry Zucker, "Endowment Funds," from Council of Jewish Federations and Welfare Funds Meeting on Endowment and Trust Funds, at National Conference of Jewish Communal Service, June 4, 1963, Folder 1159, Box 49, Jewish Community Federation of Cleveland Records, Series II: Endowment Funds 1936–1990, Western Reserve Historical Society, Cleveland, Ohio.

control in its 2017 annual report, up from $1 billion just a decade earlier. In the charitable world, donor-advised funds had become big business, managed by commercial and public charitable entities, invested in high-earning stock portfolios, and used to support countless charitable causes. The historical shifts and individual acts of legal interpretation that willed them into being were overshadowed by how massive these funds became—and as that history faded, so too did the ability to imagine a different course for capital or power.[45]

The astronomical growth in philanthropic assets held in donor-advised funds contributed to massive changes to American philanthropic practice by the end of the twentieth century that all reflected the politics and economics of the private market. Across the United States by 2017, donor-advised funds, roughly a half-million separate accounts, held more than $100 billion in charitable assets, while the total number of private foundations, just over eighty thousand, held $855 billion in charitable assets. Individuals' freedom to use their private capital as proxy for public freedom was a prized and lasting component of Reagan's re-articulation of the American dream. That the American state would use its power of taxation to subsidize individuals' freedom was just one manifestation of the political collateral it took for private market politics to appear possible, desirable, and, even, inevitable. By the late twentieth century, the American state was the single largest backer of the market it had claimed to free from regulation and state control in the 1980s.[46]

The practices of American philanthropy reinforced the concentrations of power and capital enabled by privatization politics. With more access to capital than ever, the American Jewish philanthropic complex grew alongside American philanthropy, nurtured by a state that invested its power and, thus, the power of the public in private organs. The American Jewish philanthropic complex's growth and high returns became predicated on a stripped-down communal process that ceded itself to an individualized vision for charitable allocation and expansion. Never a perfect process, earlier versions of American Jewish communal philanthropy had at least attempted to use immediate capital distribution as a tool to spread power, even if just a few voices often controlled allocation decisions. But this vision for communal philanthropy would not survive the transformations in American political economy or the changes in American Jews' capital and political positions. The question at the turn of the millennium was just how concentrated the political and economic capital of the American Jewish philanthropic complex could become before its density would prove more of a liability than an asset.

8

The Complex

ON DECEMBER 11, 2008, FBI agents entered Bernard (Bernie) Madoff's Upper East Side apartment and arrested him on the charge of securities fraud. Although the Securities and Exchange Commission had investigated Madoff years earlier, his investment funds' unusually consistent returns during the subprime crisis and market downturn in 2008 had raised new suspicion. Throughout that fall, federal investigators gathered evidence that the seventy-year-old, Jewish, Queens-born financier had been running a sham investment operation, capturing capital from investors, falsely reporting returns, and using investors' money to pay those who wanted to cash in. In early December, aware that law enforcement was closing in on him, Madoff confessed to his sons, who turned him in to the authorities. Within days of his arrest, fund holders learned they had lost everything to Madoff's $50 billion-plus Ponzi scheme.[1]

Headlining newspapers and cable news for months, the Madoff story was as financially complex as it was pathos-filled. Few reporters could resist chronicling one of the most poignant sides of the story: the flocks of philanthropic organizations crippled by Madoff's swindle. They focused on the hospitals, universities, charities, and, especially, Jewish nonprofits that had put their trust and investment portfolios in Madoff's hands. Not only had Madoff wrecked individuals' futures, and not only had he ruined corporate banks, he had also damaged the public good, deceiving those who stewarded it with the promise that he could safeguard and grow their endowments, all the while using their money for his personal gain and to repay other investors. For many years, his theft had paid off, as the endowments he invested, just like the personal and corporate fortunes he managed, reported healthy growth on paper. Philanthropic organizations were in many ways his perfect clients and accessories. Fiscal prudence kept most from dipping into their endowments, beyond a portion of their returns, so paper growth was all that mattered.[2]

Madoff would be tried and sentenced to 150 years in prison, but his fraud had succeeded because, criminality aside, it looked awfully similar to late-twentieth-century capitalism. Short sales and futures and tranches made investment practices inscrutable to most investors, yet the rhetoric of freedom—the promise of Reagan's America—endowed capital growth with patriotic fervor. Market freedom, shorn of state regulation, had come to stand in for democratic political freedom: as long as the market was free, Americans would be free.[3]

Contrary to the language Americans had been sold, the market was not free for all to access its goods equally. Instead, for every mortgage bundled together and sliced up for resale or every carried interest dollar treated not as income but rather as capital gains (taxed at a lower rate than income), or a whole array of other financial transactions, the American state meted out benefits, with those at the top receiving enrichment out of reach to others. Perhaps beneficiaries of state largesse would direct their privilege downward, through job creation, consumption, or philanthropy, but even these voluntary acts of redistribution accrued private financial benefit through state subsidy. This was a formula for capital growth through inequality.[4]

Madoff's criminal conduct put his practices beyond the pale of what the American investment economy tolerated. He acted criminally and knowingly deceived his investors and government investigators. Yet what hurt his victims most was not the crime—which had been going on for decades, certainly to his benefit but also to that of his investors—as much as its exposure. When Madoff's investment empire fell, it revealed the capital void at the center of his fraud: there simply was not enough money. And, at least momentarily, it exposed the hollow prize of putting the public good in the trust of capitalism.[5]

As news of the significant losses sustained by Jewish individuals and institutions gained coverage, some commentators suggested that in addition to his fraudulent financial behavior, Madoff was also guilty of an "affinity scam," or "affinity fraud." Starting with his own family, his children, his nieces and nephews, and extending outward to his social circle assembled in country clubs in New York and Florida, Madoff had exploited his personal networks, many of which were firmly ensconced in the Jewish world, and had traded on his reputation as an active Jewish philanthropist.[6]

Articles listed the major Jewish donors, the Jewish family foundations, the federations and Jewish community foundations, and the Jewish nonprofits immediately ravaged by Madoff's arrest. The hits came quickly: just a few days after the FBI agents stormed his apartment, reports revealed that Steven

Spielberg, Elie Wiesel, Mortimer Zuckerman, Jacob Ezra Merkin. Norman
Braman, and Stanley Chais all lost substantial personal wealth, some of which
had been earmarked for Jewish charitable causes; that the Chais Family, Julian J. Levitt, and Charles I. and Mary Kaplan foundations were forced to close
and several others dramatically depleted; that Yeshiva University hemor-
rhaged in excess of $100 million from its endowment; that Hadassah and the
American Jewish Congress lost millions; and that Los Angeles's Jewish Community Foundation's investment pool was down by tens of millions. These
were the calculable losses, but their ripple effects were much harder to measure. Even organizations, such as New York's federation, that did not have endowment dollars invested in Madoff's funds relied on donors and foundations
that did. Various reports tried to assign a dollar figure, ranging anywhere from
$600 million to $2.5 billion depending how one took the sum of the future, to
the losses endured by Jewish philanthropic organizations.[7]

By the end of December, the Jewish animus directed toward Madoff
reached a fever pitch, with rabbis and Jewish leaders consigning Madoff to "a
special circle of hell" and spinning other Dantean fantasies. Rabbi David
Wolpe of Los Angeles fumed, "It is not possible for him to atone for all the
damage he did, and I don't even think there is a punishment that is commensurate with the crime, for the wreckage of lives that he's left behind. The only
thing he could do, for the rest of his life, is work for redemption that he would
never achieve." Jewish leaders blamed Madoff for more than immediate and
future financial losses to the Jewish community; they blamed him for the loss
of face he caused American Jews. In Wolpe's words, "[W]hen a Jew does this,
Jews feel ashamed by proxy." In addition to their embarrassment, some Jews
also felt fear. The Anti-Defamation League tracked an increase in online antisemitic comments, many of which used Madoff's arrest to advance conspiracy
theories that tied duplicitous financial behavior to Jews' plots for global
dominance.[8]

Madoff was so quickly demonized that, far from serving as a bellwether of
the pitfalls of putting the public good in the trust of putative market freedom,
he was regarded as an outlier. Although some immediate reports speculated
that donors and philanthropic organizations would feel compelled to reassess
their financial practices, including their reliance on endowments and investment capital, in just a few months, these predictions proved shortsighted. Re-
portedly, representatives from about three dozen of the largest Jewish private
foundations met less than two weeks after Madoff's arrest to coordinate a plan
to help organizations rebuild from their losses. Much like the American

government that year, they would use bailouts—what one report called "bridge financing"—to help Jewish communal life return to normalcy, before the full extent of Madoff's crimes had even been exposed.[9]

In surveying American Jewish philanthropy from the 1990s to the early decades of the new millennium, one sees more continuity than rupture and more ossification than mutability. The hardening of the American Jewish philanthropy complex was a direct result of its historical formation and, now, its embeddedness in the political economy of late-twentieth- and early-twenty-first-century American capitalism. The public good—the desideratum of democracy—had become stitched to market-driven financial practices and privatization through philanthropy. Complexes are strongest when they reinforce themselves. Even as some of the particular elements of Jewish philanthropy appeared benighted at the end of the twentieth century, the complex was not.

That Bernie Madoff's crime, which in material and spiritual ways challenged American Jewish philanthropy, was so quickly absorbed by the complex is one indication of its durability. The complex echoed and affirmed guiding practices of late-twentieth-century American political economy, in its reliance on market growth and private capital and power. And it wove that political economy into distinctly Jewish concerns rendered through the language of identity, survival, and continuity. The ability to warehouse and grow capital had become the central instrument for supporting Jewish identity and ensuring its survival.

By the turn of the millennium, glaring inequities in American life, emerging from decades of upwardly redistributive laws and policies, imprinted themselves on American Jewish philanthropy's answers to existential Jewish questions. For all of the blame, anger, and distress precipitated by the Madoff crisis, American Jewish organizations and their leaders continued to believe, as they had been trained to think over the last three decades, that philanthropic growth and accumulation was the best and only guarantor of an American Jewish future.

———

Studies of American Jewish philanthropy from the 1980s and 1990s consistently observed a decline in charitable giving to Jewish organizations and interpreted this pattern as a reflection of waning Jewish identity. Writing in the *American Jewish Year Book* in 1980, sociologist Steven M. Cohen reported that, according to data comparing Boston Jews' giving patterns in 1965 to their patterns in 1975, "philanthropic activity is becoming increasingly confined to those Jews who regularly act out their Jewishness." Turning to the language of finance, he concluded, "It is clear that Jewish involvement has become philanthropy's capital stock, and that that stock is badly in need of replenishment." Cohen advised that such revitalization could happen only if demographic trends of intermarriage and low fertility rates were reversed, an admonishment that would dominate the sociologist's normative statements in decades to come, and he speculated that this would occur only if more Jews learned to value their "Jewishness."[10]

Cohen was not alone in suggesting that the returns from Jewish philanthropy's investment in identity would, in turn, fuel more philanthropy. An essay in a 1991 volume on Jewish philanthropy charted the relationship between Jewish identity and philanthropy and concluded, based on the authors' survey of Jews in Northern New Jersey, "Building Jewish identity over a long time period certainly will have positive effects on Jewish philanthropy." Likewise, a 1994 article concluded that "investment in Jewish identity-building processes, particularly Jewish education and trips to Israel for young people," was the best hope for strengthening Jewish philanthropy.[11]

Many decades earlier, in the post–World War II years, American Jewish philanthropic leaders had landed upon Jewish identity as a central object for their institutions' reinvention, at a moment when Jews' increased sense of comfort in the United States posed a threat to those Jewish institutions that had been established and funded to meet Jews' pressing material needs. Thanks to the expansion of the American social welfare state, a greater number of philanthropic organizations could contemplate the possibility of investing in Jewish identity, in part through diverting funds that otherwise might have been necessary to meet urgent material needs. This had created a ripe environment for the rise of endowments, which promised perpetual growth, even as they held back capital from immediate circulation. By the final decades of the twentieth century, the language of Jewish identity had become inseparable from the logic of Jewish philanthropy, with one validating the other in a continuous loop. Cohen put it clearly in his 1980 article: "Questions about the future of Jewish giving, then, are in reality questions about the future of organized Jewry."[12]

From the standpoint of the late twentieth century, many commentators believed that of most consequence to the future of Jewish giving and organized Jewry was the striking growth of Jewish private family foundations. Mirroring

broad trends in American philanthropy, the number of Jewish private charitable foundations steadily increased starting in the mid-1970s and then rose
precipitously in the 1990s. Empirical data on Jewish private family foundations
were riddled with definitional problems, primarily, how one should determine
whether a private foundation should be classed as Jewish. Even so, a report
from the mid-1990s placed the number of Jewish private family foundations
at 3,000, while one less than a decade later set it at 10,000.[13]

Unlike a Jewish federation that had to court donors and so might feel restrained from suggesting that philanthropic gifts ought to have identity consequences and identity ought to fuel philanthropy, private family foundations
possessed different mechanisms of control that allowed them to assert the
relationship more forcefully. In the early 1990s, the Arie and Ida Crown Memorial Fund, the private foundation established in Chicago in 1947 and capi-
talized through new contributions and investment income over the interven-
ing half-century, sought to bind identity to philanthropy in the most formalistic
way possible: through its bylaws. Significantly older than most Jewish family
foundations, Crown had amended its bylaws several times over to change its
name, modify its array of officers and the timing of meetings, and respond to
revisions to the tax code. But as the Crown family's philanthropic holdings
were transferred from generation to generation, the bylaws also served to ar-
ticulate a vision of the ties between philanthropy and Jewish identity.

In 1993, through a bylaw amendment, the Crown Fund obligated itself to
distributing at least 50% of its total grants "to organizations which, in the opinion of the board of directors, are Jewish organizations." The new spending rule
revealed rising concern among board members that, unless governed by such
a rule, the foundation's mission might drift away from its original focus on
Jewish philanthropy. Aware that the line between a Jewish and not Jewish
organization could be fuzzy, the framers of the amendment mandated that the
board's determination would be "final and binding."[14]

With such clear power assigned to the board, the amended bylaws also set
out new criteria for service on the board: "No person shall be eligible to serve
as a director unless such person has demonstrated his or her Jewish identity
through his or her personal religious observance, synagogue membership,
organizational affiliation, or in some other manner that shows his or her ties
to the Jewish community and to Judaism." Relying on the language of identity,
the clause continued that if, over the course of time, a director's "Jewish identity" became "questionable" and he or she was no longer "identifiable as a Jew,"
that person would be expected to resign from the board. Not satisfied to leave

identity in the hands of the individual, however, the clause further specified, "A person shall conclusively be deemed ineligible . . . if any six (6) of the nine (9) oldest then living descendants of HENRY CROWN and IRVING CROWN deliver to such person, and to the President of the Corporation a written statement that, in their good faith opinion, such person does not possess a Jewish identity, setting forth the basis for their opinion."[15]

Turning to the tool they possessed to try to shape an uncertain future, the second generation of Crowns—Henry's two living sons and Irving's daughter—used their family foundation's bylaws to weave philanthropy and Jewish identity together into a structure of discipline. Over the past five years, the patresfamilias of the Crown family, Irving and Henry, had both died, likely fueling the effort to amend the foundation's legal instrument and tighten its discipline over the future board. Just as their fathers could no longer direct what happened to the money they had put in the philanthropic foundation, so too would the second generation lose control of it to the inevitable force of mortality.[16]

Of course, as the act of crafting new legal parameters to guide the foundation proved, bylaws were living documents and could be revised according to their own procedures away from their original intent. If 75% of the board willed it, almost any element of Crown's bylaws could be changed, as long as the alteration did not breach state or federal laws. But so adamant was the second generation of the Crown family to maintain the Jewish focus of their foundation and the Jewish identity of their family long into the future, they mandated that the new amendments introduced in the early 1990s required unanimous consent to change. The board members of the Crown foundation embraced tactics of self-policing and family surveillance as necessary means for guarding their family's Jewish future, measured by its philanthropic and identity commitments. The framers of the new bylaws maintained that without identifiably Jewish descendants, money set aside to support Jewish life and to sustain the Jewish identity of the Crown family in perpetuity would face the same hard truths of human mortality: we cannot outlive ourselves.[17]

In the same years that the Crown foundation's board approved the identity clause, Jewish communal organizations and social researchers, some of whom were retained by those same organizations, reported a Jewish identity crisis, illustrated most starkly by intermarriage data. Throughout the 1980s, the Council of Jewish Federations coordinated demographic surveys of American Jews and channeled funds from Mandell (Bill) L. Berman, a Detroit-born housing developer and philanthropist, to endow the Berman North American

Jewish Data Bank at the Graduate School and University Center of the City University of New York. In 1990, a multi-phased survey generated a vast store of data from a sampling of American Jews, but the data point most widely broadcast was the intermarriage rate, reported at 52%. Even as researchers would contest the exact percentage, none could dispute that the rate of inter-marriage had increased over the past decades, a state of affairs that drew a new level of attention to the terms of and funding for Jewish identity. Begin-ning in the 1970s, Jewish social researchers and leaders had started to use the words "survival" and "continuity" to describe the stakes of their enterprises, whether studying Jewish demographic patterns or trying to develop pro-grams to influence those patterns. By the 1990s, Jewish continuity reigned supreme in the lexicon of Jewish communal priorities, and researchers and leaders tended to pit it against intermarriage, imagined as the ultimate disrup-tion to Jewish continuity.[18]

In the bylaws of the Crown foundation, however, the rigid approach to Jewish identity threatened to undermine its philanthropic commitment to continuity—its own and that of the Jewish people. By 2009, the foundation board backtracked on its Jewish identity test, instead crafting a more flexible kinship model to pair with its investment in philanthropic perpetuity as a path-way for Jewish continuity. The newly revised bylaws distinguished among generations as well as between "Crown Members" (that is, "living descendants of Henry Crown and Irving Crown who have reached age 25") and "Spouse Members" ("who have reached age 25 and have been married to such Crown Member for at least one year"), apportioning each with slightly different rights and responsibilities. Removed was any mention of Jewishness as the grounds for membership or forced resignation. In its place, the board prioritized kin-ship lines, while maintaining the rule that 50% of its grants be allocated to Jewish initiatives. Notably, the board remained fixed on an identity-based fi-nancial strategy of capitalizing Jewish projects through a perpetual foundation, regardless of the marital and affiliation choices that Crown descendants might make. Jewish continuity could be achieved in capital terms, even as the board struggled to understand its human terms.[19]

By 2016, the Crown family controlled roughly $1 billion in charitable assets. Yet only two-thirds of this capital resided in its family foundation, with the other one-third held in a structure defined in tax code as a "supporting organization." Much like donor-advised funds, supporting organizations emerged from the 1969 Tax Reform Act as vehicles for extending public charitable benefits to a wide array of charitable capital. In the case of a supporting organization, in order to receive the preferred tax treatment, its purposes had to be limited to the mission of the public charity that housed it, and its decision-making authority was split between representatives from the public charity (who maintained a controlling number of seats on the board) and members of the family. In 1985, the Crown family had established the Crown Family Foundation as a supporting organization "to support and carry out the exempt purposes of the Jewish Federation of Metropolitan Chicago and the Jewish Fund of Metropolitan Chicago." The bylaws for the family's private foundation, although only governing that entity, specified in the early 1990s that the 50% clause could be fulfilled by grants made from any charitable entities "recognized by the Board of Directors as part of the Crown Family's organized philanthropy," and clarified in 2009 that this included supporting organizations. (In 2004, members of the Crown family established a second, much smaller supporting organization, also held at the Chicago federation.)[20]

Bound by its own legal instrument to make half of its grants to Jewish organizations, the Crown family's decision to house some of its philanthropic assets in a public charity, the Chicago federation, with a specifically Jewish mission made good sense. The capital placed in the supporting organization would gain the standing and benefits of public charitable capital and could be used to fulfill the bylaw requirements. And, surely, for Chicago's federation the arrangement was a great boon. Not only could it calculate the supporting organization's distributions as part of its total annual grants, it also saw its endowment total swell with the addition of the supporting organization's assets.

By 2014, Crown-designated capital constituted approximately one-third of the Chicago federation's endowment. The astounding growth that the federation's endowment experienced, from $10 million at midcentury to $32 million in 1975 and, eventually in 2014, about $1 billion, with $600 million in supporting foundations and $140 million in donor-advised funds, would have been impossible without Crown contributions. Stewards of Chicago's endowment were quick to point out that more than 10%, including about $8.5 million of the allocations from donor-advised funds and supporting organizations, went directly to support the federation's annual campaign, though they also noted that in raw dollars, more money from these funds supported non-Jewish than Jewish organizations. While philanthropic capital held in Chicago's federation was irrevocably charitable and legally the property of the federation, a great deal of it also was recognizably Crown capital, often disbursed with the Crown name attached to it and, certainly, perceived by federation professionals as indicating the sway of the Crown family over their organization.[21]

By the late 1990s and early 2000s, Jewish federations became reliant upon the same philanthropic vehicles that also challenged their power. In 1999, a professor who had studied trends in Jewish philanthropy over the last decade cowrote an article with a federation staff member on "new funding streams" for federations. The two noted that although the last annual campaign had raised a total of $756 million across all Jewish federations in the United States, the revenue from it, once the benchmark for Jewish fund-raising, was being steadily eclipsed by the capital that federations maintained in endowments and, especially, donor-advised funds and supporting foundations. According to the authors' calculations, the holdings in these new financial structures not only surpassed annual campaign dollars many times over but also grew at a much faster rate and thus would continue to comprise a greater and greater share of federation assets. In the future, these funds might keep federations solvent, even, according to the authors, "as merely conduits for the largesse of the wealthiest Jews." The future of Jewish federations kept afloat not by mass communal giving but rather by stores of private capital would not be all that different from the Crown board's eventual decision to put more stock in financial practices and less in identity tests as the primary mechanism for Jewish continuity.[22]

———

Despite the differences in tax treatment, the distance between private foundations and public charities appeared to be shrinking at the turn of the millennium, as both charitable forms increasingly bore the marks of private control and capital accumulation. In the midst of this realignment, Jewish philanthropic leaders tried to understand how the growing power of individual donors, especially an elite group of very wealthy Jewish families, many of whom, like the Crowns, held private family foundations and a variety of other philanthropic vehicles, could be harnessed to advance what they had worked to define as consensus Jewish interests. Without the federation to set priorities, they worried that the Jewish philanthropic sector would splinter and fade.

In response to fears about the diminishment of Jewish philanthropy despite unprecedented wealth among American Jews, a small group of philanthropists and foundation professionals established a coalition in 1990 to structure private Jewish giving. Called the Jewish Funders Network, its mission statement called for the coordination of new nodes of Jewish philanthropic power "to share ideas, resources, connections, and methods" and to "foster cooperation."

The founders of the Jewish Funders Network opted for a broad definition of Jewish philanthropy that could range from non-Jewish support for causes that served Jewish interests to Jewish support for causes that were not explicitly Jewish, but that reflected the Jewish value of "Tikkun Olam," defined as "the responsibility of Jews to make the world a better place." Finally, its founders declared their aspirations not only to coordinate Jewish philanthropy more efficiently and to use an explicitly progressive vision to broaden what constituted Jewish philanthropy, but also to change the fundamental nature of philanthropy by employing "democratic" means to bring recipient communities into funding decisions.[23]

Observers noted the progressive and anti-establishment sensibility that drove the first phase of the Jewish Funders Network. An article from the late 1990s explained, "[T]he network originally provided a meeting ground for a small group of private funders interested in supporting progressive secular and Jewish causes, such as Arab-Jewish dialogue, Jewish women's history projects, innovative Jewish and interdenominational education, environmental conservation in Israel." Its first conference, held in January 1991, included sessions that brought attention to how Jewish funders could help solve the AIDS crisis; craft a Jewish response to oil dependency; address homelessness and poverty, especially among women and children, in the face of government cutbacks; and support dialogue and peace work between Jews and Arabs.[24]

In 1998, Marc Kramer, the chair of the board, described the Jewish Funders Network as "hit[ting] a vital nerve" among "the next generation of funders, many of whom are somewhat alienated from traditional ways of giving, or the philanthropic system." Donors drawn to the organization "have not felt connected to the Jewish establishment, have not been interested in or engaged by the federation system." "A very attractive place for progressive funders to come," in Kramer's description, the Jewish Funders Network offered more left-leaning and less institutionally tied funders everything they believed the federation was not.[25]

Yet for all of Kramer's effort to position the Jewish Funders Network as an alternative site for progressive Jewish philanthropists, Evan Mendelson, the newly hired executive director and first full-time staff person for the organization, prudently assured reporters in 1998 that the organization was transforming to serve a broad constituency. She emphasized, "There is much less of a specific ideological basis today." Under her leadership, the organization instituted a membership policy allowing foundations or individuals that pledged at least $20,000 yearly to charitable giving to join the network, and, by the late 1990s, it had approximately 260 members.[26]

Over time, instead of pinning its identity on its progressive impulses, the organization redefined its mission as seeking to improve Jewish funders' philanthropic strategy, a purportedly politically neutral goal. Backpedaling from leftist politics, Mendelson sought to divide foundations and federations along the poles of innovation and tradition. She described foundations as "risk-takers" and "change agents," able to tap into models from the for-profit world, and characterized federations as "structures," less entrepreneurial and often burdened with unsexy but essential communal tasks. The Jewish Funders Network appreciated federations' structural work, but its commitment was to the foundation world, where it hoped to foster the divide Mendelson described by encouraging Jewish foundations to self-identity as innovators.[27]

While still driven by his own anti-establishment commitments, Kramer led the way in formulating market-driven innovation as the new mission for the Jewish Funders Network. In 1999, he and a friend, Harvard Business School professor Michael Porter, published a seminal article in the *Harvard Business Review* entitled "Philanthropy's New Agenda: Creating Value." They argued that the massive growth in charitable foundations over the last two decades obligated foundations to carry broader social responsibilities than ever. With assets that had increased more than 1000% in just twenty years, "Foundations can and should lead social progress." Notably, the authors' outline for social progress was rooted in process, measurement, and calibration, not policy reform or stated political ideology.[28]

For Kramer and Porter, philanthropy had no greater goal than "to create value." Although they appreciated the double entendre, their conception of value emerged from a capitalist framework. Philanthropic foundations, like private businesses, could succeed only through the conservation of their worth; that is, they had to create more value than they expended. "A foundation creates values," they explained, "when it achieves an equivalent social benefit with fewer dollars or creates greater social benefit for comparable cost." And just like businesses, foundations could build value by investing in strategies to make each dollar they held worth more, even without traditional consumer-driven modes of profit generation. (The word "strategy" appeared 32 times in the nine-page article.)[29]

As the Jewish Funders Network expanded, it ceded its progressive and anti-establishment goals to a vision of progress through market-based strategy and innovation. In a show of its turn away from partisan progressive politics, the board hired Mark Charendoff, a man with right-of-center politics, as its new president and CEO in 2001 to replace Evan Mendelson. He pledged himself to helping the more than nine hundred individuals and three hundred foundations that were members at the beginning of his tenure to use "their wealth more strategically." The first conference over which he presided included presentations from the managing director of the Global Foundation Group at JP Morgan Chase and Jeffrey Swartz, the CEO of Timberland.[30]

Unlike in its early years, when it struggled to stay afloat, the organization under Charendoff's leadership became a destination for the most prominent American Jewish funders and their foundations. Through a new membership structure, they could pledge hundreds of thousands of dollars over multiyear stretches to support the Jewish Funders Network. Charendoff perceived a direct correlation between the organization's financial growth and its abandonment of its left-leaning and anti-establishment identity. Large funders, who in his estimation would not have been interested in the earlier incarnation of the Jewish Funders Network, were attracted to its commitment to strategy and innovation, ideas familiar to many of them from their own professional worlds. And they welcomed the opportunity to spend time with their wealthy peers at annual conferences and special events reserved for high-level funders only.[31]

As so-called mega-donors, wealthy men like Michael Steinhardt, Charles Bronfman, and Leslie Wexner, who controlled their own private family foundations, joined the ranks of the Jewish Funders Network, the organization ironically threatened federations more than when it had defined itself as countercultural and critical of established federations. Alongside its growth, it built the infrastructure, including research reports and records, to magnify the trend of private Jewish charitable dollars flowing outside of federation channels. Studies from the early 2000s helped create the perception of a stark line of division between federations and Jewish foundations. Researchers still acknowledged the challenge of categorizing Jewish foundations and used a variety of formulas to do so, but with the Jewish Funders Network in place, they could rely on its membership rolls and data as definitive of Jewish foundations and then track those foundations as gaining ground within the Jewish philanthropic sector.[32]

Still, whatever competition existed between the federations and private foundations, the two philanthropic vehicles were increasingly unified under a market-based logic of measurable value creation. Jeffrey Solomon, president of the Andrea and Charles Bronfman Philanthropies and the former chief financial officer for the New York federation, noted in 2005 that for all of their divergences, federations and foundations could act in tandem. Echoing the distinction that the first executive director of the Jewish Funders Network had drawn, Solomon suggested that foundations' innovation and federations' structures together could insure that as wealth transferred to a new generation, it would not be transferred away from Jewish life.[33]

That same year, a small group of high-level foundation and federation leaders gathered in Tarrytown, New York, to inaugurate an annual convening guided by shared priorities and potential collaborations. Similarly, a 2007 report funded by the United Jewish Communities (an organization formed in 1999 from a merger of the Council of Jewish Federations and the United Jewish Appeal, renamed in 2009 as the Jewish Federations of North America), sought to "foster strategic alignment between federations and foundations" with the same ends in mind: to capture Jewish philanthropic dollars, wherever they happened to reside, for shared Jewish interests. A new class of experts—data collectors, consultants, and the executive directors or presidents of large foundations, many of whom, like Solomon, had started their careers working at federations—helped steward Jewish foundations and federations toward a common pursuit, made all the easier by their shared financial practices.[34]

Since its founding in the early 1990s, the Jewish Funders Network had transformed from an avowedly countercultural organization to one that represented the very core of Jewish philanthropic culture. In part, this occurred because of its success bringing new strategies, such as coordinated efforts to share ideas and, even, funding ventures among private philanthropists, into the center of Jewish philanthropic life. But far more consequential was its embrace of Kramer's market-based vision of value generation as the fundamental obligation of philanthropy. This capitalist objective shored up innovation, strategy, and efforts to spark younger givers under a framework of capital growth and accumulation, and it hardened the American Jewish philanthropic complex through a process of replication. Funders and professionals learned that they were part of a sector because they had common objectives, but they also learned how to remake themselves to fit into the sector. The Jewish Funders Network served to socialize high-rolling philanthropists and their professional handlers to fund together and, as the saying goes, to play together. Later, its efforts would be augmented by those of a handful of other institutions that similarly aimed to coordinate Jewish philanthropy by creating catalogues, curating conferences, and supporting fellows whose projects showcased the fruits of Jewish philanthropy. Despite the diversity of projects that might emerge from these efforts, the most significant product was an isomorphic logic—that every node in the system shared an underlying structure and, thus, validated and naturalized that structure.[35]

By the beginning of the new millennium, Jewish private foundations had strengthened, not threatened, the American Jewish philanthropic complex. Shaped and nourished by the political economy of the late-twentieth-century state, foundations and federations and the various tax structures within them, such as supporting organizations and donor-advised funds, were all vehicles for the accumulation and growth of charitable capital, an abstraction from the circulation of actual capital. Charitable capital could do public good by simply existing and, especially for Jewish organizations committed to the language of Jewish survival and continuity, could generate value through its promise of perpetual growth and eternity.

———

No product of American Jewish philanthropy so perfectly represented the power of the American Jewish philanthropic complex by the end of the twentieth century as did Birthright, a program originated in the late 1990s to offer every Jewish young person a free trip to Israel. Its goals, structure, and reputation gained fuel from the complex and, in turn, powered it. Explicitly not political, while tied closely to advocating Jewish and American support for Israel, it amplified the depoliticized politics of American philanthropy. Furthermore, embedded in the market logic of charitable capital that paid little heed to the difference between federations or foundations, Birthright validated financial instruments as the arbiters of value, feeding a complex that calculated its worth by measurements of growth and accumulation, whether of dollars or markers of Jewish identity. Fixed on Jewish identity and continuity as its products, it distilled into the span of a ten-day trip the most significant trends in American Jewish philanthropy since the post–World War II years.

Framed as a unified endeavor of the Jewish people, Birthright drew its vitality from a Jewish philanthropic complex so tightly constructed as to make it credible that a singular Jewish people would finance an identity-producing but politically neutral trip to Israel. American Jews began to travel on organized youth tours to Israel almost immediately after the establishment of the Jewish state. However, whereas religious institutions (generally denominationally specific youth groups) or ideological institutions (usually American Zionist groups espousing different political philosophies) had sponsored the vast

majority of those tours, the individuals and groups that took credit for founding Birthright all imagined it as a tour suitable for every young American Jew,
with a low barrier for entry: it would be free to the participant and would not
exert any ideological pressure on young people to immigrate to Israel.[36]

Birthright's multiple points of origin highlight the constituent parts of the
philanthropic complex. According to ethnographer Shaul Kelner, Israel's dep-
uty foreign minister Yossi Beilin first floated the idea in a talk he delivered at
the 1994 General Assembly, the annual gathering of Jewish federations. In
considering how American Jews could maintain a close relationship with Israel, he suggested that "every young Jew [should] receive a birthday card from
the local Federation on his or her seventeenth birthday with a coupon for
travel and accommodations in Israel during the next summer vacation."
Throwing down the gauntlet to the professional and philanthropic leaders of
the Jewish federation system, Beilin may have thought it strategic to get buy-in
from what some federation leaders persisted in calling "the central address" of
American Jewish life. (Historically, Jewish federations had focused on domestic fund-raising, leaving the task of raising money for Israel to the United Jewish Appeal; however, beginning in the 1980s, the already blurred line between
the two started to fade as the institutions merged on the local and, eventually,
national level.) As Kelner explains, however, many federation leaders in fact
resented the foreign minister's proposal to reallocate funds directed to social
services in Israel to this new travel program. The narrative that Israel needed
American cash in order to function, despite many indications to the contrary,
continued to be part of federations' fund-raising tactics. For an Israeli governmental official to shrug off his country's dependence on American Jewish
money could strain donors' credulity when it came to federations' call for
donations.[37]

Private funders, however, were not beholden to the same narrative of Israel's
economic dependence and vulnerability as federations and did not have donors
to court. A different origin story of Birthright begins with those private funders
and their family foundations. Michael Steinhardt, a successful hedge fund
manager with a personal net worth of $300 million when he established a
private foundation (his second) in 1994, wrote in his autobiography, *No Bull*,
that he conceived of the idea on a picturesque Jerusalem evening in 1997. Steinhardt and his friend Charles Bronfman, who managed the Seagram liquor
empire with his brother, Edgar, and in 1986 had established the Andrea and
Charles Bronfman Philanthropies, strolled together that evening. Moved by
the city and the evening, Steinhardt recalled proposing to Bronfman that they

create "a universal trip whereby every Jew, aged 18 to 26, would have, as a rite of passage, a 10-day trip to Israel." Bronfman already supported a youth-travel program called Israel Experience, but according to Steinhardt, he immediately saw the wisdom of remaking and expanding that program. That very evening, the two pledged $5 million each to build the program.[38]

Its genesis tales, variously set in the public charity and private foundation worlds and peopled by an Israeli government official, American Jewish communal leaders, and phenomenally wealthy private American citizens, indicate the commanding power that Birthright gained as a product of the American Jewish philanthropic complex. When it launched in 1999, its funding model combined each plotline, with the estimated $210 million necessary to launch it split among private Jewish philanthropists, the Israeli government (through the Jewish Agency and Keren Hayesod), and federations. In 2001, the Birthright Israel Foundation incorporated as its own charitable organization with the capacity to absorb far larger gifts than most Jewish nonprofits, other than universities and hospitals, many of which by this point were connected to Jewish life in name and history only.[39]

In addition to the work of creating the tours—finding young people to staff them, planning itineraries, managing an application process for participants— the founders of Birthright almost immediately created the infrastructure to measure its value, taking their cue from people like the Jewish Funders Network's Marc Kramer and others who suggested that measuring and creating value were shared pursuits. In 2005, Steinhardt gave $12 million to Brandeis University to establish the Steinhardt Social Research Institute. Although its researchers produced a range of studies to fulfill the institute's mission "to provid[e] unbiased, high-quality data about contemporary Jewry," Birthright was its core area of exploration, with studies of the program released at least annually and sometimes more frequently.[40]

Thanks to reams of social scientific data produced about Birthright, its supporters were able to track not only the numbers of participants but also how participants changed their behavior and Jewish observances in the wake of the trip. Of most consequence, as the data piled up and years passed, social researchers suggested that rates of intermarriage with non-Jews were measurably lower for participants than nonparticipants, a tangible form of evidence that the program's goals of strengthening Jewish identity and fostering Jewish continuity were being attained. These data, in turn, helped Birthright make fundraising pitches. Investments in Birthright yielded the return of Jewish continuity.[41]

The American Jewish philanthropic complex and Birthright seemed to fit together seamlessly. Yet, the fit between the two was so perfect that just as the perceived strength of one fortified the other, perceived flaws in one also exposed the shortcomings of the other. With growing fervor, voices from within and outside of the Jewish community started to scrutinize Birthright's political positions, its financial practices, and its ways of creating and measuring Jewish value through identity and continuity. Mounting criticism of Birthright inexorably exposed these very same questions within the broader Jewish philanthropic world and amplified critiques of American philanthropy that had grown more vociferous since the 2008 economic recession.[42]

In 2007, Sheldon Adelson, a Boston-born Jewish man who built a fortune from casino development, donated a total of $30 million to Birthright through his private family foundation, enabling the program to expand its operations by tens of thousands of students annually. Few other Jewish organizations, aside from university programs and Israeli medical institutions (which were treated as "Jewish" organizations according to most surveys of Jewish philanthropy) would have had the capacity to absorb such a large gift. That same year, *Forbes* ranked Adelson the third-wealthiest person in the United States and sixth-wealthiest in the world, with a net worth of $26.5 billion. Known for his support of Republican politicians and conservative causes in the United States and Israel, Adelson's largest charitable expenditures in the beginning of the 2000s were not to those political causes but rather to Birthright. According to one review of its tax returns, the Adelson Family Foundation donated a total of $123 million to Birthright from its first large gift in 2007 through 2011, accounting for 40% of the total money raised by Birthright over that same time period.[43]

The fact that one donor's foundation bankrolled such a substantial proportion of the program's budget raised questions in some observers' minds about the relationship between Adelson's conservative politics and the program's stated political neutrality. Hoping to get ahead of the concerns, the research team at the Steinhardt Social Research Institute initiated a 2014 study titled "Does Taglit-Birthright Israel Foster Long-Distance Nationalism?" Noting Birthright's guidelines that eschewed any political position and embraced "a balanced presentation of alternative views on complex issues," and highlighting a 2011 policy change that disallowed the practice of partnering with advocacy organizations for particular tour groups, the authors set out to test whether Birthright's claims to political neutrality were true or if rising criticism of Birthright's "right-wing political bias" had basis in fact. From their storehouse of survey data, the researchers concluded, "Taglit [Birthright's Hebrew name, literally, "discovery"] achieves its declared aim of fostering forms of homeland attachment that are politically neutral in the Israeli context." Yet empirical data could not stem the tide of rising criticism about the political and economic structure of a program—and an entire philanthropic sector—framed by a legal mandate to disavow its politics and funded through financial practices that empowered private wealth concentration with the subsidy of the American public.[44]

Philip Klutznick or Max Fisher, to be certain, had never concealed their party loyalties, nor had the scores of other Jewish philanthropists who filled the ranks of the Republican Jewish Coalition in the 1980s, but all had performed a depoliticized version of their politics when it came to asserting Jewish interests. In their communal roles, they had invoked consensus and nonpartisanship, adhering to the framework of tax law to dodge the deeply political nature of their advocacy. And even in their openly political positions, as political donors or advisors, they had protected a place for Jewish consensus as if it were removed from the business of politics. This had always been a performance, more or less credible at varying moments. But Adelson refused to adhere to the script. In early 2012, he told *Forbes* that although he was against people using their wealth to control elections, "as long as it's doable I'm going to do it." Thanks to shifts in American campaign finance law two years prior, even if wealth could not control elections, it could influence them more than it had in the past, as individuals and large corporations were no longer limited in their ability to fund political candidates, so long as they channeled their money through organizations (often called Super PACs) separate from candidates' campaigns.[45]

At a gathering in 2012 called Tribefest, an annual federation-sponsored conference for young adults held that year in Adelson's hometown, Las Vegas, the casino magnate flouted the long-established practice among Jewish philanthropists of acting as if a barrier separated their partisan politics from their Jewish communal interests. Entering a session in progress that had been organized as a debate between the executive director of the Republican Jewish Coalition and the president of the National Jewish Democratic Council, Adelson interrupted the speakers and launched into a tirade against President Obama. An anonymous source told a reporter that "the only reason Adelson was able to monopolize the conversation . . . was because he 'owned the room, literally.'"[46]

In 2015, Open Hillel, an organization created two years earlier to protest the restrictions that Hillel placed on its university chapters' Israel programming,

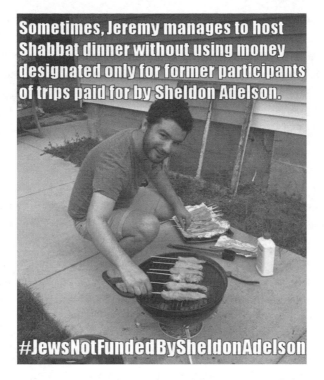

FIGURE 8.1. Image from Open Hillel's #JewsNotFundedBy
SheldonAdelson campaign, posted on Tumblr, September 1, 2015.
Courtesy of Jeremy Swack.

used the hashtag #JewsNotFundedBySheldonAdelson to expose the hold that
Adelson exercised over American Jewish life and chided Jewish organizations
for believing they could take his money without political consequence. Indeed, Open Hillel and several new countercultural Jewish organizations, including IfNotNow, suggested that the Jewish communal world was not simply
buffeted by its largest donors; rather, it shared its major donors' politics in
equal measure to its donors' share in it.[47]

Because Adelson's foundation bankrolled such a substantial percentage of
Birthright; because, especially with changes to campaign finance law, his political donations could significantly advance the Republican party's agenda;
and because he openly aligned himself with a right-wing Israeli agenda, critics
of the American Jewish philanthropic scene pounced on him with particular
ferocity. In his actions and statements, Adelson begged the question of how
American Jewish philanthropy could possibly stand aloof from politics.

Whether Adelson actually compelled Birthright to embrace a certain political agenda may have been important to the program's supporters or critics. But that American Jewish philanthropy was, itself, a political creature concerned with the distribution and accumulation of power, and that those who operated within the American Jewish philanthropic world exercised profound political influence to present a set of putatively consensus Jewish interests, were truths that predated and exceeded Adelson or Birthright.

———

Small fissures in the American Jewish philanthropic complex were most threatening to its integrity when they exposed cleavages that ran deeper than the complex itself. This had appeared to be the case in the few weeks after Madoff's 2008 arrest, yet Jewish communal leaders quickly smoothed over the cracks, drawing upon similar efforts at the level of American state policy to rebuild confidence in private finance and capitalist growth after a period of financial crisis. Adelson's prominent support for rightist political agendas in the United States and Israel—an extension of the machine that Max Fisher and others beginning in the 1970s had built to organize American Jewish communal interests around conservative politics—drew scrutiny because it threatened the depoliticized politics of American Jewish philanthropy and exposed the extent to which monied interests appeared to be driving American politics, more generally, to the right. Yet aside from a few voices, castigated by many Jewish leaders as naively youthful, overly radical, or unsparingly critical of Jewish life, Adelson's philanthropic capital hardly stimulated a communal reckoning about the deeply political nature of its philanthropic system, just as Madoff's criminality barely skimmed the surface of questions about the market-driven model of philanthropy.

Again, in 2018 and 2019, a deep cleavage might have cracked the American Jewish philanthropic complex, as Michael Steinhardt, the prominent Jewish philanthropist, and Steven M. Cohen, the sociologist frequently contracted by Jewish philanthropists and philanthropic organizations to evaluate their continuity- and identity-oriented work, faced allegations of sexual misconduct. Just as Madoff's arrest had exposed how embedded Jewish philanthropic practices were in American finance and capitalism, and Adelson's political visibility exposed the intersections of Jewish philanthropic power and American political power, the allegations leveled against Cohen and Steinhardt seemed to implicate the central ideology of Jewish identity and continuity in a broad pattern of gender inequality and oppression.[48]

In the era of #MeToo, when women and investigative journalists shined a spotlight on high-profile cases of workplace sexual misconduct and exposed the rampant sexual intimidation, exploitation, harassment, and assault that buttressed systems of gender inequality, the allegations against Cohen and Steinhardt rippled across Jewish and non-Jewish conversations about sexual politics. Women came forward to talk about times when these two men violated their sexual autonomy and attempted to control their bodies with words and actions in professional settings. Although the substance of the specific allegations varied, both cases revealed a culture of tolerance for their alleged misdeeds, which had been the subject of rumors and, in Steinhardt's case, an actual policy barring female staff members of Hillel, where Steinhardt served on the board and donated significant funds, from meeting alone with the philanthropist.[49]

Some responses to these revelations suggested that each man was individually responsible for his malfeasance—reminiscent of responses to Madoff—but others, including my own, asked whether the logic and structure of American Jewish philanthropy itself was implicated in creating hostile work environments for women and, more broadly, advancing a gender politics predicated upon women's subservience and inequality. According to reports, both men had brought inappropriate attention to women's marital status, their fertility, and their bodies, whether in front of large audiences or in workplace situations. The allegations against them, like their investment in marriage and reproduction as the heart of Jewish continuity programs, seemed to indicate their belief that women's sexuality could be controlled to serve the Jewish public good; that is, as if it, too, were a form of capital that could be measured and valued, as much for public benefit as, perhaps, private gain.[50]

Whether Jewish communal responses to these allegations—and new ones that grabbed headlines, such as the nature of billionaire philanthropist Leslie Wexner's ties to convicted sex criminal Jeffrey Epstein—would pry open and expose the fissures that over the past decade had appeared in the American Jewish philanthropic complex remained an unresolved question. By and large, Jewish communal responses to allegations of philanthropists' wrongdoing continued to draw focus to individuals, echoing the wider American conversation about tainted philanthropic gifts, highlighted most strikingly in the case of arts and culture institutions deciding to blackball the Sackler family after allegations emerged in 2018 that it had helped cause and then profited from the opioid epidemic.

This line of response—to focus attention on individuals, whether for their misdeeds or their virtues—posed little threat to the American Jewish philanthropic complex. Indeed, it strengthened it. As long as criticism was directed against individuals and not the financial and political structure that empowered them to act, it was difficult to see how any substantial change would be affected. Nonetheless, a set of reformers with strikingly different visions for the future of American Jewish philanthropy, American democracy, and American capitalism emerged in the early decades of the twenty-first century, suggesting that just as the complex was a product of its history, so too would it change with history.[51]

Reform

Three Snapshots

I.

In the late 1990s, a small group of young people began to meet to discuss their common struggle with economic prosperity. Born into families with substantial wealth and set to inherit a portion of it in the near future, these mainly twenty-somethings were plagued with discomfort and, for some, shame about the privilege and power they possessed. Before long, they established an organization called Resource Generation. Over the first decade of its existence, Resource Generation organizers convened monthly gatherings in several cities, held weekend workshops and training sessions, published pamphlets and books, collaborated with progressive philanthropic organizations, created cross-class giving circles, hired a small staff, and formed a board. In 2012, 1,200-people strong, it defined its mission as helping "young people with wealth bring all they have and all they are to the social change movements and issues they care about. We organize to transform philanthropy, policy, and institutions, and leverage our collective power to make lasting structural change."[1]

Not a Jewish organization, Resource Generation nonetheless included a substantial core of Jewish founders and members. Members spent a great deal of time reflecting on the identity politics of their wealth: what factors had allowed them to benefit from economic security, and how did their social locations help or hinder their ability to attain the mission of "lasting structural change"? According to an ethnographic study written by a self-identified member, "Resource Generation can be thought of as a caucus space in which young people with wealth can talk about their own positionality and are able to understand some of the side effects of their class privilege through a process of learning from and with other people who have class privilege." As part of a "critical consciousness"-raising process, some of the members organized a Jewish "praxis group" to explore the intersection between class privilege and Jewishness. They sought to recognize the historical and familial factors that made it difficult to wrest themselves away from viewing accumulated capital as a source of existential protection—and, in doing so, hoped to free themselves from the cycle of using power over resources, labor, and land as a hedge against imagined vulnerability.[2]

A member of the Jewish praxis group, Margot Seigle, eventually published a blog post in 2016 entitled, "Walking the Wealthy & Jewish Tight Rope." She began her reflections, "I grew up believing that the majority of wealthy people were Jews, that this was something to hide, and that therefore I should do my best not to let anyone know I was Jewish or wealthy." In diary-like fashion, she catalogued the experiences that taught her to understand her Jewishness and wealth as sources of shame: her recognition that where she grew up the few Jews she knew were also the wealthiest ones; her discomfort about her lavish bat mitzvah celebration; her realization that her last name shouted her affluence in her home community; and her run-in with a classmate in a college seminar who castigated all Jews for being powerful and privileged. In 2009, her father forwarded her an email about a Resource Generation conference: "I am immediately turned off. A retreat for rich kids like me at a JEWISH retreat center? You must be kidding, I think. That sounds like my worst nightmare. I immediately decline the invite." The next year, she decided to give the conference a try, in part because it was not being held at a Jewish conference center. She was "blown away," and felt such a sense of belonging that she even self-identified as Jewish by sitting at a designated "Shabbat dinner table." In her telling, this was the start of her journey away from the tightrope upon which she had walked so precariously for so long. Instead of trying to balance on a thin filament where she could hide her Jewishness and her wealth, she stepped into a new and broader understanding of both of them. She began to learn how wealth and Jewishness shaped her. This consciousness allowed her to forge a new way forward, unburdening herself of the shame she had carried for many years—in large part, by releasing her wealth to causes that would spread justice.[3]

For Seigle, who described herself on her website as "a white, cisgender, genderqueer female identified owning class queer ashkenazi Jew," Resource Generation provided a context in which it was appropriate to talk about wealth as a core component of identity and, in her case, of her Jewish identity. But this "critical consciousness" phase was just the first step of a process that she, similar to other members of Resource Generation, underwent to learn how to transform their wealth from a deeply lodged condition of their individual existence to a tool for social transformation. Six years after her first Resource Generation meeting, Seigle wrote with confidence, "I move boldly as a donor, giving away more than I am told is 'safe' and giving it to communities and projects that are deemed too risky." Already divested of one-third of her inheritance, she anticipated a time when she could feel a sense of safety without the crutch of "excess wealth."[4]

Through her involvement with Resource Generation, as well as several politically and economically radical Jewish groups, Seigle discovered that the parts of herself she had been brought up to hide and that had caused her to feel paralyzed in the narrow straits of humiliation could be sources of personal and social liberation. She explained, "I navigate the contradictions of being a Jew with wealth by being visible as a wealthy Jew who advocates for the redistribution of wealth and rejects narratives that say we hold all the power." In my conversations with Jewish members (and former members, since technically membership is open only to those who are thirty-five and under), I learned that many shared Seigle's experiences. As if speaking from a script, they described, first, gaining awareness that their access to wealth and their Jewishness were bound together in a web of shame and insecurity, and then realizing that to release themselves from equating wealth with safety and Jewishness with vulnerability, they had to step outside of many conventional structures of American Jewish life, including its communal and philanthropic institutions and, sometimes, their own families.[5]

As Resource Generation expanded, establishing local chapters, publishing materials, and collaborating with other progressive philanthropic organizations, it sought to upend the hierarchies and power structures its members often reported experiencing in their families' philanthropic activities. It pledged itself to "social justice philanthropy" that "strive[s] to include the people who are impacted by . . . injustices as decision-makers." It oriented its work around a set of guiding principles that mandated focusing on "root causes" of injustice, including "the people who are impacted by those injustices as leaders and decision-makers," and increasing the accessibility and diversity of the philanthropic field. If wealth could help solve the problems of injustice, then wealth itself would have to stop operating unjustly.[6]

FIGURE C.1. Margot Seigle, left, People's Climate Change March, New York City, 2014. Photo by Meredith Cohen, courtesy of Margot Seigle.

As testament to the depth of its commitment to changing the way wealth functioned, Resource Generation members educated themselves about American tax policy and even lobbied Congress. In 2013, it convened a "National Tax Organizing Team" that wrote a "Tax Justice Platform." The preamble asserted, "Taxes are the best way we have of turning private wealth into public good" and noted that as much as Resource Generation's efforts to encourage members to give "large portions of our wealth away to grassroots social justice movements" mattered, they paled in comparison to the large-scale change that a more redistributive tax policy could precipitate. Compiling suggestions from several progressive economic organizations, the Resource Generation platform was broadly ambitious, though light on specific policy recommendations.[7]

As tax reform legislation that ran contrary to Resource Generation's platform came before Congress in 2017 and 2018, members wrote blog posts, created hashtags (for example, #TrumpTaxScam), and joined protests. In April 2017, the day before a national tax demonstration, the organization issued a press release: "Rich Millennials Join Trump Tax March, Demand End to Corrupt Tax System that Favors Rich."[8]

II.

In December 2017, an organization called JLens Investor Network, founded five years earlier, convened a day-long Jewish Impact Investing Summit in New York City. Cosponsored by a range of Jewish philanthropic entities, from federations to private family foundations and the Jewish Funders Network, as well as major American foundations such as the Ford Foundation, JLens gathered an audience of more than three hundred people to learn how impact investing could benefit the Jewish community. Speaker after speaker made the case that impact investing, also sometimes called "mission-related investing," was an untapped resource for financing Jewish priorities. The method was simple: beyond giving direct grants, Jewish nonprofit organizations and, for that matter, for-profit organizations could advance Jewish interests by investing their assets in funds with values or missions consistent with their own.[9]

Imagine, JLens's founder and executive director Julie Hammerman proposed to the audience, if all of the assets—and not just those earmarked for grant-making—held by Jewish organizations were harnessed to "our broad-based communal agenda." Suddenly, capital growth itself could be put to work. Instead of that growth providing only a narrow stream of active mission-based capital, the very process of growth would capitalize a Jewish communal agenda. Michael Lustig, a former investment manager at BlackRock and an active lay leader for New York's federation, explained to the audience that by impact investing, "You are combining the best aspects of entrepreneurial capitalism, and you're harnessing it for doing a social good."[10]

Two years earlier, in 2015, JLens had devised a "Jewish Advocacy Strategy" to guide Jewish organizations and investors toward its impact investing vision. The strategy consisted of an investment portfolio with "300 large-cap US public companies" that all conformed to JLens's definition of companies friendly to the Jewish communal agenda. Different from other investment portfolios, this one turned its shareholders into advocates for "Jewish values" as defined by "six pillars," each rooted in—and authenticated by—a Hebrew phrase drawn from a traditional Jewish text: obligation to investors, to society, to the worker, to the environment, to coexistence, and finally a sixth described simply as "support for Israel" (*Yishuv Eretz Yisrael*). Through a screening process of the five hundred largest publicly traded companies, JLens would determine the extent to which companies achieved these values, using a scale from *met-zuyan* (Hebrew for "excellent") to *treif* (translated in JLens material as "not a fit"),

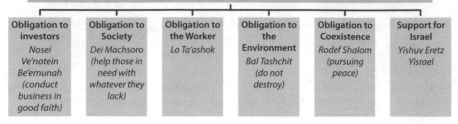

Six pillars of Judaism's framework of *mitzvot* (obligations) guide JLens' evaluation of companies and investor advocacy priorities					
Obligation to investors	**Obligation to Society**	**Obligation to the Worker**	**Obligation to the Environment**	**Obligation to Coexistence**	**Support for Israel**
Nosei Ve'notein Be'emunah (conduct business in good faith)	*Dei Machsoro (help those in need with whatever they lack)*	*Lo Ta'ashok*	*Bal Tashchit (do not destroy)*	*Rodef Shalom (pursuing peace)*	*Yishuv Eretz Yisrael*

FIGURE C.2. JLens's Six Pillars chart, https://www.jlensnetwork.org/jewishadvocacystrategy, November 2019. Reprinted with permission from JLens Jewish Advocacy Strategy.

and then would exclude companies that did not achieve at least a *tov* (good) rating from the portfolio.[11]

A midday panel at the 2017 conference addressed the sixth pillar, "support for Israel." Introducing the panel, executive director Hammerman drew immediate attention to the BDS (boycott, divestment, and sanctions practiced against Israel) movement, characterizing it as "economic warfare against Israel" and later explaining that BDS activists "weaponized" the investment economy against Israel by pressuring companies to divest from Israeli-held companies. Panelists, including a member of Israel's Ministry of Strategic Affairs and representatives from organizations devoted to monitoring and fighting anti-Israel activity, explained that Jewish philanthropic organizations and private investors alike could use their shareholder power to retaliate against BDS. In other words, their investments could also be used as weapons, just trained on different targets: companies that divested from Israel.[12]

A year after the conference, when Airbnb, a popular room and home rental service valued at approximately $38 billion in 2018, announced it would scrub its listings of properties located in West Bank settlements, JLens rebuked the company for "acquiescing to BDS." Once again, it described BDS as "economic warfare" and asserted, "Most leaders in the US and around the world oppose BDS and consider it a discriminatory anti-Semitic movement." JLens's statement suggested that only through a counter-strategy—its own Jewish Advocacy Strategy—could companies be armed to resist "biased campaigns with ulterior political motives."[13]

The language of warfare and weaponry was more than just metaphorical. A few months before the Airbnb controversy, JLens had explained that while it excluded civilian firearms manufacturers from its Jewish values portfolio, it would invest in companies "that provide military firearms based on the principles of self-defense." As it did in many of its materials, JLens drew upon traditional Jewish texts and Hebrew phrases to legitimate its decision. Thus, it explained that its application of "Jewish wisdom" led it to declaim the sale of firearms to civilians but to support companies that sold "weapons to Jewish militias or to governments ... to protect Jews and other citizens." JLens directed investors to use the power of their capital both to punish companies that divested from Israel or otherwise eschewed investing in it and to capitalize companies that armed the country.[14]

From the 2015 creation of its portfolio to 2017, JLens reported a tripling of its investment assets. In a short time, federations, Jewish community foundations, private foundations, and donor-advised funds, as well as individual investors, had signed onto the strategy with at least the minimum required investment of $1 million. (Donor-advised funds could meet the threshold as part of an institution, so each fund did not necessarily invest the full $1 million.) In addition to leveraging their investments to "ensure values alignment" from companies, shareholders were rewarded with returns consistent with the standard S&P 500 index.[15]

By channeling primarily Jewish philanthropic capital into a values-based fund that captured investment income to grow steadily, funders could achieve goals that they might otherwise pursue only through grants and program-building. In this way, philanthropic entities with significant capital power—in endowments, donor-advised funds, supporting foundations, or private foundations—could widen the scope of their power. Instead of divesting themselves of wealth or power, through a more vigorous pace of grant allocation, they could invest in their own power, enhancing it through on-mission investment strategies with favorable returns.

III.

In early 2019, as a shutdown of the US government approached a record-setting number of days, Sue Reinhold drafted a note to the holders of the largest endowment funds that she managed for the San Francisco federation. Setting out the dire circumstances that federal employees in Northern California were experiencing, she proposed that her clients consider lending a portion of their philanthropic capital at 0% interest to help meet furloughed workers' immediate needs.[16]

Combining empirical, ethical, and financial logics, Reinhold set out the case for her plan that ran counter to common Jewish philanthropic practice. She began with the numbers: "While together our donor advisors grant over $175 million into the community every year, our donor advisors also have committed over $2 billion to philanthropy that we steward for you." In simple terms, this meant that approximately $1.8 billion annually was not put into philanthropic circulation. Often regarded as the principal or corpus, preserved to invest, generate returns, and allow perpetual capital growth, these assets—or some portion of them—could also be considered, in Reinhold's words, "found money." For JLens, this found money transformed into impact investing capital, while for Resource Generation the same found money was meant to be released quickly to communities that needed resources. Reinhold saw wisdom in impact investing, but she also gathered insight from more radical economic practices to put capital into circulation through its rapid redistribution. Blurring the ethical and empirical, Reinhold suggested that during desperate times, her large-fund holders might feel an obligation not to leave so much capital "on the sidelines awaiting your grantmaking in future years."[17]

Reinhold's ethical claim, issued in a gentle way—after all, the note was meant to be sent to her clients and some of the federation's most significant donors—and her empirical observation served as the ballast for her financial proposition: to create fund-based loans to furloughed workers. Attempting to sell the plan, she explained that while creditors always take on risk, "angel grantors" had agreed to "backstop" or guarantee up to 10% of the principal value of any loan in the case of default. Furthermore, San Francisco's federation would work with Hebrew Free Loan, an established community agency, allowing lenders to rest assured that the default rate would be low. Finally, whatever losses her fund holders incurred could be accounted for as a philanthropic expenditure, that is, as a normal grant.[18]

Reinhold, the founder and former managing partner of a highly lucrative financial advisory firm, understood that San Francisco's federation had hired her to manage its endowment funds because they valued those funds and the donors who maintained and enriched them. But much like the founders of JLens and Resource Generation, Reinhold perceived incredible sums of potential energy stored in accumulated philanthropic capital, just waiting to be unleashed. Whereas Resource Generation subscribers sought to liberate as much of that potential energy as possible to redistribute capital across communities that experienced injustice, JLens advised conserving the potential energy as a form of power, to advocate for corporate values and to meet organizations' missions. Reinhold sought a middle ground, pulling on the language of impact investment while offering a clear-eyed analysis of the redistributive goals that were sacrificed for the sake of philanthropic accumulation.

Even before the government shutdown, Reinhold had paid close attention to the historical trends of Jewish philanthropy and the ways those trends might be steered in new directions. In a 2018 address to her investment managers that she then crafted into a blog post, she explained, "While umbrella giving in the form of Jewish Federations and the United Way were in the 20th century the predominant means of giving—money in, money out propositions, year to year—we are now living in the *age of philanthropic capital*. There is a LOT of money siloed away irrevocably to philanthropy, and for more and more donors it is being put into semi-permanent or permanent storage." Reinhold and her team knew intimately those vast sums of philanthropic capital; just under 9% of the $2 billion they managed in supporting foundations and donor-advised funds had been expended as grants over the last year.[19]

At a Jewish Funders Network conference in 2019, Reinhold related that her friends from her old line of work—"the buy side" of investment services—had summed up her new job as "an AUM [assets under management] play." But for Reinhold, the fact that their glib encapsulation of her job was so accurate rankled her, and she found herself asking again and again, "What is that capital doing while it is in storage?" Of course, the same question had animated Resource Generation and JLens. But Reinhold was neither content to view portfolio investments as the extent of good that warehoused philanthropic capital could do nor convinced that simply releasing philanthropic capital would make a difference in solving broad social problems or addressing Jewish needs. Instead, for her, the heart of the matter was how to balance long-range sustainability with capital circulation. Wriggling out from under the AUM model, she instructed her team of investment managers, readers of her blog, and the audience at the Jewish Funders Network conference to embrace "a new metric: AIC . . . Assets in Community."[20]

In the case of the furloughed workers, to achieve the transformation from assets under management to assets in community, Reinhold had proposed lending philanthropic capital to struggling local agencies at below-market rates and to low-income communities at 0% interest. Although the plan never materialized—because the government shutdown ended just as Reinhold was finalizing it—her idea staked out the ground between Resource Generation's distribution model and JLens's impact investment model. Reinhold calculated the returns on her plan as the sum of the loan repayments plus the on-mission good the money did in the community. By shifting attention toward capital's movement through communities, Reinhold sought to value philanthropic capital by its circulation patterns through communities, back into accumulation-based structures, and then out into the world again.[21]

––––––

The reformers profiled here all believed that something was amiss. In their own fashion, they sought to remake the system, whether to make it more thoroughly democratic (as in Resource Generation), more completely capitalist (as in JLens), or to rebalance it somewhere in the middle (as in Reinhold's vision). No matter how imperfect their solutions, they recognized that any effort to improve Jewish philanthropy demanded a consideration of its place within American political economy broadly understood.

As this book has argued, philanthropy in the United States developed over the twentieth century as a creature of capitalism and a tool for democracy. In its various efforts to shape philanthropy, American state structures sought to balance private and public interests. To expect philanthropy to serve exclusively democratic interests, as perhaps the members of Resource Generation hoped it could, was to seek its demise—since without the engine of capitalist class differentiation, philanthropic capital simply would not exist. And to edge it ever more closely toward capitalism, as JLens and other impact investment models tried, would similarly undo its logic—since without the aspirations of using philanthropy to serve the goal of a more democratic, justly provisioned public, the line between philanthropic capital and other forms of private capital would diminish. Reinhold appreciated the middle ground and hoped that new approaches to capital circulation and accumulation could keep the philanthropic system intact while freeing it from replicating and reinforcing inequality.

Yet the reality by the early decades of the twenty-first century was an American philanthropic system that, much like the American state, seemed to be choosing capitalism over democracy at every turn. Whether a middle-ground approach could right the balance was as much of an open question as a rarely asked one. Instead, from many quarters of American life, Jewish and not, a sense of complacency, inexorability, or, in some cases, celebration reigned when it came to regarding the sway that private money held over our country's public process.

By tracing the history of the American Jewish philanthropic complex, I have pointed to the American laws and policies woven into it and, likewise, threaded through relentless American endeavors to prove that private interests might serve the public good. Those laws and policies have allowed for some of the most triumphant moments of altruism, while also hardening the most persistent forms of exclusion and inequality.

We would be naïve to think that, for whatever its achievements or short-comings, American Jewish philanthropy stands alone or eternal. It has not existed as it does today in perpetuity or in isolation. An awareness of this fact carries the obligation that we act as if change is possible.

That change must begin with an accounting of the past. The historical for-mation of the American Jewish philanthropic complex provides just such an accounting by showing the steady interaction between American state laws and policies, on one hand, and Jewish philanthropic structures, on the other. From the evolving policies governing collective associations, to the shifting regulatory apparatus applied to them, to the various schemes of revenue ex-traction and subsidy that state bodies devised to manage associations, to the political postures nourished and disavowed through legal frameworks of phi-lanthropy, American Jewish philanthropy existed within the tangled threads of American statecraft, while also responding to specific Jewish histories, anx-ieties, and needs.

The contests between democratic forms of governance and capitalist prac-tice that American Jewish philanthropic organizations experienced over the twentieth century, thus, were hardly internal matters alone. Rather, the terms of these contests—the available options, the most attractive and elegant resolutions—revealed the embeddedness of Jewish philanthropy within the political economy of the American state. Jewish philanthropic leaders and in-stitutions responded to but also helped craft the laws and policies that governed them. I have chronicled the rise of an American Jewish philanthropic complex to mark this mutually sustaining, though hardly exclusive, relationship.

By the final decades of the twentieth century, far from appearing as the sum of these historical variables, the American Jewish philanthropic complex that emerged often appeared timeless and inevitable, a perception bolstered by those institutions and individuals most invested in it. By offering this history of the contingencies and constituent parts of the complex, I hope to have chal-lenged such an unyielding perception of the past and its hold on our present and future. Other scholars may build on—or debate—my categories of analy-sis and delve into dimensions I sidelined.

But beyond these scholarly aims, I also hope the history I have chronicled will stand as a defense of broad and bold thinking about future change. I say this not as a revolutionary, but rather, I think, as a realist.

From studying the history of American Jewish philanthropy, I have learned to appreciate the interrelationship of individuals, institutions, policies, laws, and structures. As I dug into the archives, read minutes and financial statements, tried to discern the history of tax policies, and followed the correspondence between lawyers and legislators, I realized that a topic I had first approached as a relatively bound and narrow one was, in fact, related to the very largest and most basic questions about how people can live together: how should resources be owned and shared; how should authority be exercised, maintained, and checked; and how can individuals, institutions, and government make progress toward better answers that improve the lives of more people?

These are big and hard questions, and no single individual, institution, politician, or lawmaker will solve them. But this does not mean we—the reader, the scholar, the person affiliated with American Jewish communities, the US citizen or resident, all of us who dwell in this world—can desist from asking them loudly and often. To do anything less is to deny the complex history our past has bequeathed to us.

ACKNOWLEDGMENTS

THIS BOOK started with a footnote and a friendship. The footnote origin story is straightforward, if a little, well, academic. In January 2013, I was completing work on a book about Jews and urbanism and trying to track down a reference. I hoped to find the book that offered a broad analysis of American Jews' historical relationship to philanthropy. My search didn't lead me to the footnote I wanted, but it did direct me to the idea for my next book.

Had it not been for my college friend Chris Herron, however, my quest for a footnote may have trailed off long before it became a book. The same day I searched for that citation, I happened to Google Chat with Chris. I mentioned to him what I was working on, only because I knew he would enjoy mocking me for feeling so frustrated by a footnote. The truth is, although we had stayed in touch after college, I had not exactly kept up with his various career moves. But when he reminded me that he was now working at a venture philanthropy fund, I was more curious about his work than I apparently had ever been. From that day forward, he and I traded countless texts and emails and had long conversations about the philosophical, political, and practical dimensions of philanthropy. (For the record, he was unable to furnish me with my original footnote, though he helped with some others in this book.) At some point along the way, I realized we were really talking about what it meant to live well—and unwell—in this world.

In March 2017, Chris died from brain cancer. For a few months after his death, I thought I would never finish this book because to do so was to confront a new grief: the end of what I had come to consider our shared endeavor. In the final days of writing this book, I have felt that loss, stacked on top of the rest. But I have also received an unexpected gift amidst my grief. As I read over these pages—and when I quiet the din of my inner critic—here and there I catch the voice of my old friend, who was dear to me and so many others.

Footnotes and the departed may be first in my list of acknowledgments, but thankfully, they do not stand alone. This book is built upon the good work of archivists, who safeguard the materials of the past and relayed them to me in boxes, folders, digital scans, and copies—and, often, pointed me toward files I had no idea I needed until I saw them. Ann Sindelar at Western Reserve Historical Society; Aimee Ergas, a collections archivist at the Walter P. Reuther Library at Wayne State University; Melanie Meyers, the director of collections at the American Jewish Historical Society; as well as archivists at the Universities of Chicago and Michigan, the Jacob Rader Marcus Center of the American Jewish Archives, and the Crown Family Foundation all assisted me in my search to understand American Jewish philanthropy. I am hopeful that this book helps convince more private family foundations of the value in preserving their records so that future historians can learn from them, and I am grateful to Annie Polland, my friend and the visionary executive director of the American Jewish Historical Society, and to the Jewish Funders Network for pursuing this task.

My research benefited from several institutions that invested in it. Temple University provided me with a year-long fellowship, including a semester of teaching relief, at its Center for the Humanities and, also, a grant from the Office of the Vice President for Research. Multiple other universities and conferences gave me opportunities to share my work along the way, forcing me to commit research to paper and exposing me to eager and erudite audiences with whom to discuss it. Indiana University, Northwestern University, the University of California, Los Angeles, the University of Hartford, the University of Michigan, and the University of Wisconsin are among the schools that all served as excellent hosts. The Association for Jewish Studies, in particular, has long been a fruitful environment for me to explore new ideas.

Additionally, journals and press outlets published my articles, similarly offering me the chance to share work and receive feedback on it. I am particularly grateful to the editors and reviewers at the *American Historical Review* for their thorough response to several drafts of a manuscript that eventually appeared as "How Americans Give: The Financialization of American Jewish Philanthropy," 122, no. 5 (December 2017): 1459–1489. My thanks as well for their permission to reprint sections of that article here. I am similarly grateful to editors at the academic journals *Jewish Social Studies* and *Religion and American Culture*, as well as to those who encouraged me to publish for the broader readerships of the *Forward*, the *Jewish Week*, and the *Washington Post*.

Foremost among the institutions that enabled me to write this book is Princeton University Press and my incomparable editor there, Fred Appel. From the day I first mentioned the idea for this book to him, he has been a steadfast champion of my research, providing sound advice and many lovely lunches. I thank him and the production team at Princeton for giving me the privilege to publish a book. All errors that remain here are solely my fault, but they are far fewer thanks to the sharp eyes of these skilled professionals.

My scholarly community expanded as I worked on this book, and I am profoundly grateful to have been on the receiving end of so much expertise and support. For teaching me how to read tax law and turning me into an evangelist for its historical significance, my profound thanks to two law professors, Ray Madoff and Kathy Mandelbaum. Kathy gave me the incredible gift of her nonprofit law course and answered my questions as I made my way through the materials, and then steadily sent me new articles. Ray ushered me into a community of legal scholars of philanthropy through the Boston College Law School Forum on Philanthropy and the Public Good. When she invited me to write a history of donor-advised funds, she provided me with her unrivaled expertise and gave me the confidence to interpret the historical meaning of tax code. Ben Soskis, a skilled writer and historian, has made me feel at home in the world of philanthropic studies and unstintingly offered compelling feedback on chapters and drafts. Through Ray and Ben, I met Rob Reich, who generously sent me his work and read mine and also included me in a conference he organized through Stanford University's Center for Philanthropy and Civil Society.

Alongside scholars of philanthropy, philanthropic practitioners also came to play a crucial role in my quest to understand American Jewish philanthropy. I have listed their names and, when appropriate, cited them throughout the book, but I want to offer special thanks to a few. Jeffrey Solomon, the president of the now shuttered Andrea and Charles Bronfman Philanthropies, was among the first philanthropic professionals with whom I spoke and immediately impressed me with his candid and incisive reflections on the sector. He introduced me to his colleagues far and wide, and for this I am deeply appreciative. Neel Hajra, the CEO of the Ann Arbor Community Foundation and lecturer at the University of Michigan's Ford School of Public Policy, gave me access to his course on the nonprofit sector, read my articles, and offered his sharp perspective to me. Margot Seigle, who appears in the book's conclusion, shared her story and wisdom with me and introduced me to other Resource Generation members. Sue Reinhold, who also appears in my conclusion, has become one of my most trusted interlocutors. I continue to learn from her anthropological perspective, her deep knowledge of finance, and her sheer concern for the well-being of humanity. I also extend thanks to Yehuda Sarna and the community he has created through the Applied Research Collective for American Jewry at New York University. Gratitude as well to Elka Abrahamson, Cindy Chazan, and the Wexner Foundation for caring about the conversations I have wanted to have.

Even as this book pushed me to learn new fields, meet new people, and reinvent my scholarly interests, it also allowed me to cherish more than ever the friends and colleagues who steadfastly provide support and good company no matter how fickle my interests. I met Deborah Dash Moore when I was a graduate student, and I simply cannot imagine my professional life without her. She is my model of scholarly integrity, generosity, and intellectual engagement. Bryant Simon, my colleague at Temple, helps me remember why I got into this game. With his vivid turns of phrase, his ability to see patterns in chaos, and his love of the puzzle, he makes history matter and is a solid gold friend.

For sharing in my enthusiasm about this research, for asking excellent questions, for reading drafts, and for producing their own scholarship that informs how I think about the past and present, I have so many other wonderful people to thank, including: Mara Benjamin, Rachel Deblinger, Danielle Durchslag, Josh Friedman, Karla Goldman, Warren Hoffman, Ari Kelman, Shaul Kelner, Moshe Kornfeld, Josh Lambert, Jon Levisohn, Lital Levy, Jim Loeffler, Shaul Magid, Tony Michels, David Myers, Julia Ott, Avinoam Patt, Moses Pava, Derek Penslar, Noam Pianko, Annie Polland, Riv-Ellen Prell, Kate Rosenblatt, David Sorkin, Ronit Stahl, Sarah Stein, Elli Stern, Rafi Stern, Britt Tevis, Beth Wenger, Barry Wimpfheimer, and Olivier Zunz. Matt Berkman contributed research and editing assistance, in addition to writing a marvelous dissertation that has shaped my thinking about the politics of Jewish philanthropy. Thank you, as well, to Peter Ganong for creating the graphs in the book. Additionally, I am grateful to Steve Weitzman for his unbridled enthusiasm about my work and for his vision to build a broad field of inquiry around the study of Jewish philanthropy. As always, I owe a great debt to my graduate school teachers, Jon Butler and Paula Hyman (z"l), whose sense of the obligations of history and the historian remain present in my mind.

Colleagues at Temple have fostered a supportive intellectual environment. I offer thanks in particular to Rebecca Alpert, Richard Deeg, Petra Goedde, Rita Krueger, Laura Levitt, Jay Lockenour, Harvey Neptune, Mónica Ricketts, Jessica Choppin Roney, and Eileen Ryan. In my role as director of the Feinstein Center for American Jewish History at Temple, I have worked closely with Ariella Werden-Greenfield, a scholar in her own right and a wonderful colleague. I am also thankful to my undergraduate and graduate students at

Temple. Two sets of students—those who took a seminar I offered at Princeton in the spring of 2018 and the group who enrolled in my honors seminar at Temple the following fall—deserve special mention for working alongside me so as to understand the themes of power and powerlessness in Jewish history.

My work on this book changed in 2016, as I tried to make sense of one of the most cynical and hopeless moments I have ever witnessed in American politics. For helping me imagine that there is a way forward and that democratic aspirations still matter, I am deeply grateful to my friend Mindy Brown, a fierce political organizer, an extraordinary proofreader for this project and so many others, and the only person I know who can absolutely nail an Ottolenghi recipe. I also consider myself lucky to be part of a group of Jewish studies scholars who established the Jewish Studies Activist Network as an act of hope and a practical way to channel some of our despair. Finally, for inspiring me with their activism, their intellect, and their incredible hospitality, I am grateful to Catherine Rottenberg (who is also the very best draft reader I know) and Neve Gordon.

For becoming the kinds of friends who are family, I thank my Germantown Jewish Centre community, Germantown Friends School families, and people from so many other walks of life who show up for me and my family. For making me want to do nothing less than figure out the world and for making life today seem as hilarious as it is alarming, thanks especially to Lisa Davidson, Alice Huang, JooYun Kim, Marion Menzin, Tom Nassim, Reepa Shah, Chip Turner, and Bree Wilde.

My earliest notions about capitalism came from observing my parents, Sandy and Lee Corwin. They both worked in the public sector—as a special education teacher at public schools and a psychologist at state institutions—and belonged to unions. They talked frankly to my brothers and me about money, cringed at conspicuous consumption, and taught us to think carefully about resource distribution—even when all I wanted to do was go shopping at the mall. I may not have always appreciated their analysis of capitalism, but I have long drawn strength from their unfaltering love and support.

My family has listened to me talk about my work, but, more important, they have also given me reason to ignore it. My three brothers—Alex, Eric, and Ivan—are always up for the debate, no matter how large or small the issue at hand. I am lucky to have such formidable sparring partners and also to have my world expand through their wonderful spouses and children. Indeed, the fact that our family is always growing—with new partners, children, and pets—provides me with the most reliable sense I know of stability and hope. Goldie Newman, my grandmother, steadfastly ties us all together and has passed down the tradition of huge, food-filled, multi-day holiday celebrations. Her embrace is boundless; from the youngest baby to the finnickiest toddler to the coolest teenager to the most tentative new boyfriend or girlfriend, Bubbie draws everyone in and out with her warmth and intelligence. My in-laws, Sandra Berman and Joe Ohren and Marvin and Donna Berman, are woven into my family and also have made me part of their families with incredible love.

At the very center of all of these circles of community, colleagues, friends, and family is my husband, Dan, and our two children, Ella and Simon. Each and every day, I am grateful for Dan's unparalleled focus, his mastery of balance, his quick wit, and his even swifter sense of what to say to make people feel easy and free. He has shared these extraordinary gifts with me and also conveyed them to our children. For as many nicknames as I have for Dan, Ella, and Simon, I find words inadequate to tell them how much I love them. (The three of them will also insist that I thank our dog, Vento, so I will simply say that he and I have shared more walks than most.) When I am with Dan and the kids, I feel like there's no place I would rather be and also that there's no place we can't go.

Philadelphia, Thanksgiving, 2019

ARCHIVES AND ABBREVIATIONS

Berman Collection: Unprocessed, Bentley Historical Library, University of Michigan, Ann Arbor, Michigan

Big Apple Tzedekah Cooperative Records, MS-606, The Jacob Rader Marcus Center of the American Jewish Archives, Hebrew Union College–Jewish Institute of Religion, Cincinnati, Ohio

Crown Papers: Crown Family Philanthropies, on special request from archivist, Chicago, Illinois

Fed-Cleveland: Cleveland Federation Papers, MS 4835, Western Reserve Historical Society, Cleveland, Ohio

JFN: Jewish Funders Network papers, furnished to author directly from Jewish Funders Network, New York, New York

MF Papers: Max Fisher Papers, UP002350, Walter P. Reuther Library, Wayne State University, Detroit, Michigan

NFJC: National Foundation for Jewish Culture, I-527, American Jewish Historical Society at the Center for Jewish History, New York, New York

NS Papers: Norman Sugarman Papers, P-633, American Jewish Historical Society at the Center for Jewish History, New York, New York

PK Papers: Philip M. Klutznick Papers, Special Collections Research Center, University of Chicago Library, Chicago, Illinois

PS Papers: Philip Slomovitz Papers, UP001494, Walter P. Reuther Library, Wayne State University, Detroit, Michigan

UJA-FedNY: United Jewish Appeal-Federation of New York Collection, 1909–2004, Center for Jewish History, New York, New York

AUTHOR'S INTERVIEWS

Naomi Adler, CEO of Jewish Federation of Greater Philadelphia, Philadelphia, Pennsylvania, February 17, 2015

Adina Dubin Barkinskiy, Program Director, Morningstar Foundation, Washington, DC, February 17, 2016

Sandy Cardin, President, Schusterman Foundation, offices in Atlanta, Georgia; Jerusalem, Israel; New York, New York; San Francisco, California; Tulsa, Oklahoma; and Washington, DC, August 12, 2014

Mark Charendoff, former President and CEO, Jewish Funders Network, and President, Maimonides Fund, New York, New York, June 2, 2014

Karyn Cohen, Director, Jacobson Foundation, Boston, Massachusetts, November 5, 2014

Sue Dickman, Executive Vice President and CEO of the Jewish Communal Fund, New York, New York, October 22, 2014

Alisa Doctoroff, former President, UJA-Federation, New York, New York, August 11, 2016

Charles "Chip" Edelsberg, former Executive Director, Jim Joseph Foundation, San Francisco, California, October 2, 2015

Jim Farley, President and CEO, Leichtag Foundation, Encinitas, California, February 27, 2015

David Gedzelman, President and CEO, Steinhardt Foundation for Jewish Life, New York, New York, February 23, 2015

Sharna Goldseker, Executive Director, 21/64, formerly part of Andrea and Charles Bronfman Philanthropies, New York, New York, June 26, 2014

Sally Gottesman, Board Member, Paula and Jerry Gottesman Foundation, a supporting foundation held at the Jewish Community Foundation and Jewish Federation of Greater MetroWest NJ, Whippany, New Jersey, January 22, 2015

Julie Hammerman, Executive Director, JLens Investor Network, New York, New York, and San Francisco, California, April 15, 2015

Felicia Herman, Executive Director, Natan, New York, New York, July 17, 2014

Joseph Imberman, Associate Vice President of Planned Giving and Endowments, Jewish Federations of North America, New York, New York, Oct 3, 2014

Jonathan Jacoby, Director of Operations, New Israel Fund, Southern California; and formerly Senior Vice President, Jewish Federation of Greater Los Angeles, Los Angeles, California, March 6, 2015

Jamie Jaffee, Managing Partner, Philanthropic Initiative, Boston Foundation, Boston, Massachusetts, September 12, 2014

Martin Kaminer, Kaminer Family Foundation and Bikkurim, New York, New York, January 7, 2015

Marjory Kaplan, Executive Director, Jewish Community Foundation of San Francisco, San Francisco, California, November 14, 2014

Donald Kent, Principal at Bernstein Global Wealth Management, formerly Director of Planned Giving and Endowment, Council of Jewish Federations, New York, New York, January 13, 2015; April 10, 2015; February 2, 2016

Shawn Landres, CEO and Director of Research, Jumpstart, Santa Monica, California, August 26, 2014

Jeff Levin, Chief Resource Development Officer, Greater Miami Jewish Federation, Miami, Florida, October 21, 2014

Norman Lipoff, former Chair of Council of Jewish Federations National Endowment Committee, New York, New York, January 17, 2017

Lesley Said Matsa, Program Officer, Crown Family Philanthropies, Chicago, Illinois, June 30, 2017

Adin Miller, Senior Director of Community Impact and Innovations at the Jewish Community Federation and Endowment Fund, San Francisco, California, March 6, 2015

Lisa Farber Miller, Senior Program Officer, Rose Community Foundation, Denver, Colorado, October 16, 2014

Rachel Monroe, President, Weinberg Foundation, Owings Mills, Maryland, September 22, 2014

Larry Moses, former President, Wexner Foundation, New Albany, Ohio, February 11, 2015

Steve Nasatir, President, Jewish United Fund/Federation of Metropolitan Chicago, Chicago, Illinois, December 9, 2014

Yossi Prager, President, AVI CHAI Foundation, New York, New York, January 7, 2014

Andrew Rehfeld, CEO of Jewish Federation of St. Louis, St. Louis, Missouri, May 5, 2015

Sue Reinhold, Managing Director of Philanthropy, Jewish Community Federation and Endowment Fund, San Francisco, California, November 16, 2018

David Rosenn, Executive Director, Hebrew Free Loan Society, New York, New York, January 10, 2018

Jennifer Hoos Rothberg, Executive Director, Einhorn Family Charitable Trust, New York, New York, August 28, 2015

Jay Ruderman, President, Ruderman Family Foundation, Newton, Massachusetts, January 6, 2016

John Ruskay, former CEO of the UJA-Federation, New York, New York, December 18, 2014

Adene Sacks, former Program Officer, Jim Joseph Foundation, San Francisco, California, May 29, 2015

Julie Sandorf, President, Revson Foundation, New York, New York, January 6, 2015

Sarai Brachman Shoup, former Director, Mandell L. and Madeleine H. Berman Foundation, Ann Arbor, Michigan, August 23, 2017

Barry Shrage, President, Combined Jewish Philanthropies, Boston, Massachusetts, August 6, 2014

Jacob Solomon, President/CEO, Greater Miami Federation, Miami, Florida, March 2, 2015

Jeffrey Solomon, former President, Andrea and Charles Bronfman Philanthropies, New York, New York, July 10, 2014

Andrés Spokoiny, President and CEO, Jewish Funders Network, New York, New York, May 7, 2015

Rachel Sternberg, Senior Vice President of Annual Campaign, Jewish United Fund/Federation of Metropolitan Chicago, Chicago, Illinois, November 12, 2014

Marc Terrill, CEO, The Associated: Jewish Community Federation of Baltimore, Baltimore, Maryland, October 2, 2014

Resource Generation Interviews

Rachel Adler, June 13, 2017

Gabe Kravitz, July 14, 2017

Sara Narva, June 28, 2017

Karen Pittelman, June 12, 2017

Kate Poole, June 26, 2017

Jessica Rosenberg, June 13, 2017

Margot Seigle, November 4, 2014, October 8, 2015

Naomi Sobel, June 12, 2017

Jessie Spector, Executive Director, August 4, 2014

Samantha Waxman, June 12, 2017, June 29, 2017

NOTES

Introduction: The State of Philanthropy

1. Josh Nathan-Kazis, "26 Billion Bucks: The Jewish Charity Industry Uncovered," *Forward*, March 24, 2014, at http://forward.com/articles/194978/-billion-bucks-the-jewish-charity-industry-unco/. As described in the articles, this figure did not include synagogue assets, which are not required to be reported in tax filings, and other philanthropic funds not readily identifiable as Jewish. On the calculation of the $46.3 billion figure, including a discussion on how to define and value Jewish philanthropy, see Hanna Shaul Bar Nissim and Matthew A. Brookner, "Ethno-Religious Philanthropy: Lessons from a Study of United States Jewish Philanthropy," *Contemporary Jewry* 39, no. 1 (March 2019): 38. The authors note that their figure accounts for grants larger than $500,000 made by Jewish funding organizations from 2000 to 2015.

2. Eisenhower was hardly a detractor of private enterprise, but he worried about the disproportionate influence private interests (especially defense contractors) could wield over government (especially military personnel) without the proper forms of restraint and discipline. For an encapsulation of his philosophy, see Robert Griffith, "Dwight D. Eisenhower and the Corporate Commonwealth," *American Historical Review* 87, no. 1 (February 1982): 87–122.

3. The books that have most influenced my thinking about this period of American expansion include Eric Foner, *Reconstruction: America's Unfinished Revolution, 1863–1877* (New York: Harper and Row, 1988); Steven Hahn, *A Nation Under Our Feet: Black Political Struggles in the Rural South, from Slavery to the Great Migration* (Cambridge, MA: Belknap Press of Harvard University Press, 2003); Matthew Frye Jacobson, *Whiteness of a Different Color* (Cambridge, MA: Harvard University Press, 1998); Martha Jones, *Birthright Citizens: A History of Race and Rights in Antebellum America* (New York: Cambridge University Press, 2018); Jackson Lears, *Rebirth of a Nation: The Making of Modern America, 1870–1920* (New York: Harper Collins, 2009); Eli Lederhendler, *Jewish Immigrants and American Capitalism, 1880–1920* (New York: Cambridge University Press, 2009); and Natalia Molina, *How Race Is Made in America: Immigration, Citizenship, and the Historical Power of Racial Scripts* (Berkeley: University of California Press, 2014).

4. For a few reflections on the centrality of this paradigm, see Michael S. Alexander, "The Exilic Imperative of American Jewry," *Religions* 9, no. 12 (2018): 412, https://doi.org/10.3390/rel9120412; Hasia Diner, *How America Met the Jews* (Providence, RI: Brown Judaic Studies, 2017); and Jonathan D. Sarna, "The Cult of Synthesis in American Jewish Culture," *Jewish Social Studies* 5 (1998/99): 52–79. Situated in a volume that pays attention to state structures and citizenship, Ira Katznelson's essay on Jews and American liberalism suggests the value of looking

at American state policy, but for the most part comes down on the side of seeing Jewish emancipation as an uncomplicated affair in the United States that allowed Jews to operate as individuals with minimal state interference. Jews' perception of antisemitism in the United States, he argues, was often triggered and amplified by their far more treacherous experiences with it elsewhere. Ira Katznelson, "Jews on the Margins of American Liberalism," in Pierre Birnbaum and Ira Katznelson, eds., *Paths of Emancipation: Jews, States, and Citizenship* (Princeton, NJ: Princeton University Press, 1995). For two companion articles that take to task this exceptionalist approach to emancipation and the American state, see Tony Michels, "Is America 'Different'? A Critique of American Jewish Exceptionalism," and David Sorkin, "Is American Jewry Exceptional? Comparing Jewish Emancipation in Europe and America," *American Jewish History* 96, no. 3 (September 2010): 175–200 (Sorkin) and 201–204 (Michels). Also see David Sorkin, *Jewish Emancipation: A History Across Five Centuries* (Princeton, NJ: Princeton University Press, 2019), ch. 27. For an indication that the field is starting to change and ask more sophisticated questions about American Jews' relationship to the state, see Kirsten Fermaglich, *A Rosenberg by Any Other Name: A History of Jewish Name Changing in America* (New York: New York University Press, 2018).

5. William J. Novak, "The Myth of the 'Weak' American State," *American Historical Review* 113, no. 3 (June 2008): 752–772. For some of the most influential scholarship that has repositioned the American state in this way, see Margot Canaday, *The Straight State: Sexuality and Citizenship in Twentieth-Century America* (Princeton, NJ: Princeton University Press, 2009); Nathan Connolly, *A World More Concrete: Real Estate and the Remaking of Jim Crow South Florida* (Chicago: University of Chicago Press, 2014); Jennifer Mittelstadt, *The Rise of the Military Welfare State* (Cambridge, MA: Harvard University Press, 2015); Molina, *How Race Is Made in America*; and Robert Self, *All in the Family: The Realignment of American Democracy since the 1960s* (New York: Hill & Wang, 2012).

6. Theda Skocpol, Introduction to "Politics Symposium: Why Political Scientists Should Study Organized Philanthropy," *PS: Political Science & Politics* 49, no. 3 (July 2016): 433.

7. Daniel Elazar, *Community and Polity: The Organizational Dynamics of American Jewry* (Philadelphia: Jewish Publication Society, 1995 [1976]), 7, 10; and Jonathan S. Woocher, *Sacred Survival: The Civil Religion of American Jews* (Bloomington: Indiana University Press, 1986), 20. See also Daniel Elazar, *People and Polity: The Organizational Dynamics of World Jewry* (Detroit, MI: Wayne State University Press, 1989). A recent and significant addition to the literature on American Jewish philanthropy, unsurprisingly also written by a political scientist with a historical bent, is Matthew Berkman, "Coercive Consensus: Jewish Federations, Ethnic Representation, and the Roots of American Jewish Politics" (PhD diss., University of Pennsylvania, 2018). Aside from these works, the only other book that has considered American Jewish philanthropy in a broad and interpretive way was written by a journalist: J. J. Goldberg, *Jewish Power: Inside the Jewish Establishment* (Reading, MA: Addison-Wesley, 1996).

8. See Jonathan Krasner, "The Place of Tikkun Olam in American Jewish Life," *Jewish Political Studies Review* 24, no. 3/4 (Fall 2013): 59–98. In most cases, when historians have studied American Jewish philanthropy, they have written institutional histories, focusing on the structure and evolution of one particular institution—and these are cited throughout the book. Although broad histories of American Jewry address the topic of Jewish philanthropy, they do so obliquely—and, often, as proof of American Jews' exceptional adaptation to and success in the United States. For two examples of this, see Hasia Diner, *The Jews of the United States,*

1654–2000 (Berkeley: University of California Press, 2004); Hasia Diner, Eli Faber, Henry Feingold, Edward Shapiro, and Gerald Sorin, *The Jewish People in America*, 5 vols. (Baltimore, MD: Johns Hopkins University Press, 1992); and Jonathan Sarna, *American Judaism: A History* (New Haven, CT: Yale University Press, 2004). Anthologies presenting similar synthetic treatments of American Jewish history also weave discussions about Jewish philanthropy throughout multiple chapters but tend not to address it as a subject itself. See, for example, Marc Lee Raphael, ed., *The Columbia History of Jews and Judaism in America* (New York: Columbia University Press, 2008); and Jonathan Sarna, *The American Jewish Experience* (New York: Holmes and Meier, 1986). Finally, a number of studies have situated Jewish philanthropy in other national contexts and illustrate its contextual and comparative patterns. See, for example, Nancy Green, "To Give and Receive: Philanthropy and Collective Responsibility among Jews in Paris, 1880–1914," in Peter Mandler, ed., *The Uses of Charity: The Poor on Relief in the Nineteenth-Century Metropolis* (Philadelphia: University of Pennsylvania Press, 1990); Rainer Liedtke, *Jewish Welfare in Hamburg and Manchester, c. 1850–1914* (Oxford: Clarendon Press, 1998); and Mordechai Rozin, *The Rich and the Poor: Jewish Philanthropy and Social Control in Nineteenth-Century London* (Brighton: Sussex Academic Press, 1999).

9. Some of the newest and most exciting scholarship on Jewish philanthropy highlights its transnational nature. See Jaclyn Granick, "Waging Relief: The Politics and Logistics of American Jewish War Relief in Europe and the Near East (1914–1918)," *First World War Studies* 5, no. 1 (2014): 55–68; and Rebecca Kobrin, "American Jewish Philanthropy, Polish Jewry, and the Crisis of 1929," in Hasia Diner and Gennady Estraikh, eds., *1929: Mapping the Jewish World* (New York: New York University Press, 2013), 73–92.

10. On foundationalist historical claims, see Joan W. Scott, "The Evidence of Experience," *Critical Inquiry* 17, no. 5 (Summer 1991): 777.

11. For a rich discussion of these dynamics, see Rebecca Kobrin and Adam Teller, "Introduction: Purchasing Power: The Economics of Modern Jewish History," in Kobrin and Teller, eds., *Purchasing Power: The Economics of Modern Jewish History* (Philadelphia: University of Pennsylvania Press, 2015), 1–24.

12. Derek Penslar, "The Origins of Jewish Political Economy," *Jewish Social Studies* 3, no. 3 (Spring–Summer 1997): 35, 54; and Adam Sutcliffe, "Anxieties of Distinctiveness: Walter Sombart's *The Jews and Modern Capitalism* and the Politics of Jewish Economic History," in *Purchasing Power*, 256–257. For a sampling of the recent turn toward thinking about Jews and economic power, especially through the lens of capitalism, see Cornelia Aust, *The Jewish Economic Elite: Making Modern Europe* (Bloomington: Indiana University Press, 2018); Michael Cohen, *Cotton Capitalists: Jewish Entrepreneurship in the Reconstruction Era* (New York: New York University Press, 2017); Abigail Green, *Moses Montefiore: Jewish Liberator, Imperial Hero* (Cambridge, MA: Belknap Press of Harvard University Press, 2010); Jonathan Karp, *The Politics of Jewish Commerce: Economic Thought and Emancipation in Europe, 1638–1848* (New York: Cambridge University Press, 2008), 27–45; Rebecca Kobrin, ed., *Chosen Capital: The Jewish Encounter with American Capitalism* (New Brunswick, NJ: Rutgers University Press, 2012); Lederhendler, *Jewish Immigrants and American Capitalism, 1880–1920*; Adam Mendelsohn, *Rag Race: How Jews Sewed Their Way to Success in America and the British Empire* (New York: New York University Press, 2015); Jerry Muller, *Capitalism and the Jews* (Princeton, NJ: Princeton University Press, 2010); Derek Penslar, *Shylock's Children: Economics and Jewish Identity in Modern Europe*

(Berkeley: University of California Press, 2001); Yuri Slezkine, *The Jewish Century* (Princeton, NJ: Princeton University Press, 2004); Glenda Sluga, "'Who Hold the Balance of the World?' Bankers at the Congress of Vienna, and in International History," *American Historical Review* 1222, no. 5 (December 2017): 1403–1430; and Adam Teller, *Money, Power, and Influence in Eighteenth-Century Lithuania: The Jews of the Radziwill Estates* (Stanford, CA: Stanford University Press, 2016).

13. For attempts to track the concept of "power" across Jewish history, see David Biale, *Power and Powerlessness in Jewish History* (New York: Schocken Books, 1986); and Ruth Wisse, *Jews and Power* (New York: Schocken Books, 2007). Some historians and critics have used the term "Jewish power" to address American Jews' status and standing. See, for example, Henry Feingold, *Jewish Power in America: Myth and Reality* (New Brunswick, NJ: Transaction Press, 2008); and J. J. Goldberg, *Jewish Power*. Finally, my thinking here about how to deploy Jewishness as a category analysis, which would be different from describing something called "Jewish power," but instead would analyze power through a Jewish lens, has been influenced by Lisa Silverman, "Beyond Antisemitism: A Critical Approach to German Jewish Cultural History," in William Collins Donahue and Martha Helfer, eds., *Nexus: Essays in German Jewish Studies*, vol. 1 (Rochester, NY: Camden House, 2011), 27–45. I also explore this point in Lila Corwin Berman, "Jewish History Beyond the Jewish People," *AJS Review* 42, no. 2 (November 2018): 269–292.

Chapter 1: Associations

1. Harry Lurie, "Is Democracy Possible in Jewish Community Life?" *Journal of Jewish Communal Service* 22, no. 2 (1945): 131.

2. Alexis de Tocqueville, *Democracy in America, Volume 1* (Urbana, IL: Project Gutenberg, 2006), ch. 12, www.gutenberg.org/files/815/815-h/815-h.htm; Alexis de Tocqueville, *Democracy in America, Volume 2* (Urbana, IL: Project Gutenberg, 2006), sec. 2, chs. 5 and 8, http://www.gutenberg .org/files/816/816-h/816-h.htm.

3. On Tocqueville's centrality to narratives of American exceptionalism, see William J. Novak, "The Myth of the 'Weak' American State," *American Historical Review* 113, no. 3 (June 2008): 752–772; Mahmood Mamdani, "Settler Colonialism: Then and Now," *Critical Inquiry* 41, no. 3 (Spring 2015): 596–614; and Rogers M. Smith, "Beyond Tocqueville, Myrdal, and Hartz: The Multiple Traditions in America," *American Political Science Review* 87, no. 3 (September 1993): 549–566. Also see Harold Hongju Koh, "On American Exceptionalism," *Stanford Law Review* 55, no. 5 (May 2003): 1479–1527; Seymour Martin Lipset, *American Exceptionalism: A Double-Edged Sword* (New York: W.W. Norton, 1997); Byron E. Shafer, ed., *Is America Different? A New Look at American Exceptionalism* (New York: Oxford University Press, 1991); and Ian Tyrrell, "American Exceptionalism in an Age of International History," *American Historical Review* 96, no. 4 (October 1991): 1031–1055.

4. On Harry Lurie, see "Harry L. Lurie, 81, of Jewish Council," *New York Times*, June 27, 1973, https://www.nytimes.com/1973/06/27/archives/harry-l-lurie-81-of-jewish-council-founder -of-philanthropic.html. See William J. Novak, "The American Law of Association: The Legal-Political Construction of Civil Society," *Studies in American Political Development* 15 (Fall 2001): 163–188; and Theda Skocpol, *Protecting Soldiers and Mothers: The Political Origins of Social Policy in the United States* (Cambridge, MA: Harvard University Press, 1992).

5. On the history of nineteenth-century Jewish associations, see case-specific books, including Dianne Ashton, *Rebecca Gratz: Women and Judaism in Antebellum America* (Detroit, MI:

Wayne State University Press, 1998); Leon A. Jick, *The Americanization of the Synagogue, 1820–1870* (Waltham, MA: Brandeis University Press, 1976); Deborah Dash Moore, *B'nai B'rith and the Challenge of Ethnic Leadership* (Albany: SUNY Press, 1981); Faith Rogow, *Gone to Another Meeting: The National Council of Jewish Women, 1893–1993* (Tuscaloosa: University of Alabama Press, 2005); and Daniel Soyer, *Jewish Immigrant Associations and American Identity in New York, 1880–1939* (Cambridge, MA: Harvard University Press, 1997).

6. On the state-based origins of associationalism, see Robert Gross, "Giving in America: From Charity to Philanthropy," in Lawrence Friedman and Mark McGarvie, eds., *Charity, Philanthropy, and Civility in American History* (New York: Cambridge University Press, 2003), 29–30; Amy Gutmann, "Freedom of Association: An Introductory Essay," in Gutmann, ed., *Freedom of Association* (Princeton, NJ: Princeton University Press, 1998), 9; and Novak, "The American Law of Association." More generally, see Brian Balogh, *The Associational State: American Governance in the Twentieth Century* (Philadelphia: University of Pennsylvania Press, 2015), ch. 1; John Brooke, "Ancient Lodges and Self-Created Societies: Voluntary Association and the Public Sphere in the Early Republic," in Ronald Hoffman and Peter J. Albert, eds., *Launching the "Extended Republic": The Federalist Era,* (Charlottesville: University of Virginia Press, 1996): 273–359; Kathleen McCarthy, *American Creed: Philanthropy and the Rise of Civil Society* (Chicago: University of Chicago Press, 2003); and Johann Neem, *Creating a Nation of Joiners: Democracy and Civil Society in Early National Massachusetts* (Cambridge, MA: Harvard University Press 2008), introduction.

7. Sarah Barringer Gordon, "The First Disestablishment: Limits on Church Power and Property Before the Civil War," *University of Pennsylvania Law Review* 162, no. 1 (December 2013): 316. Novak makes the same point in "The American Law of Association," 182. Also see Steven Green, *The Second Disestablishment: Church and State in Nineteenth-Century America* (New York: Oxford University Press, 2010).

8. Jonathan Levy, "Altruism and the Origins of Nonprofit Philanthropy," in Rob Reich, Chiara Cordelli, and Lucy Bernholz, eds., *Philanthropy in Democratic Societies: History, Institutions, Values* (Chicago: University of Chicago Press, 2016), 28–29.

9. *Trustees of Dartmouth College v. Woodward* 17 U.S. (4 Wheat.) 518 (1819); and Mark McGarvie, "The *Dartmouth College* Case and the Legal Design of Civil Society," in Lawrence Friedman and Mark McGarvie, eds., *Charity, Philanthropy, and Civility in American History* (New York: Cambridge University Press, 2003), 91–106.

10. Levy, "Altruism and the Origins of Nonprofit Philanthropy."

11. On incorporation law as a protector of diverse opinions or faiths, see Sarah Barringer Gordon, "The African Supplement: Religion, Race, and Corporate Law in Early National America," *William and Mary Quarterly* 72, no. 3 (July 2015): 385–422; and Jonathan Sarna, "The Debate Over Mixed Seating in the American Synagogue," in Jack Wertheimer, ed., *The American Synagogue: A Sanctuary Transformed* (New York: Cambridge University Press, 1987), 363–394. On the expansion and diversification of American Christianity, see Jon Butler, *Awash in a Sea of Faith: Christianizing the American People* (Cambridge, MA: Harvard University Press, 1992); and Nathan Hatch, *The Democratization of American Christianity* (New Haven, CT: Yale University Press, 1989). On patterns of nineteenth-century synagogue growth, see Shari Rabin, *Jews on the Frontier: Religion and Mobility in Nineteenth-Century America* (New York: New York University Press, 2017), 39–42; and Sarna, *American Judaism*, 58–61.

12. John Witte, Jr., "Tax Exemption of Church Property: Historical Anomaly or Valid Constitutional Practice?" *Southern California Law Review* 64, no. 2 (January 1991): 363–414.

13. Witte, "Tax Exemption of Church Property." See also John R. Brancato, "Characterization in Religious Property Tax-Exemption: What Is Religion—A Survey and a Proposed Definition and Approach," *Notre Dame Law Review* 44, no. 1 (1969): 60–80; and John Witte, Jr., "'A Most Mild and Equitable Establishment of Religion': John Adams and the Massachusetts Experiment," *Journal of Church and State* 41, no. 2 (March 1999): 213–252.

14. Witte, "Tax Exemption of Church Property," 389; Rabin, *Jews on the Frontier*, 43; and Hamilton Andrews Hill, "The Exemption of Church Property from Taxation," Paper read before the American Statistical Association, May 5, 1876 (Boston: A. Williams and Company, 1976), 16 (reports total valuation at $87.3 million in 1850 and $171.4 million in 1860).

15. Gordon, "The First Disestablishment," 317. On the ways in which the state makes certain practices, behaviors, and statuses visible, see Margot Canaday, *The Straight State: Sexuality and Citizenship in Twentieth-Century America* (Princeton, NJ: Princeton University Press, 2009); and James C. Scott, *Seeing Like a State: How Certain Schemes to Improve the Human Condition Have Failed* (New Haven, CT: Yale University Press, 1998).

16. Levy, "Altruism and the Origins of Nonprofit Philanthropy," 29–31.

17. See Ajay Mehrotra, *Making the Modern American Fiscal State: Law, Politics, and the Rise of Progressive Taxation, 1877–1929* (New York: Cambridge University Press, 2013), 39–44, 127–130.

18. Mehrotra, *Making the Modern American Fiscal State*, 148. On progressive reform efforts, see Bruce A. Ackerman, Stephen M. Engel, and Stephen Skowronek, eds., *The Progressives' Century: Political Reform, Constitutional Government, and the Modern American State* (New Haven, CT: Yale University Press, 2016); Robert Johnston, *The Radical Middle Class: Populist Democracy and the Question of Capitalism in Progressive Era Portland, Oregon* (Princeton, NJ: Princeton University Press, 2003); Michael McGerr, *A Fierce Discontent: The Rise and Fall of the Progressive Movement in America, 1870–1920* (New York: Free Press, 2003); and Daniel Rodgers, *Atlantic Crossings: Social Politics in a Progressive Age* (Cambridge, MA: Belknap Press of Harvard University Press, 1998). On the comparative contexts of European and American progressive reform and taxation, see James Kloppenberg, *Uncertain Victory: Social Democracy and Progressivism in European and American Thought, 1870–1920* (New York: Oxford University Press, 1986), ch. 9.

19. Mehrotra, *Making the Modern American Fiscal State*, 299–300.

20. Act of Aug. 27, 1894, ch. 349, § 32, 28 Stat. 509, 556. The Supreme Court determined the act was unconstitutional in *Pollack v. Farmers' Loan and Trust Company*, 158 U.S. 601 (1895). See W. Elliot Brownlee, *Federal Taxation in America: A Short History* (New York: Cambridge University Press, 2004), 53–72. On the history of the charitable deduction, including the steady increase of the maximum charitable deduction from 15% of one's income in 1917 to 50%, where it has held steady since 1969, see Mehrotra, *Making the Modern American Fiscal State*, 298–307; and Vada Waters Lindsey, "The Charitable Contribution Deduction: A Historical Review and a Look to the Future," *Nebraska Law Review* 81, 3 (2002): 1056–1096.

21. On Jews' low rate of congregational membership in the nineteenth century, see Hasia Diner, *The Jews of the United States, 1654–2000* (Berkeley: University of California Press, 2004), 131.

22. Soyer, *Jewish Immigrant Associations*, 1, 43–44. Also see Dash Moore, *B'nai B'rith*. On the proliferation of American associations generally, see Theda Skocpol, Marshall Ganz, and Ziad Munson, "A Nation of Organizers: The Institutional Origins of Civic Voluntarism in the United States," *American Political Science Review* 94, no. 3 (September 2000): 527–546; Brian Balogh, *A Government Out of Sight: The Mystery of National Authority in Nineteenth-Century America* (New York: Cambridge University Press, 2009), ch. 9.

23. See Idana Goldberg, "Gender, Religion and the Jewish Public Sphere in Mid-Nineteenth Century America" (PhD diss., University of Pennsylvania, 2004); Karla Goldman, *Beyond the Synagogue Gallery: Finding a Place for Women in American Judaism* (Cambridge, MA: Harvard University Press, 2000); Deborah Skolnick-Einhorn, "Power of the Purse: Social Change in Jewish Women's Philanthropy" (PhD diss., Brandeis University, 2012), 15–20; and Beth Wenger, "Federation Men: The Masculine World of New York Jewish Philanthropy," *American Jewish History* 101, no. 3 (2017): 377–399. On the gendered patterns of American benevolent work more generally, see Lori Ginzberg, *Women and the Work of Benevolence: Morality, Politics, and Class in the Nineteenth-Century United States* (New Haven, CT: Yale University Press, 1992).

24. Wenger, "Federation Men," 381. On the struggles between agencies and federation boosters, see Matthew Berkman, "Transforming Philanthropy: Finance and Institutional Evolution at the Jewish Federation of New York, 1917–1986," *Jewish Social Studies* 22, 2 (Winter 2017): 146–195.

25. Skocpol, Ganz, and Munson, "A Nation of Organizers," 541. See also McGerr, *A Fierce Discontent*.

26. McGerr, *A Fierce Discontent*, 68. On Jews and socialism, see Tony Michels, *A Fire in Their Hearts: Yiddish Socialists in New York* (Cambridge, MA: Harvard University Press, 2005).

27. Annie Polland and Daniel Soyer, *Emerging Metropolis: New York Jews in the Age of Immigration, 1840–1920* (New York: New York University Press, 2012), 57–63. On the broader context of Protestant social gospel reform, see Christopher Hodge Evans, *The Social Gospel in American Religion: A History* (New York: New York University Press, 2017).

28. See William A. Braverman, "The Emergence of a Unified Community, 1880–1917," and Leon A. Jick, "From Margin to Mainstream, 1917–1967," in Jonathan Sarna, Ellen Smith, and Scott-Martin Kosofsky, eds., *The Jews of Boston* (New Haven, CT: Yale University Press, 2005).

29. Arthur Goren, *New York Jews and the Quest for Community: The Kehillah Experiment, 1908–1922* (New York: Columbia University Press, 1970). For the classic history of Jewish life in Cleveland, see Lloyd Gartner, *History of the Jews of Cleveland* (Cleveland, OH: Western Reserve Historical Society, 1978). On the history of Jewish federations, see Daniel J. Elazar, *Community and Polity: The Organizational Dynamics of American Jewry* (New York: Jewish Publication Society, 1995), 211–218 (includes a catalogue of each federation and its founding date); Marc Lee Raphael, *A History of the United Jewish Appeal* (Chico, CA: Scholars' Press, 1982); Chaim Waxman, "American Jewish Philanthropy, Direct Giving, and the Unity of the Jewish Community," in Yossi Prager, ed., *Toward a Renewed Ethic of Jewish Philanthropy* (New York: Ktav, 2010), 53–78; and Jonathan S. Woocher, *Sacred Survival: The Civil Religion of American Jews* (Bloomington: Indiana University Press, 1986), ch. 2.

30. Daniel Walkowitz, *Working with Class: Social Workers and the Politics of Middle-Class Identity* (Chapel Hill: University of North Carolina Press, 1999). On the community chest movement and United Way, see Emily Barman, *Contesting Communities: The Transformation of Workplace Charity* (Stanford, CA: Stanford University Press, 2006); and Eleanor Brilliant, *The United Way: Dilemmas of Organized Charity* (New York: Columbia University Press, 1990). On Catholic Charities, see Dorothy Brown and Elizabeth McKeown, *The Poor Belong to Us: Catholic Charities and American Welfare* (Cambridge, MA: Harvard University Press, 1997); J. Bryan Hehir, ed., *Catholic Charities USA: 100 Years at the Intersection of Charity and Justice* (Collegeville, MN: Liturgical Press, 2010); Mary Oates, *The Catholic Philanthropic Tradition in America* (Bloomington: Indiana University Press, 1995); and John O'Grady, *Catholic Charities in the United States* (New York: Arno Press, 1931).

31. William Hutchinson, *Errand to the World: American Protestant Thought and Foreign Missions* (Chicago: University of Chicago Press, 1987); Akira Iriye, "A Century of NGOs," *Diplomatic History* 23, no. 3 (July 1999): 421–435; Matthew Frye Jacobson, *Special Sorrows* (Berkeley: University of California Press, 2002); and Melani McAlister, *The Kingdom of God Has No Borders: A Global History of American Evangelicals* (New York: Oxford University Press, 2018).

32. Avinoam Patt, Atina Grossman, Linda G. Levi, and Maud S. Mandel, eds., *The JDC at 100: A Century of Humanitarianism* (Detroit, MI: Wayne State University Press, 2019); and Yehuda Bauer, *American Jewry and the Holocaust: The American Jewish Joint Distribution Committee, 1939–1945* (Detroit, MI: Wayne State University Press, 1981). On the Alliance Israélite Universelle, see Lisa Moses Leff, *Sacred Bonds of Solidarity: The Rise of Internationalism in Nineteenth-Century France* (Stanford, CA: Stanford University Press, 2006), and on Jewish international philanthropy more broadly, see Jonathan Dekel-Chen, "Philanthropy, Diplomacy, and Jewish Internationalism," in Mitchell Hart and Tony Michels, eds., *The Cambridge History of Judaism, The Modern World, 1815–2000*, vol. 8 (New York: Cambridge University Press, 2017). On the phenomenon of diasporic nationalism, see Jacobson, *Special Sorrows*; and Rebecca Kobrin, *Jewish Bialystok and Its Diaspora* (Bloomington: Indiana University Press, 2010).

33. Report quoted in Harry Lurie, *A Heritage Affirmed: The Jewish Federation Movement in America* (Philadelphia: Jewish Publication Society, 1961), 57.

34. Lurie, *A Heritage Affirmed*, 57.

35. Rob Reich, "On the Role of Foundations in Democracies," in Reich et al., *Philanthropy in Democratic Societies*, 67. On early-twentieth-century foundations, see Rob Reich, *Just Giving: Why Philanthropy Is Failing Democracy and How It Can Do Better* (Princeton, NJ: Princeton University Press, 2018); Benjamin Soskis, "The Pre- and Early History of American Corporate Philanthropy," History of Corporate Responsibility Project Working Paper, no. 3 (Minneapolis, MN: Center for Ethical Business Culture, 2010); and Olivier Zunz, *Philanthropy in America: A History* (Princeton, NJ: Princeton University Press, 2012).

36. Reich, *Just Giving*, ch. 1. On the theory of "core technologies" of organizations, see Berkman, "Transforming Philanthropy," 148.

37. Jonathan D. Sarna, "The Cult of Synthesis in American Jewish Culture," *Jewish Social Studies* 5 (1998/99): 52–79.

38. Tyrrell, "American Exceptionalism in an Age of International History." On narratives of American progress and their ties to capitalism, see Eli Cook, *The Pricing of Progress: Economic Indicators and the Capitalization of American Life* (Cambridge, MA: Harvard University Press, 2017).

Chapter 2: Regulations

1. U.S. Commission on Industrial Relations, "Final Report and Testimony," submitted to Congress, 1916, vol. 8, 7430, at https://archive.org/stream/industrialrelato3manlgoog#page /n450/mode/2up. On the Commission on Industrial Relations, often referred to as the Walsh Commission after the labor lawyer Frank Walsh, see F. Emerson Andrews, *Philanthropic Foundation* (New York: Russell Sage Foundation, 1956), 342–343; and Judith Sealander, *Private Wealth and Public Life: Foundation Philanthropy and the Reshaping of American Social Policy from the Progressive Era to the New Deal* (Baltimore, MD: Johns Hopkins University Press, 1997), 228–234.

2. U.S. Commission on Industrial Relations, "Final Report and Testimony."

3. U.S. Commission on Industrial Relations, "Final Report and Testimony."

4. Sarah Igo, *The Known Citizen: A History of Privacy in Modern America* (Cambridge, MA: Harvard University Press, 2018).

5. On the Federal Reserve Bank, see Peter Conti-Brown, *The Power and Independence of the Federal Reserve* (Princeton, NJ: Princeton University Press, 2016), ch. 1; Roger Lowenstein, *America's Bank: The Epic Struggle to Create the Federal Reserve* (New York: Penguin Press, 2015); and David M. P. Freund, "State Building for a Free Market: The Great Depression and the Rise of Monetary Orthodoxy," in Brent Cebul, Lily Geismer, and Mason Williams, eds., *Shaped by the State: Toward a New Political History of the Twentieth Century* (Chicago: University of Chicago Press, 2019).

6. On Untermyer, see "Untermyer Dead in his 82d Year: Long Had Been Ill," *New York Times*, March 17, 1940. Also see "Nation Mourns Samuel Untermyer, Noted Attorney, Jewish Leader, Dead at 82," *Jewish Telegraphic Agency*, March 18, 1940, at https://www.jta.org/1940/03/18 /archive/nation-mourns-samuel-untermyer-noted-attorney-jewish-leader-dead-at-82. Untermyer's papers are held at the Jacob Rader Marcus Center of the American Jewish Archives, and the finding aid has a biographic sketch; see http://collections.americanjewisharchives.org/ms /ms0251/ms0251.html.

7. Olivier Zunz, *Philanthropy in America: A History* (Princeton, NJ: Princeton University Press, 2012), 22. On large early-twentieth-century foundations, see Barry Karl and Stanley Katz, "The American Private Philanthropic Foundation and the Public Sphere, 1890–1930," *Minerva* 19, no. 2 (1981): 236–270; and Inderjeet Parmar, *Foundations of the American Century: The Ford, Carnegie, and Rockefeller Foundations in the Rise of American Power* (New York: Columbia University Press, 2014).

8. Board of Trustees, Dec. 12, 1921, 4–5. All board meetings can be found in Subgroup I, Series 1, Subseries a, Subsubseries i, United Jewish Appeal-Federation of New York Collection, 1909–2004, Center for Jewish History, New York City (online access), hereafter UJA-FedNY. For the Resolution of the Law Committee proposing the incorporation of the Federation for the Support of Jewish Philanthropic Societies of New York City in the state of New York, see Minutes of the Meeting of the Organization Committee, Dec. 20, 1916, appendix A, UJA-FedNY. On the Jewish Federation of New York City, see Matthew Berkman, "Transforming Philanthropy: Finance and Evolution at the Jewish Federation of New York, 1917–1986," *Jewish Social Studies* 22, 2 (2017): 146–195; Charles Liebman, "Leadership and Decision-making in a Jewish Federation: The New York Federation of Jewish Philanthropies," *American Jewish Year Book* vol. 79 (Philadelphia: Jewish Publication Society, 1979), 3–76; and Beth Wenger, "Federation Men: The Masculine World of New York Jewish Philanthropy," *American Jewish History* 101, no. 3 (2017): 377–399.

9. On Catholic Charities' eschewal of endowment practices, see Mary Oates, *The Catholic Philanthropic Tradition in America* (Bloomington: Indiana University Press, 1995), 99–106.

10. Jens Beckert, *Inherited Wealth,* translated by Thomas Dunlap (Princeton, NJ: Princeton University Press, 2008), 174–185; T. J. Jackson Lears, *Rebirth of a Nation: The Making of Modern America, 1877–1920* (New York: Harper Collins, 2009); and Michael McGerr, *A Fierce Discontent: The Rise and Fall of the Progressive Movement in America, 1870–1920* (New York: Oxford University Press, 2003).

11. On the agencies served, see Harry Lurie, *A Heritage Affirmed: The Jewish Federation Movement in America* (Philadelphia: Jewish Publication Society of America, 1961), 78. On populist

animus against wealth accumulation, see Charles Postel, *The Populist Vision* (New York: Oxford University Press, 2007).

12. Board of Trustees, Nov. 14, 1921, 4, UJA-FedNY.

13. "J. H. Schiff's Will; Its Text in Full," *New York Times*, Oct. 6, 1920, 11. On Schiff, see Naomi Wiener Cohen, *Jacob H. Schiff: A Study in American Jewish Leadership* (Hanover, NH: Brandeis University Press, 1999).

14. Boris Bogen, *Jewish Philanthropy: An Exposition of Principles and Methods of Jewish Social Service in the United States* (Montclair, NJ: Patterson Smith,1969 [1917]), 42.

15. Board of Trustees, Nov. 14, 1921, 6–7, UJA-FedNY. On Leo Arnstein, who also served on the board of Mt. Sinai Hospital, one of the earliest affiliated agencies of the New York Federation, see *Decennial Record of the Class of 1896, Yale College* (New York: De Vine Press, 1907), 188–189; and "Leo Arnstein Is Elected to Central Bank Board," *Jewish Telegraphic Agency*, Nov. 15, 1934, at https://www.jta.org/1934/11/15/archive/leo-arnstein-is-elected-to-central-bank-board.

16. Board of Trustees, Dec. 12, 1921, 6, 12–13, UJA-FedNY.

17. Board of Trustees, May 23, 1927, 11; and Board of Trustees, Jan. 13, 1930, 7–10, UJA-FedNY.

18. Board of Trustees, Jan. 16, 1922, 9, UJA-FedNY.

19. Board of Trustees, Jan. 16, 1922, 9, UJA-FedNY.

20. Julia Ott, *When Wall Street Met Main Street: The Quest for an Investors' Democracy* (Cambridge, MA: Harvard University Press, 2011).

21. Board of Trustees, Jan. 8, 1923, 10, UJA-FedNY. For an example of a financial report, see Board of Trustees, Dec. 11, 1922, 3, "Report of the Finance Committee," UJA-FedNY.

22. Revenue Act of 1918, §231(6). https://babel.hathitrust.org/cgi/pt?id=c001.ark:/13960/t4xho5z7f;view=1up;seq=51, on 41–42 here.

23. Board of Trustees, Sept. 26, 1923, 2–3; and Board of Trustees, Dec. 10, 1923, 2–3, UJA-FedNY.

24. Board of Trustees, May 11, 1925, 11–26, UJA-FedNY.

25. Board of Trustees, May 11, 1925, 11–26, UJA-FedNY.

26. On these challenges to economic regulation, see Angus Burgin, *The Great Persuasion: Reinventing Free Markets since the Depression* (Cambridge, MA: Harvard University Press, 2012); Jacob Hacker, *The Divided Welfare State: The Battle over Public and Private Social Benefits in the United States* (New York: Cambridge University Press, 2002); Jennifer Klein, *For All These Rights: Business, Labor, and the Shaping of America's Public-Private Welfare State* (Princeton, NJ: Princeton University Press, 2006); Nancy MacLean, *Democracy in Chains: The Deep History of the Radical Right's Stealth Plan for America* (New York: Viking, 2017); and Kim Phillips-Fein, *Invisible Hands: The Businessmen's Crusade Against the New Deal* (New York: W.W. Norton, 2010).

27. Herman Jacobs, "Historical and Critical Survey of the Federation of Jewish Charities Movement, and a Sketch of the Federation of Jewish Charities of San Francisco," Master's thesis, Training School for Jewish Social Work, New York, 1926, table 1, p. 81, SC 11662, American Jewish Archives, Cincinnati, OH. For the comparison to community chest budgets, see Eleanor Brilliant, *The United Way: Dilemmas of Organized Charity* (New York: Columbia University Press, 1990), 23.

28. Herman Lissner, "Plan for Money Raising for Federation for the Support of Jewish Philanthropic Societies of New York," Feb. 25, 1926, 15–16, UJA-FedNY. Minutes of the Week-End

Conference of the Councilors of the Business Men's Council of Fed at Briarcliff Lodge, Feb. 27 and 28, 1926, 5, UJA-FedNY. On New York's budget, see Jacobs, "Historical and Critical Survey of the Federation of Jewish Charities Movement." His numbers may be somewhat inflated, since New York reported its total budget in 1929 as $3.8 million. See Board of Trustees, Jan. 14, 1929, UJA-FedNY.

29. Board of Trustees, May 23, 1927, 9–10, UJA-FedNY. On Stroock, see "Honor Sol Stroock, New President of Federation," *Jewish Telegraphic Agency*, Dec. 14, 1926, at https://www.jta.org /1926/12/14/archive/honor-sol-stroock-new-president-of-Federation.

30. Bogen, *Jewish Philanthropy*, 42.

31. On Rosenwald, see Peter Ascoli, *Julius Rosenwald: The Man Who Built Sears Roebuck and Advanced the Cause of Black Education in the American South* (Bloomington: Indiana University Press, 2006); Tobias Brinkmann, *Sundays at Sinai* (Chicago: University of Chicago Press, 2012), 228–229; Evelyn Brody, "Charitable Endowments and the Democratization of Dynasty," *Arizona Law Review* 39 (Fall 1997): 873–948; and Hasia Diner, *Julius Rosenwald: Repairing the World* (New Haven, CT: Yale University Press, 2017). Also see *Rosenwald: The Remarkable Story of a Jewish Partnership with African American Communities*, written, produced, and directed by Aviva Kempner (Washington, DC: Ciesla Foundation, 2015), film.

32. Ascoli, *Julius Rosenwald*, 97–98, 124.

33. Edwin Rogers Embree and Julia Waxman, *Investment in People: The Story of the Julius Rosenwald Fund* (New York: Harper and Brothers, 1949).

34. Julius Rosenwald, "The Burden of Wealth," *Saturday Evening Post*, Jan. 5, 1929, 13.

35. Rosenwald, "The Burden of Wealth," 12, 136. On the slogan's creation, see Ascoli, *Julius Rosenwald*, 131.

36. Rosenwald, "The Burden of Wealth," 136. On the schools, see *Rosenwald*, film.

37. Klein, *For All These Rights*. On the Great Depression and the regulations that followed, see Alan Brinkley, *The End of Reform: New Deal Liberalism in Recession and War* (New York: Alfred A. Knopf, 1995); Lizabeth Cohen, *Making a New Deal: Industrial Workers in Chicago, 1919–1939* (New York: Cambridge University Press, 1990); Jefferson Cowie, *The Great Exception: The New Deal and the Limits of American Politics* (Princeton, NJ: Princeton University Press, 2016); and Steve Fraser and Gary Gerstle, eds., *The Rise and Fall of the New Deal Order, 1930–1980* (Princeton, NJ: Princeton University Press, 1989).

38. Board of Trustees, March 24, 1930, 5–6, UJA-FedNY. For the vote to approve the Distribution Committee's budget, see Board of Trustees, March 31, 1930, 9, UJA-FedNY.

39. B. M. Selekman, "The Federation in the Changing American Scene," *American Jewish Year Book*, vol. 35 (Philadelphia: Jewish Publication Society, 1934), 68. Board of Trustees, April 18, 1932; and April 24, 1933, UJA-FedNY. On the effects of the Great Depression on Jewish organizational life in New York City, see Beth Wenger, *New York Jews and the Great Depression: Uncertain Promise* (New Haven, CT: Yale University Press, 1996).

40. On Rosenwald's work with President Hoover, see Zunz, *Philanthropy in America*, 106–125.

41. Board of Trustees, Oct. 9, 1933, 4, UJA-FedNY. Zunz, *Philanthropy in America*, 127.

42. Selekman, "The Federation in the Changing American Scene," 69.

43. As Beth Wenger shows, three-quarters of New York Jews supported FDR in 1932, and almost 90% voted for him in 1940, "far surpassing the Democratic presidential vote of any other

ethnic group" (133). Wenger, *New York Jews and the Great Depression*. On Jewish support for the New Deal, see Leonard Dinnerstein, "Jews and the New Deal," *American Jewish History* 72, no. 4 (June 1983): 461–476. Many scholars have also noted FDR's ambivalent relationship to American Jews and his misguided decisions in the face of Nazi aggression. See Richard Breitman and Allan Lichtman, *FDR and the Jews* (Cambridge, MA: Belknap Press of Harvard University Press, 2013).

44. Selekman, "The Federation in the Changing American Scene," 70.

45. Phillips-Fein, *Invisible Hands*, 8–9.

Chapter 3: Property

1. Salo Baron, "Modern Capitalism and Jewish Fate," *Menorah Journal* (Summer 1942): 124–126, 136–137. On Baron, see Robert Liberles, *Salo Wittmayer Baron: Architect of Modern Jewish History* (New York: New York University Press, 1995). On the *Menorah Journal*, see Daniel Greene, *The Jewish Origins of Cultural Pluralism: The Menorah Association and American Diversity* (Bloomington: Indiana University Press, 2011).

2. Baron, "Modern Capitalism and Jewish Fate," 116.

3. Baron, "Modern Capitalism and Jewish Fate," 137–138.

4. On earlier Jewish thought about property and materiality, see Eliyahu Stern, *Jewish Materialism: The Intellectual Revolution of the 1870s* (New Haven, CT: Yale University Press, 2018).

5. Baron, "Modern Capitalism and Jewish Fate," 137.

6. Wendy Wall, *Inventing the 'American Way': The Politics of Consensus from the New Deal to the Civil Rights Movement* (New York: Oxford University Press, 2008). The literature on contestations over private freedoms versus state power in the post–World War II era is vast. On how these contests tended to alight on ideas about property, see Lila Corwin Berman, *Metropolitan Jews: Politics, Race, and Religion in Postwar Detroit* (Chicago: University of Chicago Press, 2015); Nathan Connolly, *A World More Concrete: Real Estate and the Remaking of Jim Crow South Florida* (Chicago: University of Chicago Press, 2014); David Freund, *Colored Property: State Policy and Racial Politics in Suburban America* (Chicago: University of Chicago Press, 2007); Lisa McGirr, *Suburban Warriors: The Origins of the New American Right* (Princeton, NJ: Princeton University Press, 2001); Robert Self, *American Babylon: Race and the Struggle for Postwar Oakland* (Princeton, NJ: Princeton University Press, 2003); and Thomas Sugrue, *The Origins of the Urban Crisis: Race and Inequality in Postwar Detroit* (Princeton, NJ: Princeton University Press, 1996).

7. Historians are beginning to trace the roots of 1970s economic transformations, including the rise of neoliberalism, to the immediate post–World War II period. For an excellent statement of this intervention into the scholarship on neoliberalism, see Brent Cebul, Lily Geismer, and Mason B. Williams, "Beyond Red and Blue: Crisis and Continuity in Twentieth-Century U.S. Political History," in Cebul, Geismer, and Williams, eds., *Shaped by the State: Toward a New Political History of the Twentieth Century* (Chicago: University of Chicago Press, 2019), 8–9; and Suleiman Osman, "Glocal America: The Politics of Scale in the 1970s," in Cebul et al., *Shaped by the State*.

8. Board of Trustees, Jan. 17, 1944, UJA-FedNY.

9. Julia Ott, *When Wall Street Met Main Street: The Question for an Investors' Democracy* (Cambridge, MA: Harvard University Press, 2011).

10. Rachel Deblinger, "'In a World Still Trembling': American Jewish Philanthropy and the Shaping of Holocaust Survivor Narratives in Postwar America (1945–1953)" (PhD diss., UCLA, 2014).

11. For reports on the success of the campaigns, see Board of Trustees, March 8, 1943, 7–8; and Board of Trustees, April 10, 1944, 7–8, UJA-FedNY. On Goetz, see "Norman S. Goetz, Lawyer 60 Years," *New York Times*, March 6, 1972, at https://www.nytimes.com/1972/03/06/archives/normansgoetz-lawyer-60-years-prominentfigure-in-jewish.html. On the fiscal crises that New York's federation faced in its earlier years, see Matthew Berkman, "Transforming Philanthropy: Finance and Institutional Evolution at the Jewish Federation of New York, 1917–1986," *Jewish Social Studies* 22, 2 (Winter 2017): 156–160.

12. Sidney Cohen, "Trends in Fundraising," *Journal of Jewish Communal Service* 23, no. 1 (Sept. 1946): 78–79. For Goetz's suggestion, see Board of Trustees, March 8, 1943, UJA-FedNY, 16.

13. Board of Trustees, April 10, 1944, UJA-FedNY, 20. The executive director, Joseph Willen, also referred to the reserve money as a "sacred trust." See Board of Trustees, Feb. 14, 1944, UJA-FedNY, 2.

14. Board of Trustees, April 10, 1944, UJA-FedNY, 14. On Joseph Willen, the executive vice president, see "Joseph Willen Is Dead; A Jewish Fundraiser," *New York Times*, July 10, 1985, at https://www.nytimes.com/1985/07/10/nyregion/joseph-willen-is-dead-a-jewish-fund-raiser.html.

15. Board of Trustees, Oct. 14, 1946, 5, 6, UJA-FedNY.

16. Board of Trustees, Jan. 13, 1947, 20, UJA-FedNY.

17. Board of Trustees, Jan. 13, 1947, 19, 26; and Board of Trustees, Feb. 10, 1947, 3, UJA-FedNY.

18. Board of Trustees, Feb. 14, 1944, 2; and Board of Trustees, April 10, 1944, 9, 14, UJA-FedNY.

19. For tax tables from the 1950s, see "US Federal Individual Income Tax Rates History, 1862–2013," compiled by the Tax Foundation, Aug. 22, 2017 at https://taxfoundation.org/us-federal-individual-income-tax-rates-history-1913-2013-nominal-and-inflation-adjusted-brackets/. For the sake of comparison, in 2018, the top marginal rate was 37%. W. Elliot Brownlee, *Federal Taxation in America: A Short History* (New York: Cambridge University Press, 2004), 115–116; and Joel Slemrod, "The Economics of Taxing the Rich," in Joel Slemrod, ed., *Does Atlas Shrug? The Economic Consequences of Taxing the Rich* (Cambridge, MA: Harvard University Press, 2000), 3.

20. On taxation as a pivot point in the contests between democracy and capitalism, see Ajay Mehrotra, *Making the Modern American Fiscal State: Law, Politics, and the Rise of Progressive Taxation, 1877–1929* (New York: Cambridge University Press, 2013), introduction.

21. Quoted in Berrien Eaton, Jr., "Charitable Foundations and Related Matters under the 1950 Revenue Act: Part I," *Virginia Law Review* 37, no. 1 (Jan 1951): 3.

22. Herman T. Reiling, "Federal Taxation: What Is a Charitable Organization?" *American Bar Association Journal* 44 (June 1958): 529–530.

23. On the growth of federations, see Daniel J. Elazar, *Community and Polity: The Organizational Dynamics of American Jewry* (New York: Jewish Publication Society, 1995), 211–218; and Shaul Kelner, "Religious Ambivalence in Jewish American Philanthropy," in Thomas J. Davis, ed., *Religion in Philanthropic Organizations* (Bloomington: Indiana University Press,

2013), 31. On the United Way, see Emily Barman, *Contesting Communities: The Transformation of Workplace Charity* (Stanford, CA: Stanford University Press, 2006); and Eleanor Brilliant, *The United Way: Dilemmas of Organized Charity* (New York: Columbia University Press, 1990). On Catholic Charities, see Dorothy Brown and Elizabeth McKeown, *The Poor Belong to Us: Catholics Charities and American Welfare* (Cambridge, MA: Harvard University Press, 1997); J. Bryan Hehir, ed., *Catholic Charities USA: 100 Years at the Intersection of Charity and Justice* (Collegeville, MN: Liturgical Press, 2010); Mary Oates, *The Catholic Philanthropic Tradition in America* (Bloomington: Indiana University Press, 1995); and John O'Grady, *Catholic Charities in the United States* (New York: Arno Press, 1931).

24. On the Ford Foundation and comparative foundation and university endowment data, see Inderjeet Parmar, *Foundations of the American Century: The Ford, Carnegie, and Rockefeller Foundations in the Rise of American Power* (New York: Columbia University Press, 2011); Francis X. Sutton, "The Ford Foundation: The Early Years," *Daedalus* 116, no. 1 (1987): 41–91; and Olivier Zunz, *Philanthropy in America: A History* (Princeton, NJ: Princeton University Press, 2012), 173–174. On the number of foundations, see Eaton, "Charitable Foundations," 812.

25. Articles of Incorporation of the Crown Foundation under the General Not for Profit Corporation Act, Dec. 13, 1947, in author's possession from Crown Foundation Archives, Chicago, Illinois, hereafter Crown Papers. On its allocations, see Minutes of the Special Meeting of the Board of Directors of the Arie Crown Memorial Fund, Jan. 12, 1949, Crown Papers. On the name changes, see State of Illinois Office of the Secretary of State, Amendment to Articles of Incorporation, Dec. 30, 1947; and State of Illinois Office of the Secretary of State, Amendment to the Articles of Incorporation, May 21, 1959, Crown Papers.

26. On early cash and stock gifts, see Minutes of the Special Meeting of the Board of Directors and of the Members of the Arie Crown Memorial Fund, Jan. 12, 1949, Crown Papers. On the president's authorization to sell securities, see Minutes of the Special Meeting of the Board of Directors of the Arie Crown Memorial Fund, Aug. 11, 1949, Crown Papers. The charter members of the foundation were three of Arie and Ida Crown's sons, two of their grandchildren (both Henry Crown's sons), Milton Falkoff, the comptroller of the family's building supply company, and Harry Wyatt, a lawyer who served as the trustee for funds that Henry gave to children. See Minutes of a Special Meeting of the Board of Directors, Oct. 11, 1954, Crown Papers; and *Crown v. Commissioner* 67 T.C. 1060 (1977), at https://www.leagle.com/decision/1977112767cjtc106011040 for information on some of the board members.

27. On Henry Crown's investment in the Empire State Building in the early 1950s, see "Big Purchase," *New Yorker*, Jan. 8, 1955: 20–21; and Joan Cook, "Henry Crown, Industrialist, Dies; Billionaire, 94, Rose from Poverty," *New York Times*, Aug. 16, 1990, at https://www.nytimes.com /1990/08/16/obituaries/henry-crown-industrialist-dies-billionaire-94-rose-from-poverty-by -joan-cook.html. On the Crown Foundation's sale of shares in the Empire State Building Corporation, see Minutes of a Special Meeting of the Board of Directors, Nov. 24, 1953; and Minutes of a Special Meeting of the Board of Directors, Jan. 29, 1954, Crown Papers.

28. "Big Purchase," *New Yorker*, Jan. 8, 1955, 21; and Cook, "Henry Crown, Industrialist, Dies." Because I was given access to foundation records redacted of all financial details, I could not measure the ratio between the property transferred into the foundation and the property distributed through grants. As of its 2016 tax filings, the Arie and Ida Crown Memorial Fund had $774 million in assets and distributed roughly 5% of these assets, as legally mandated. See Arie

and Ida Crown Memorial 2016, 990-PF. As of 1985, the Crown family created a separate public charity, classified as a supporting organization, "to support and carry out the exempt purposes of the Jewish Federation of Metropolitan Chicago and the Jewish United Fund of Metropolitan Chicago," and as of the 2016 filing deadline, that fund held $227 million. See Crown Family Foundation 2015, 990.

29. For an excellent article that makes this point, see Ritu Birla, "C=f(P): The Trust, 'General Public Utility', and Charity as a Function of Profit in India," *Modern Asian Studies* 52, 1 (2018): 132–162.

30. Eaton, "Charitable Foundations," 810.

31. On the Revenue Act of 1950, see Boris Bittker and George Rahdert, "The Exemption of Nonprofit Organizations from Federal Income Taxation," *Yale Law Journal* 85, no. 3 (Jan. 1976): 336; and Eaton, "Charitable Foundations and Related Matters," 23–50.

32. Board of Trustees, April 10, 1944, UJA-FedNY, 17.

33. On the "subsidiarity" idea, see Axel Schäfer, *Piety and Public Funding: Evangelicals and the State in Modern America* (Philadelphia: University of Pennsylvania Press, 2012), 24. For variations on this same idea of state assistance, see Brian Balogh, *The Associational State: American Governance in the Twentieth Century* (Philadelphia: University of Pennsylvania Press, 2015); Suzanne Mettler, *The Submerged State: How Invisible Government Policies Undermine American Democracy* (Chicago: University of Chicago Press, 2011); and Sarah Milov, *The Cigarette: A Political History* (Cambridge, MA: Harvard University Press, 2019), ch. 4. Also see Jeffry Frieden, *Global Capitalism: Its Fall and Rise in the Twentieth Century* (New York: W.W. Norton, 2006).

Chapter 4: Taxation

1. House Resolution 561, 82nd Congress, 2nd Session, "Resolution," in *Hearings before the Select Committee to Investigate Tax-Exempt Foundations and Comparable Organizations*, 1, quoted in Peter Dobkin Hall, *Inventing the Nonprofit Sector and Other Essays on Philanthropy, Voluntarism, and Nonprofit Organizations* (Baltimore, MD: Johns Hopkins University Press, 1992), 67–69. For background on the investigation, see F. Emerson Andrews, *Foundation Watcher* (Lancaster, PA: Franklin and Marshall College, 1973), 132–147; and Olivier Zunz, *Philanthropy in America: A History* (Princeton, NJ: Princeton University Press, 2012), 193–194.

2. Brief biographical sketch of Norman Sugarman, provided by Paul Feinberg, copy in author's possession.

3. Sugarman, "Tax Laws Relating to Exempt Organizations," Statement on June 2, 1954, at the Hearings on "Tax Exempt Foundations" before the Special Committee (Reece Committee) to Investigate Tax Exempt Foundations and Comparable Organizations, House of Representatives, 83rd Congress, 2nd Session on H.R. 217, Part 1, 24, Articles and Addresses, vol. 1, 1939–1951, Box 1, Norman Sugarman Papers, P-633, American Jewish Historical Society, at the Center for Jewish History, New York, NY, hereafter NS Papers. On the Reece Committee and the Cox Committee that preceded it, see Eleanor Brilliant, *Private Charity and Public Inquiry: A History of the Filer and Peterson Commissions* (Bloomington: Indiana University Press, 2000), ch. 2; Hall, *Inventing the Nonprofit Sector*, 66–71; Alice O'Connor, "The Politics of Rich and Rich: Postwar Investigations of Foundations and the Rise of the Philanthropic Right," in Nelson Lichtenstein, ed., *American Capitalism: Social Thought and Political Economy in the Twentieth Century*

(Philadelphia: University of Pennsylvania Press, 2006), 228–248; and Zunz, *Philanthropy in America*, 146. On McCarthyism more generally, see Jennifer Delton, *Rethinking the 1950s: How Anticommunism and the Cold War Made America Liberal* (New York: Cambridge University Press, 2013); and Ellen Schrecker, *Many Are the Crimes: McCarthyism in America* (Princeton, NJ: Princeton University Press, 1999).

4. Identical quotations from Sugarman, "Laws and Regulations Relative to Tax Exempt Organizations," Statement on Nov. 19, 1952 at Hearings on Tax Exempt Foundations, before Select Committee to Investigate Tax Exempt Foundations and Comparable Organizations (Congressman Cox, Chairman), House of Representatives, 82nd Congress, 2nd Session, H.R. 561, 5; and Sugarman, "Tax Laws Relating to Exempt Organizations," Statement on June 2, 1954 at the Hearings on "Tax Exempt Foundations" before the Special Committee to Investigate Tax Exempt Foundations and Comparable Organizations, House of Representatives, 83rd Congress, 2nd Session on H.R. 217, 9; both in Articles and Addresses, vol. 1, 1939–1951, Box 1, NS Papers.

5. On this shift, see Angus Burgin, *The Great Persuasion: Reinventing Free Markets since the Depression* (Cambridge, MA: Harvard University Press, 2012); Jennifer Klein, *For All These Rights: Business, Labor, and the Shaping of America's Public-Private Welfare State* (Princeton, NJ: Princeton University Press, 2006); and Kim Phillips-Fein, *Invisible Hands: The Businessmen's Crusade Against the New Deal* (New York: W.W. Norton, 2009).

6. Britt Tevis, "May It Please the Court: Jewish Lawyers and the Democratization of American Law" (PhD diss., University of Wisconsin, 2016). On Treasury lawyers as "essential intermediar[ies]," see Ajay Mehrotra, *Making the Modern American Fiscal State: Law, Politics, and the Rise of Progressive Taxation, 1877–1929* (New York: Cambridge University Press, 2013), 311.

7. Norman Sugarman, Oral Statement to the Senate Finance Committee on behalf of the Council of Jewish Federations, Inc., Concerning the Revenue Act of 1978 (J.R. 13511), reported in the Bureau of National Affairs Daily Report for Executives #169, Aug. 30, 1978, 11, Articles and Addresses, Vol. 8, 1978–1979, Box 3, NS Papers.

8. Jon Teaford, *Cities of the Heartland: The Rise and Fall of the Industrial Midwest* (Bloomington: Indiana University Press, 1993).

9. On the Cleveland Foundation, see Diana Tittle, *Rebuilding Cleveland: The Cleveland Foundation and Its Evolving Urban Strategy* (Columbus: Ohio State University Press, 1992); Zunz, *Philanthropy in America*, 54–55; and "Goff's Vision: The World's First Permanent but Flexible 'Community Savings Account,'" at http://www.clevelandfoundation100.org/foundation-of -change/invention/goffs-vision/. On Cleveland, see W. Dennis Keating and David Perry, eds., *Cleveland: A Metropolitan Reader* (Kent, OH: Kent State University Press, 1995), especially part 5, "Governance: Public and Private"; Carol Poh Miller and Robert Wheeler, *A Concise History of Cleveland* (Bloomington: Indiana University Press, 1997); and Teaford, *Cities of the Heartland*. Also see Lloyd Gartner, *History of the Jews of Cleveland* (Cleveland, OH: Western Reserve Historical Society, 1978).

10. This history is recounted in "A Recap of the Development of the Policy Statement of the Endowment Fund Committee Concerning the Administration of Endowment Funds," May 6, 1965, Box 48, Folder 1138, Cleveland Federation Papers, MS 4835, Western Reserve Historical Society, Cleveland, Ohio, hereafter Fed-Cleveland.

11. Rudi Walter and Henry Zucker, "Study of Endowment Fund Programs of Thirteen Large City Jewish Federations," prepared for the Endowment Fund Committee of the Jewish

Community Federation of Cleveland, Nov. 1959, Folder 1214, Box 52, Fed-Cleveland. This study includes a summary of the 1954 program. The cities included in the study were Baltimore, Boston, Chicago, Cleveland, Detroit, Los Angeles (studied as two entities because it was home to a community council and a federation that both held endowments), New York City, Newark, Philadelphia, Pittsburgh, St. Louis, and San Francisco. After Cleveland, the cities with the highest increase in endowment size were (in order of growth) Detroit, Chicago, and St. Louis.

12. Walter and Zucker, "Study of Endowment Fund Programs of Thirteen Large City Jewish Federations," 13.

13. Report of the Finance and Investment Committee to the Board of Trustees of the Jewish Community Federation of Cleveland, Nov. 5, 1958, Folder 108, Box 7, MS 4563, Fed-Cleveland.

14. Memo from Executive Committee to Board of Trustees of the Jewish Community Federation, re: Administration of Federation's Endowment Fund, March 25, 1959, Folder 1196, Box 51, Fed-Cleveland, which quotes from March 26, 1958, statement of purpose of Endowment Committee presented to Board of Trustees.

15. Memo from Executive Committee to Board of Trustees of the Jewish Community Federation, re: Administration of Federation's Endowment Fund.

16. Purpose of Endowment, Oct. 1, 1958, printed in Memo from Executive Committee to the Board of Trustees of the Jewish Community Federation, re: Administration of Federation's Endowment Fund.

17. Letter from Rudi Walter and Henry Zucker to Frank Joseph, Nov. 1, 1959, included in Walter and Zucker, "Study of Endowment Fund Programs of Thirteen Large City Jewish Federations."

18. The presenters from 1955 to 1974 were all male. See List of Tax Seminar Programs, Oct. 16, 1975, Folder 1196, Box 51, Fed-Cleveland. Memo from Frank Joseph, chairman of Endowment Fund Committee, Oct. 29, 1959, with "Handbook for Attorneys" attached, Folder 1196, Box 51, Fed-Cleveland. Letter from Norman Sugarman (lists himself as chairman of editorial committee of the "Handbook for Attorneys") to editorial committee members, Nov. 6, 1959, Folder 1214, Box 52, Fed-Cleveland.

19. David Myers, "A Federation Endowment Program with Special Reference to Trust Fund," Nov. 19, 1961, Folder 1159, Box 49, Fed-Cleveland. Walter and Zucker, "Study of Endowment Fund Programs of Thirteen Large City Jewish Federations," which includes Letter from Rudi Walter and Henry Zucker to Frank Joseph, Nov. 1, 1959. There is a dearth of research on the history of university endowments. For a few studies that help put in perspective the importance of university endowments in normalizing endowment practices, see Merle Curti and Roderick Nash, *Philanthropy in the Shaping of American Higher Education* (New Brunswick, NJ: Rutgers University Press, 1965); Roger Geiger, "After the Emergence: Voluntary Support and the Building of American Research Universities," *History of Education Quarterly* 25, no. 3 (Fall 1985): 369–381; and Henry Hansmann, "Why Do Universities Have Endowments?" *Journal of Legal Studies* 19, no. 1 (Jan. 1990): 3–42.

20. On American Jews' support for Roosevelt and his New Deal programs that required state intervention, see Beth Wenger, *New York Jews and the Great Depression: Uncertain Promise* (New Haven, CT: Yale University Press, 1996).

21. Norman Sugarman, "Charitable Giving Developments in Tax Planning and Policy," *Taxes: The Tax Magazine* (Dec. 1961): 1028, in Articles and Addresses, Vol. 4, 1961–1965, Box 2, NS papers.

22. Sugarman, "Charitable Giving Developments in Tax Planning and Policy," 1031.

23. Andrews, *Foundation Watcher*, 132–147; and Zunz, *Philanthropy in America*, 202–206.

24. Laurence Woodworth comments, "Foundations in the Eyes of the Federal Government," 16th Annual Conference of the Council on Foundations, Pittsburgh, PA, May 1965, Articles and Addresses, Vol. 4, 1961–1965, Box 2 NS Papers. On the rise of a self-identified philanthropic sector, see Peter Dobkin Hall, *Inventing the Nonprofit Sector and Other Essays on Philanthropy, Voluntarism, and Nonprofit Organizations* (Baltimore, MD: Johns Hopkins University Press, 1992), ch. 1. On the Foundation Library Center, see Andrews, *Foundation Watcher*, ch. 14.

25. Sugarman comments, "Foundations in the Eyes of the Federal Government."

26. Sugarman comments, "Foundations in the Eyes of the Federal Government"; and "State Regulation of Tax-Exempt Foundations: Panel Discussion," American Bar Association Midyear Meeting, New Orleans, Louisiana, April 1967 (reported in the Bulletin of the Section of Taxation, ABA, Vol. 20, no. 3), Articles and Addresses, Vol. 5, 1966–1970, Box 2, NS Papers. On the development of Section 501(c)(3), see Paul Arnsberger, Melissa Ludlum, Margaret Riley, and Mark Stanton, "A History of the Tax-Exempt Sector: An SOI Perspective," *Statistics of Income Bulletin* (Winter 2008).

27. Thomas Troyer, Associate Legislative Council from the Department of Treasury, on the same American Bar Association panel in April 1967, explicitly rejected the definition of exemption that released charitable entities from state control. See "State Regulation of Tax-Exempt Foundations."

28. Report to the Endowment Fund Committee Regarding Federation Trust Fund Program, April 1961, no author listed; and David Myers, "A Federation Endowment Program with Special Reference to Trust Fund," Nov. 19, 1961, Folder 1159, Box 49, Fed-Cleveland.

29. Report to the Endowment Fund Committee, April 1961.

30. Report to the Endowment Fund Committee, April 1961.

31. Henry Zucker, "Endowment Funds," from Council of Jewish Federations and Welfare Funds Meeting on Endowment and Trust Funds, at National Conference of Jewish Communal Service, June 4, 1963, Folder 1159, Box 49, Fed-Cleveland. Much of his speech was cribbed from the 1961 report that he presumably helped to write. On his 1967 report about trust funds, see Henry Zucker, "The Trust Fund Idea and Service to Independent Foundations," published as part of the Proceedings of the Institute on Endowment Funds, Jan. 24–25, 1967, sponsored by Council of Jewish Federations, Folder 1159, Box 49, Fed-Cleveland.

32. Robert Hiller, Executive Director, Associated Jewish Charities and Jewish Welfare Fund of Baltimore, "Purposes of Endowment Funds," published as part of the Proceedings of the Institute on Endowment Funds, Jan. 24–25, 1967, sponsored by the Council of Jewish Federations, Folder 1159, Box 49, Fed-Cleveland. In 1964, Rudi Walter and Henry Zucker, from Cleveland, calculated the total endowment holdings of the twelve largest federations, complementing the earlier research they had done in the late 1950s and serving as the ballast for a 1965 report from the CJFWF, the national body of the federation system. See Endowment Fund Programs of Twelve Large City Jewish Federations, Third Report, Rudi Walter and Henry Zucker, Prepared for the Endowment Fund Committee of the Jewish Community Federation of Cleveland, April 1964; and 1964 Report on Endowment Funds in Jewish Federations, Nov. 1966, produced by the Council of Jewish Federations and Welfare Funds, Folder 5, Box 12, National Foundation for Jewish Culture, I-527, housed at the American Jewish Historical Society at the Center for Jewish History, New York, NY, hereafter NFJC.

33. Henry Zucker, "The Trust Fund Idea and Service to Independent Foundations," published as part of the Proceedings of the Institute on Endowment Funds, Jan. 24–25, 1967, sponsored by Council of Jewish Federations, Folder 1159, Box 49, Fed-Cleveland.

34. Jewish Community Federation of Cleveland Endowment Fund Committee, Seminar for Stockbrokers, Nov. 29, 1967, Folder 1159, Box 49, Fed-Cleveland.

35. Norman Sugarman, "Governmental Concerns as to Foundations," address given to the Foundation Advisory Council of the Jewish Community Federation, Dec. 9, 1968, Folder 1159, Box 49, Fed-Cleveland.

Chapter 5: Politics

1. Memo from Max Fisher to Presidents, Executive Directors, CJFWF Board of Directors, re: Tax Provisions Affecting Philanthropy, Nov. 21, 1969, Folder 1182, Box 50, Fed-Cleveland.

2. Memo from John R. Brown to H. R. Haldeman, April 1, 1969, Folder 12, Box 112, Max Fisher Papers, UP002350, Walter P. Reuther Library, Wayne State University, Detroit, MI, hereafter MF Papers. Also see Peter Golden, *Quiet Diplomat: A Biography of Max Fisher* (New York: Cornwall Books, 1992).

3. On depoliticization as a governing strategy that normalizes configurations of power while emptying them of their histories and political formation, see Wendy Brown, *Regulating Aversion: Tolerance in the Age of Identity and Empire* (Princeton, NJ: Princeton University Press, 2006), 15; and Peter Burnham, "New Labour and Depoliticisation," *British Journal of Politics and International Relations* 3, no. 2 (June 2001): 128.

4. In the figures of the so-called court Jew and the intercessor or *shtadlan*, American Jews may have had models for how to operate in non-Jewish politics. While none of these models could simply be exported into American democratic politics, each suggested the utility of a circumscribed position from which Jews could exercise some political influence without posing a threat to ruling powers. Yosef Yerushalmi is best known for developing the thesis that his advisor, Salo Baron, had advanced that throughout their history of living in diaspora, Jews have tended to organize themselves around alliances with ruling powers, well represented in the figure of the *shtadlan*. See Yosef Yerushalmi, "'Servants of Kings and Not Servants of Servants': Some Aspects of Jewish Political History," first delivered as the Tenenbaum Family Lecture Series in Judaic Studies, Tam Institute for Jewish Studies, Emory University (Atlanta, 2005) and reprinted in David Myers, ed., *The Faith of Fallen Jews: Yosef Hayim Yerushalmi and the Writing of Jewish History* (Waltham, MA: Brandeis University Press, an imprint of University Press of New England, 2013). For an excellent exploration of this theme in Yerushalmi's work and its relationship to his teacher Baron as well as his effort to refute contemporary political theorist Hannah Arendt, see Lois C. Dubin, "Yosef Hayim Yerushalmi, the Royal Alliance, and Jewish Political Theory," *Jewish History* 28, no. 1 (March 2014): 51–81. Also see Scott Ury, "The Shtadlan of the Polish-Lithuanian Commonwealth: Noble Advocate or Unbridled Opportunist?" *Polin: Studies in Polish Jewry* 15 (2002): 267–300.

5. War Income Tax Revenue Act of 1917, ch. 63, § 1201 (2). For a brief description, see Vada Waters Lindsey, "The Charitable Contribution Deduction: A Historical Review and a Look to the Future," *Nebraska Law Review* 81, 1056 (2003): 1061.

6. *Slee v. Commissioner of Internal Revenue*, 42 F.2d 184 (2d Cir. 1930), https://law.justia.com /cases/federal/appellate-courts/F2/42/184/1491795/.

7. For the suggestion that this case was linked to the 1934 amendment to the tax code, see "The Revenue Code and a Charity's Politics," *Yale Law Journal* 73, no. 4 (March 1964): 666–668.

8. Norman Sugarman, "Tax Laws Relating to Exempt Organizations," Statement on June 2, 1954, at the Hearings on "Tax Exempt Foundations" before the Special Committee (Reece Committee) to Investigate Tax Exempt Foundations and Comparable Organizations, House of Representatives, 83rd Congress, 2nd Session on H.R. 217, Part 1, Articles and Addresses, Vol. 2, 1952–1954, Box 1, NS Papers.

9. Norman Sugarman, "Tax Laws Relating to Exempt Organizations." Also quoted at length in Emerson Andrews, *Philanthropic Foundations* (New York: Russell Sage Foundation, 1956), 330–333.

10. For the exact language of the amendment, see Internal Revenue Code of 1954, H.R. 8300, §501(c)(3), 163, at https://constitution.org/uslaw/sal/068A_itax.pdf. Also see James Davidson, "Why Churches Cannot Endorse or Oppose Political Candidates," *Review of Religious Research* 40, no. 1 (Sept. 1998): 18; Bruce Hopkins, *The Law of Tax-Exempt Organizations*, 10th ed. (Hoboken, NJ: Wiley, 2011), 608–609; "The Revenue Code and a Charity's Politics," *Yale Law Journal* 73, no. 4 (March 1964): 661–675. For the standard explanation of the Johnson Amendment, see Patrick L. O'Daniel, "More Honored in the Breach: A Historical Perspective of the Permeable IRS Prohibition on Campaigning by Churches," *Boston College Law Review* 42 (July 2001): 733–769; and Olivier Zunz, *Philanthropy in America: A History* (Princeton, NJ: Princeton University Press, 2012), 196. For a useful revision that sets the amendment in its longer context, see Roger Colinvaux, "Policing the Border: A History of IRS Regulation of Political Activity," *Hist-Phil*, Aug. 24, 2018, https://histphil.org/2018/08/24/policing-the-border-a-history-of-irs-regulation-of-political-activity/.

11. On Jewish leaders' efforts to replace discussions of Zionism with claims for unified Jewish support for the State of Israel, see Matthew Berkman, "Coercive Consensus: Jewish Federations, Ethnic Representation, and the Roots of American Pro-Israel Politics" (PhD diss., University of Pennsylvania, 2018), ch. 5. For a calculation of dollars raised for Palestine pre-1948, see Eric Fleisch, "Israeli NGOs and American Jewish Donors: The Structures and Dynamics of Power Sharing in a New Philanthropic Era" (PhD diss., Brandeis University, 2014), 39–40. On the United Jewish Appeal's history and the history of American Jews' philanthropic support for Israel, see Marc Lee Raphael, *A History of the United Jewish Appeal, 1939–1982* (Chico, CA: Scholars Press, 1982); Theodore Sasson, *The New Zionism* (New York: NYU Press, 2014); and David H. Shapiro, *From Philanthropy to Activism: The Political Transformation of American Zionism in the Holocaust Years, 1933–1945* (New York: Pergamon Press, 1994). On Zionism's shifting position from controversy to consensus within American Jewish life, see Judah Bernstein, "'Birthland or Fatherland': A New History of American Zionism, 1897–1929 (PhD diss., New York University, 2017); and Noam Pianko, *Zionism and the Roads Not Taken: Rawidowicz, Kaplan, Kohn* (Bloomington: Indiana University Press, 2010).

12. See Odd Arne Westad, *The Cold War: A World History* (New York: Basic Books, 2017). For reflections on NGOs and sovereignty, see Akira Iriye, "A Century of NGOs," *Diplomatic History* 23, no. 3 (Summer 1999): 421–435; Samuel Moyn, *The Last Utopia: Human Rights in History* (Cambridge, MA: Harvard University Press, 2010); and Daniel Thomas, "International NGOs, State Sovereignty, and Democratic Values," *Chicago Journal of International Law* 2, no. 2 (2001): 389–395.

13. For context on the Suez Crisis, see William Hitchcock, *The Age of Eisenhower: America and the World in the 1950s* (New York: Simon & Schuster, 2018), ch. 13; James Loeffler, *Rooted Cosmopolitans: Jews and Human Rights in the Twentieth Century* (New Haven, CT: Yale University Press, 2018), ch. 7; and William Roger Louis, "Dulles, Suez, and the British," in Richard Immerman, ed., *John Foster Dulles and the Diplomacy of the Cold War* (Princeton, NJ: Princeton University Press, 1990).

14. For a deeper discussion of the Cold War and Suez Crisis in the shifting political ideology of American Jewish communal life, see Matthew Berkman, "Coercive Consensus," chs. 5 and 6. Also see Zunz, *Philanthropy in America*, 162–164.

15. Isaac Alteras, *Eisenhower and Israel: U.S.-Israel Relations, 1953–1960* (Gainesville: University Press of Florida, 1993), ch. 9; and Zunz, *Philanthropy in America*, 164–166. On the practice of purchasing foreign bonds as a diasporic mode of philanthropic support, see Dan Lainer-Vos, "Manufacturing National Attachments: Gift-Giving, Market Exchange and the Construction of Irish and Zionist Diaspora Bonds," *Theory and Society* 41 (2012): 73–106.

16. Letter from Lawrence Laskey to Max Fisher, April 26, 1957, Folder 1, Box 214, MF Papers.

17. Dorothy Thompson, "America Demands a Single Loyalty," *Commentary* (March 1950): 210–219; and Oscar Handlin, "America Recognizes Diverse Loyalties," *Commentary* (March 1950): 220–226.

18. Letter from Philip Klutznick to Julius Berman, chair of Conference of Presidents, Dec. 3, 1984, Folder 4, Box 209, Philip M. Klutznick Papers, Special Collections Research Center, University of Chicago Library, Chicago, IL, hereafter PK Papers; and Philip Klutznick, *Angels of Vision: A Memoir of My Lives* (Chicago: Ivan R. Dee, 1991), 164–167. Also see Louis, "Dulles, Suez, and the British."

19. Letter from Klutznick to Berman, Dec. 3, 1984.

20. See Milton Goldin, *American Jews and Their Philanthropies* (New York: McMillan, 1976), 197–198; Howard Morley Sachar, *A History of the Jews in America* (New York: Vintage Books, 1992), 732–733; and Sasson, *The New Zionism*, 20–21. On the meeting with Dulles, see Klutznick, *Angels of Vision*, 164–167, 208–216.

21. Excerpt from speech republished in Philip Klutznick, "Seven Steps toward Jewish Unity," *National Jewish Monthly* 78, 1 (Sept. 1963): 22.

22. Klutznick, "Seven Steps toward Jewish Unity," 22; and Hannah Arendt, *The Origins of Totalitarianism* (New York: Harcourt, 1968 [1951]), 24–25.

23. Klutznick, *Angels of Vision*, 252–253; and Certificate, n.d., Folder 8, Box 96, PK papers.

24. Letter from Klutznick to President Kennedy, Sept. 6, 1963, Folder 8, Box 96, PK papers.

25. Letter from Fisher to Teddy Kollek, Oct. 3, 1968, Folder 30, Box 93, MF Papers.

26. Stephen Isaacs, *Jews and American Politics* (Garden City, NY: Doubleday, 1974), 120.

27. Minutes from Sept. 4, 1968, meeting; and memo from Yehuda Hellman to Fisher, Oct. 17, 1968, Folder 8, Box 156, MF Papers.

28. Memo from John R. Brown to H. R. Haldeman, April 1, 1969, MF Papers.

29. Memo from Fisher to Nixon, Oct. 9, 1969; and note from Fisher to Nixon, n.d., Folder 12, Box 112, MF Papers. The archives are full of correspondence from Jewish leaders to Nixon, copied to Fisher. On the Meir dinner, see, for example, letter from I. L. Kenan (Chairman of

AIPAC) to Nixon, Oct. 6, 1969; and letter from Irving Kane to Fisher, Oct. 1969 (in which Kane extracts from his letter to Nixon), Folder 12, Box 112, MF Papers.

30. Letter from Rabbi Samuel Silver (Temple Sinai, Stamford, CT) to Fisher, Dec. 21, 1969; and Letter from Norman Blake (Southfield, MI) to Fisher, Jan. 11, 1970, Folder 12, Box 112, MF Papers. For copies of other similar letters, see Folder 10, Box 93, and Folder 12, Box 112, MF Papers.

31. Letter from Fisher to Ben Fixman, April 2, 1970, Folder 12, Box 112, MF Papers. See Nixon's telegram to Fisher, Dec. 9, 1969, in which he relayed a message to the American Jewish Joint Distribution Committee on the occasion of its annual meeting, Folder 12, Box 112, MF Papers. Also see letter from Dwight L. Chapin, special assistant to the president, to Fisher, June 30, 1969, regarding Nixon speaking at the United Jewish Appeal national convention, Folder 12, Box 112; letter from Fisher to Nixon, July 12, 1971, asking him to speak at the General Assembly of the federation, Folder 30, Box 93, MF Papers.

32. Quoted in Nick Thimmesch, "No-Nonsense Jewish Leaders Consider Mid-East Policy," *Kansas City Times*, Jan. 13, 1970, appended to letter from Earl Tranin to Fisher, Jan. 21, 1970, Folder 12, Box 112, MF Papers. See also J. Y. Smith, "Film Producer Dore Schary, 74, Dies," *Washington Post*, July 8, 1980, at https://www.washingtonpost.com/archive/local/1980/07/08 /film-producer-dore-schary-74-dies/2568607b-4b07-421f-bb62-95e029cb60b0/?noredirect =on&utm_term=.77f9cb244e89.

33. Letter from Earl Tranin to Fisher, Jan. 21, 1970, Folder 12, Box 112, MF Papers; and quotations from Thimmesch, "No-Nonsense Jewish Leaders Consider Mid-East Policy."

34. Robert Phelps, "Mideast Lobbies: Uneven Match," *New York Times*, April 8, 1970, in Folder 1, Box 43, Philip Slomovitz Papers, UP001494, Walter P. Reuther Library, Wayne State University, Detroit, MI, hereafter PS Papers; and Letter from Philip Klutznick to Fisher, Jan. 13, 1970, Folder 10, Box 93, MF Papers.

35. On the meeting, see Irving Spiegel, "3 Jewish Leaders Meet Nixon and Ask Help in Softening 11 Leningrad Verdicts," *New York Times*, Dec. 31, 1970; and Memo from John D. Ehrlichman to Fisher, Jan. 15, 1971, Folder 13, Box 112, MF Papers. On Wexler's political loyalties, see Richard Reeves, "McGovern, Nixon and the Jewish Vote," *New York*, Aug. 14, 1972, Folder 7, Box 113, MF, and on Wexler and Schacter's political shift, see Letter from Fisher to Fred Malek, Dec. 20, 1972, Folder 7, Box 113, MF Papers. On the broad consensus among American Jews to help Jews in the Soviet Union escape from communist control, see Gal Beckerman, *When They Come for Us, We'll Be Gone: The Epic Struggle to Save Soviet Jewry* (New York: Houghton Mifflin Harcourt, 2010); and Shaul Kelner, "The American Soviet Jewry Movement's 'Uneventful' 1968: Cold War Liberalism, Human Interest, and the Politics of the Long Haul," *American Jewish History* 102, 1 (Jan. 2018): 5–35.

36. Philip Shandler, "Nixon to Give Kosher Lunch for Publishers," *The Evening Star*, March 7, 1972, Folder 13, Box 112, MF Papers. On press reports, see Terence Smith, "Nixon Aides, Seeing Big Gains, Plan a Drive for Jewish Votes," *New York Times*, July 7, 1972, 1, 11, Folder 1, Box 43, PS Papers; and Richard Reeves, "McGovern, Nixon and the Jewish Vote," *New York Times*, Aug. 14, 1972, Folder 7, Box 113, MF Papers. On Jewish votes for Nixon in 1968, which Fisher estimated to be about 17% of Jewish voters and others since have estimated to be about 15–20%, see Letter from Martin Pollner to Fisher, Jan. 9, 1970, Folder 12, Box 112, MF Papers; and Will Maslow, "Jewish Political Power: An Assessment," *American Jewish Historical Quarterly* 66, no. 2

(Dec. 1976): 349. For a political scientist's analysis of American Jews' flirtation with Republican-ism starting with Nixon and then their full-throttle return to Democratic support in the 1990s, see Kenneth Wald, *The Foundations of American Jewish Liberalism* (New York: Cambridge University Press, 2019); and for a more general discussion of American Jews' party politics, see Herbert Weisberg, *The Politics of American Jews* (Ann Arbor: University of Michigan Press, 2019).

37. Max Fisher notes, meeting at the Waldorf Astoria Hotel in New York City with President Nixon and John Mitchell, Sept. 26, 1972, Folder 13, Box 112, MF. On the political affiliation of meeting attendees, see Draft of letter from Fisher to Nixon, Oct. 6, 1972, Folder 13, Box 112, MF Papers.

38. Synopsis of Meeting with President Nixon at the Waldorf Astoria Hotel, Sept. 26, 1972, Folder 13, Box 112, MF Papers.

39. See Maslow, "Jewish Political Power," 349. On responses to the pre-election meeting with Nixon, see, for example, Letter from Rabbi Seymour Siegel (Professor of Theology, Jewish Theological Seminary) to Nixon, Oct. 2, 1972; Letter from Leonard Greenberg (West Hartford, CT) to Nixon, Oct. 16, 1972; and "Pincus Praises Nixon for His Approach to Issue of Soviet Jewry, But Stresses Struggle over Visa Fees Is Not Over," *Jewish Telegraphic Agency News Bulletin*, Oct. 3, 1972, Folder 13, Box 112, MF Papers.

40. Letter from Fisher to Fred Malek, Dec. 20, 1972, Folder 7, Box 113, MF Papers.

41. Extract from Richard Nixon memo, n.d., Folder 112, Box 12, MF papers. On Fisher's response to Nixon's antisemitic remarks, see Pete Waldmeir, "Max Backs the President," *Detroit News*, May 15, 1974, Folder 7, Box 113, MF Papers. See also Office of the White House Press Secretary, Q & A session with Max Fisher, Chairman of the Jewish Organization of Israel, and Rabbi Israel Miller, Chairman of the President's Conference of Major Jewish Organizations Following a Meeting with the President, the North Lawn, 1974 [?], Folder 7, Box 113, MF Papers.

42. Tax Proposals Affecting Philanthropy, n.d. [Aug. 1972]; and Memo from Philip Bernstein to Fisher, Dec. 12, 1972, Folder 4, Box 161, MF Papers.

43. Thomas Piketty, *Capital in the Twenty-First Century* (Cambridge, MA: Harvard University Press, 2014).

Chapter 6: Finance and Identity

1. Gary Rosenblatt, "The Life and Death of a Dream Revisited," *Journal of Jewish Communal Service* 86 nos. 1–2 (Winter-Spring 2011): 34 (reprint of an article that first appeared in *Baltimore Jewish Times*, Nov. 7, 1980). On Rosenblatt's reporting of this story, see author's conversation with Gary Rosenblatt, July 23, 2014.

2. Rosenblatt, "The Life and Death of a Dream Revisited," 35.

3. Rosenblatt, "The Life and Death of a Dream Revisited," 35.

4. Rosenblatt, "The Life and Death of a Dream Revisited," 35–36.

5. Richard L. Narva, "The Stillborn Revolution? Reforming the Philanthropies," *Response: A Contemporary Jewish Review* 6, no. 3 (Summer 1972): 19; and author's conversation with Richard Narva, Oct. 23, 2018. On Zacks's resolution, see Rosenblatt, "The Life and Death of a Dream Revisited," 36–37. On broader social criticism of the middle class and, specifically, the Jewish

middle class, see Lila Corwin Berman, "American Jews and the Ambivalence of Middle Class-ness," *American Jewish History* 93, 4 (Dec. 2007): 409–434; and Rachel Kranson, *Ambivalent Embrace: Jewish Upward Mobility in Postwar America* (Chapel Hill: University of North Carolina Press, 2017).

6. Resolution Adopted by the 38th General Assembly of the Council of Jewish Federations and Welfare Funds, "Taxes Affecting Philanthropy," Nov. 16, 1969, Boston; and Memo from Max Fisher to Presidents, Executive Directors, CJFWF Board of Directors, re: Tax Provisions Affecting Philanthropy, Nov. 21, 1969, Folder 1182, Box 50, Fed-Cleveland.

7. On the role of finance and private capital in the New Deal and the welfare state, see Angus Burgin, *The Great Persuasion: Reinventing Free Markets since the Depression* (Cambridge, MA: Harvard University Press, 2012); Jacob Hacker, *The Divided Welfare State: The Battle over Public and Private Social Benefits in the United States* (New York: Cambridge University Press, 2002); Jennifer Klein, *For All These Rights: Business, Labor, and the Shaping of America's Public-Private Welfare State* (Princeton, NJ: Princeton University Press, 2006); and Suzanne Mettler, *The Submerged State: How Invisible Government Policies Undermine American Democracy* (Chicago: University of Chicago Press, 2011). On financialization, see Larry M. Bartels, *Unequal Democracy: The Political Economy of the New Gilded Age* (Princeton, NJ: Princeton University Press, 2008); Wendy Brown, *Undoing the Demos: Neoliberalism's Stealth Revolution* (Cambridge, MA: Zone Books, 2015); Gerald Davis, *Managed by the Markets: How Finance Reshaped America* (New York: Oxford University Press, 2009); Greta Krippner, *Capitalizing on Crisis: The Political Origins of the Rise of Finance* (Cambridge, MA: Harvard University Press, 2011); Randy Martin, *Financialization of Daily Life* (Philadelphia: Temple University Press, 2002); Thomas Piketty, *Capital in the Twenty-First Century* (Cambridge, MA: Harvard University Press, 2014); Judith Stein, *Pivotal Decade: How the United States Traded Factories for Finance in the Seventies* (New Haven, CT: Yale University Press, 2010); and Benjamin Waterhouse, *Lobbying America: The Politics of Business from Nixon to NAFTA* (Princeton, NJ: Princeton University Press, 2014).

8. Board of Trustees, April 28, 1969, discussion of Report from the Committee on Communal Planning on Goals and Purpose of Federation; and Board of Trustees, Nov. 17, 1947, table showing "Total Allocations and Allocations for Cultural Recreational Activities by Jewish Federations and Welfare Funds, 1935–46," UJA-FedNY; Gerald Bubis, "The Impact of Changing Issues on Federations and Their Structures," *Jewish Political Studies Review* 7, nos. 3–4 (Fall 1995), 91; Charles Liebman, "Leadership and Decision-making in a Jewish Federation: The New York Federation of Jewish Philanthropies," *American Jewish Year Book,* vol. 79 (Philadelphia: Jewish Publication Society, 1978), 37–39; and Jack Wertheimer, "Current Trends in American Jewish Philanthropy," *American Jewish Year Book,* vol. 97 (Philadelphia: Jewish Publication Society, 1997), 85, table 2.

9. On American Jews' rising socioeconomic status and anxieties about assimilation, stoked by sociological surveys, see Berman, "American Jews and the Ambivalence of Middle Class-ness"; Lila Corwin Berman, "Blame, Boundaries, and Birthrights: Jewish Intermarriage in Mid-Century America," in Susan Glenn and Naomi Sokoloff, eds., *The Boundaries of Jewish Identity* (Seattle: University of Washington Press, 2010); Lila Corwin Berman, *Speaking of Jews: Rabbis, Intellectuals, and the Creation of an American Public Identity* (Berkeley: University of California Press, 2009); and Lila Corwin Berman, "Sociology, Jews, and Intermarriage in Twentieth-Century America," *Jewish Social Studies* 14, no. 2 (Winter 2008): 32–60; and Kranson, *Ambivalent Embrace.*

On the increase in government grants to charitable entities and these organizations' transformation into service providers, see Andrew Morris, *The Limits of Voluntarism: Charity and Welfare from the New Deal to the Great Society* (New York: Cambridge University Press, 2009); and on grants to Jewish organizations in particular, see Martha Selig, "New Dimensions in Government Funding of Voluntary Agencies: Potentials and Risks," *Journal of Jewish Communal Service* 50, no. 2 (Winter 1973): 125–135.

10. Robert Hiller and Meyer Schwartz, "Fund Raising as a Social Work Process," *Journal of Jewish Communal Service* 36, no. 1 (Fall 1959): 59; and Max Perlman, "Effects of Increased Public Funds on Jewish Federations and Agencies," *Journal of Jewish Communal Service* 34, no. 1 (Fall 1957): 21. Also see Bertram Gold, "The Urban Crisis and Its Effect Upon Jewish Communal Services," *Journal of Jewish Communal Service* 45, no. 1 (Fall 1968): 34; and Sanford Solender, "New Developments in Jewish Community Organization," *Journal of Jewish Communal Service* 24, no. 1 (Sept. 1947): 4–5. For historical framing of Jewish identity language, see Berman, *Speaking of Jews*; Jonathan Krasner, "On the Origins and Persistence of the Jewish Identity Industry in Jewish Education," in Jonathan Levisohn and Ari Kelman, eds., *Beyond Jewish Identity: Rethinking Concepts and Imagining Alternatives* (Boston, MA: Academic Studies Press, 2019); and Michael Staub, *Torn at the Roots: The Crisis of Liberalism in Postwar America* (New York: Columbia University Press, 2002). Finally, for a broader contextualization of identity discourse in American politics, see Matthew Frye Jacobson, *Roots Too: White Ethnic Revival in Post-Civil Rights America* (Cambridge, MA: Harvard University Press, 2008).

11. For a timeline of the National Foundation for Jewish Culture, see Jewish Cultural Services for the 21st Century: A Strategic Plan for the NFJC, 1991–1992, Folder 1, Box 17, NFJC. For a historical survey, see Report of the National Foundation for Jewish Culture to the Large City Budgeting Conference for the meeting of the Steering Committee, NYC, Jan. 13–15, 1962, Folder 4, Box 12, NFJC. Also see Survey Report, "National Jewish Cultural Services in America: Appraisals and Recommendations," a study conducted by the Council of Jewish Federations and Welfare Funds, survey report and recommendations approved by Board of Directors of the Council of Jewish Federations and Welfare Funds on Sept. 20, 1959, Folder 2, Box 44, NFJC.

12. Survey Report, "National Jewish Cultural Services in America: Appraisals and Recommendations.

13. Survey Report, "National Jewish Cultural Services in America: Appraisals and Recommendations."

14. Minutes of the Meeting of the Executive Committee of the NFJC, Jan. 22, 1961, Folder 4, Box 12, NFJC. On Wolf, see "Edwin Wolf 2d, 79, Rare-Books Specialist," *New York Times*, Feb. 22, 1991, at https://www.nytimes.com/1991/02/22/obituaries/edwin-wolf-2d-79-rare-books-specialist.html; and for the biographical sketch for his personal papers, which are held at the Library Company of Philadelphia, see http://dla.library.upenn.edu/dla/pacscl/detail.html?id=PACSCL_LCP_.

15. As president of Philadelphia's federation, Wolf was involved with its endowment-building efforts in the 1960s, especially its "letter of intent" program that it devised to get supporters to pledge to bequest some of their estate to the federation's endowment. See Donald Hurwitz (executive director of Philadelphia's federation), "Letter of Intent," in Proceedings of the Institute on Endowment Funds, sponsored by the Council of Jewish Federations, Jan. 24–25, 1976, Folder 1159, Box 49, Fed-Cleveland.

16. Letter from Isidore Sobeloff (Los Angeles) to Harry Baron (executive director, National Foundation for Jewish Culture), Nov. 9, 1966, Folder 5, Box 12, NFJC. Other cities' federations similarly demurred. See Letter from Louis Weintraub (San Francisco) to Julian Freeman, Sept. 28, 1966; and Letter from Sidney Posin (St. Louis) to Barron, Nov. 4, 1966, Folder 5, Box 12, NFJC. On requests for endowment funds, see Julius Paris to Gerald Soroker (Pittsburgh federation), Oct. 13, 1966, Folder 5, Box 12, NFJC. For other endowment requests, see Letter from Julian Freeman to Isidore Sobeloff, Executive Director, Jewish Federation-Council of Greater Los Angeles, Sept. 20, 1966, Folder 4, Box 12, NFJC. Freeman sent similar requests to St. Louis (letter from Julian Freeman to Morris Shenker, President, Federation of St. Louis, Sept. 22, 1966); San Francisco (letter from Freeman to Samuel Ladar, Jewish Welfare Federation of San Francisco, Marin County and the Peninsula, Sept. 20, 1966); Chicago (Freeman to Morris Glaser, President, Jewish Welfare Fund of Metropolitan Chicago, Sept. 20, 1966), Folder 5, Box 12, NFJC. The archives contain a number of reports about federation endowments, evidence that National Foundation leaders were tracking that information to help them target requests. See, for example, Endowment Development Program, June 1, 1967, Folder 4, Box 12, NFJC; "Federation Endowment Funds," n.d. [1966], Folder 5, Box 12, NFJC.

17. Toward a Proposal: A Program for the Endowment of the Arts, National Foundation for Jewish Culture, March 30, 1976, Folder 3, Box 12, NFJC. See information sheets on private family foundations, n.d. [1970], Folder 4, Box 165, NFJC.

18. My thinking on the liberal subject, individual sovereignty, and market freedom is influenced by Catherine Rottenberg, *The Rise of Neoliberal Feminism* (New York: Oxford University Press, 2018). On early and mid-twentieth-century efforts to counter the individualist logic of American liberalism, see Katherine Rosenblatt, "Cooperative Battlegrounds: Farmers, Workers, and the Search for Economic Alternatives," (PhD diss., University of Michigan, 2016).

19. "Testimony Given before the House Committee on Ways and Means in the Course of Tax Reform Hearings before that Committee," Feb. 19, 1969, reported in Congressional Digest, Articles and Addresses, Vol. 5, 1966–1970, Box 2, NS Papers. On the ways in which calls for small government in the post–New Deal period were hardly interested in shrinking government but rather hoped to refocus the largesse of the state, see Jefferson Cowie and Nick Salvatore, "The Long Exception: Rethinking the Place of the New Deal in American History," *International Labor and Working-Class History* 74 (Fall 2008): 24.

20. Statement by Council of Jewish Federations and Welfare Funds, submitted by Louis J. Fox, president to Committee on Ways and Means, House of Representatives, Re: Tax Proposals Affecting Charitable Contributions, Feb. 27, 1969, Folder 1179, Box 50, Fed-Cleveland. For Fox's talking points, see Memo from S. P. Goldberg, Director of Budget Research, to Federations and Welfare Funds, Feb. 18, 1969, Folder 1179, Box 50, Fed-Cleveland.

21. Truman quoted in Berrien Eaton, Jr., "Charitable Foundations and Related Matters under the 1950 Revenue Act: Part I," *Virginia Law Review* 37, no. 1 (Jan. 1951): 3. Also see Thomas Troyer, "The 1969 Private Foundation Law: Historical Perspective on Its Origins and Underpinnings," *The Exempt Organization Tax Review* 27, no. 1 (2000): 52–65.

22. On the coalition, see Letter from James A. Norton, Director, Cleveland Foundation, to Senator Russell Long, Chair, Senate Finance Committee, re Hearings on H.R. 13270, Sept. 19, 1969, Folder 1181, Box 50, Fed-Cleveland. For the origins of the collaboration, see Memo from S. P. Goldberg, Director of Budget Research, to Federations and Welfare Funds, Feb. 18, 1969,

Folder 1179, Box 50; and Preliminary Draft: Statement Regarding Proposed Federal Tax Legislation, attached to Letter from William Avrunin (Detroit) to Dan Rosenberg (CJFWF), Aug. 21, 1969, Folder 1180, Box 50, Fed-Cleveland.

23. On collaborations with the United Way around the 1969 Tax Reform Act, see William Avrunin, "Relationship with United Ways," *Journal of Jewish Communal Service* 49, no. 2 (Winter 1972): 119–124, here 121. On the creation of the philanthropic sector, see Emily Barman, "Classificatory Struggles in the Nonprofit Sector: The Formation of the National Taxonomy of Exempt Entities, 1969–1987," *Social Science History* 37, no. 1 (Spring 2013): 103–141; and Peter Frumkin, "The Long Recoil: Private Philanthropic Foundations and the Tax Reform Act of 1969," *American Review of Public Administration* 28, no. 3 (Sept 1998): 266–286.

24. Letter from Rudi Walter (listed here as secretary of the Endowment Fund Committee) to Bennett Yanowitz, June 4, 1969, Folder 1180, Box 50, Fed-Cleveland.

25. On the percentage of gifts of appreciated property that federations received, see Letter from Philip Bernstein (executive vice president, CJFWF) to Charles Vanik, June 5, 1969, Folder 1180, Box 50; and Memo Re Proposed Legislation Concerning Philanthropic Contributions, submitted by Samuel Silberman, June 16, 1969, Folder 1180, Box 50, Fed-Cleveland.

26. Memo from Louis J. Fox, president of CJFWF, to Presidents of Member Agencies, re: Proposed Tax Revisions Affecting Philanthropic Giving, May 14, 1969, Folder 1179, Box 50; and Letter to Board of Directors from Louis J. Fox, Sept. 16, 1969, Folder 1181, Box 50, Fed-Cleveland. On the campaign directed to Rep. Charles Vanik, see telegram from Lloyd Schwenger to Vanik, July 23, 1969, Folder 1180, Box 50, Fed-Cleveland.

27. Letter from Bennett Yanowitz to Rudi Walter, June 25, 1969, Folder 1180, Box 50, Fed-Cleveland.

28. Memo from CJFWF to Board of Directors, Presidents, Executive Directors, Campaign Services Committee, Urban Affairs & Public Welfare Committee, Aug. 15, 1969, Folder 1180, Box 50, Fed-Cleveland.

29. Guidance released from Congress after the passage of the 1969 Tax Reform Act offers a lucid discussion of the legal precedent for determining qualifying public charities and the new classification of private foundations. See "General Explanation of the Tax Reform Act of 1969," prepared by the Staff of the Joint Committee on Internal Revenue Taxation, Dec. 3, 1970, 57–58, at https://www.pgdc.com/files/generalexplanatioojcs1670_bw.pdf.

30. As a summary of the bill explained, "Heavily endowed foundations have substantial income that is not taxed." See "Summary of H.R. 13270, the Tax Reform Act of 1969 (As Passed by the House of Representatives)," Prepared by the Staffs of the Joint Committee on Internal Revenue Taxation and the Committee on Finance, Aug. 18, 1969, at http://www.jct.gov/s-61-69 .pdf, 11.

31. Letter from Bennett Yanowitz to Rudi Walter, Aug. 15, 1969, Folder 1180, Box 50, Fed-Cleveland. For similar exchanges, see Memos from Henry Zucker to Rudi Walter, Aug. 12, 1969, from Rudi Walter to Henry Zucker, Sept. 10, 1969, and from Rudi Walter to Henry Zucker, Sept. 23, 1969. Also see Letter from Julius Bisno (from Los Angeles federation) to Henry Zucker, Sept. 23, 1969, and from Henry Zucker to Julius Bisno, Sept. 26, 1969, Folder 1180, Box 50, Fed-Cleveland.

32. See Letter from Philip Bernstein (executive vice president, CJFWF) to Henry Zucker (Cleveland), Sept. 30, 1969, Folder 1181, Box 50; Memos (two of them) from Henry Zucker to

Rudi Walter, Oct. 1, 1969, Folder 1182, Box 50; and Memo from Norman Sugarman, Oct. 6, 1969, Folder 1182, Box 50, Fed-Cleveland. On Bernstein, see Philip Bernstein, *To Dwell in Unity: The Jewish Federation Movement in America Since 1960* (Philadelphia: Jewish Publication Society, 1983); and the finding aid to his papers at http://digifindingaids.cjh.org/?pID=488988.

33. Council Reports (CJFWF): The Tax Reform Act of 1969, Dec. 31, 1969 (prepared by S. P. Goldberg, Director, CJFWF Budget Research Department), Folder 1188, Box 50, Fed-Cleveland.

34. For pledges to the value of "tax equity," see Memo from Louis J. Fox (president of CJFWF) to Board of Directors, Presidents, Executive Directors, Campaign Services Committee, Urban Affairs & Public Welfare Committee, Aug. 13, 1969; Memo from Philip Bernstein (CJFWF) to Executives, re: tax legislation, Aug. 21, 1969; Letter from William Avrunin (Detroit federation) to Dan Rosenberg (CJFWF), Aug. 21, 1969, with Preliminary Draft: Statement Regarding Proposed Federal Tax Legislation, all Folder 1180, Box 50, Fed-Cleveland. Also see Statement from Council of Jewish Federations and Welfare Funds, submitted by Louis J. Fox to Senate Finance Committee, re Tax Proposals Affecting Charitable Contributions, Sept. 18, 1969; Joint Statement from United Foundation, Jewish Welfare Federation and Christian Service Department of the Archdiocese of Detroit on Proposed Federal Tax Legislation, Sept. 26, 1969; Federations and Welfare Funds, Nov. 16, 1969; Resolution Adopted by the 38th General Assembly of the Council of Jewish Federations and Welfare Funds, Nov. 16, 1969, Boston, "Taxes Affecting Philanthropy," all Folder 1181, Box 50, Fed-Cleveland.

35. Norman Sugarman, "New Opportunities in Endowment Funds," Address before the 39th Annual General Assembly of the Council of Jewish Federation and Welfare Funds, Kansas City, MO, Nov. 1970, Articles and Addresses, vol. 5, 1966–1970, Box 2, NS. I assembled a partial list of Sugarman's clients from a review of his papers.

36. For Sugarman's initial instructions, see Letter from Norman Sugarman to Henry Zucker, Jan. 23, 1970, containing a memo entitled, "Tax Reform Act of 1969: Rules and Requirements for Charitable Organizations," Folder 1183, Box 50, Fed-Cleveland. For the temporary regulations, see Procedure Announced for "Public Charities" and "Operating Foundations" to Be Recognized As Such Under The Tax Reform Act of 1969, prepared by Baker, Hostetler & Patterson, July 15, 1970, Folder 1185, Box 50, Fed-Cleveland.

37. Norman Sugarman, "Suggestion for Treasury Regulations Under Tax Reform Act of 1969," March 17, 1970; and Sugarman, "Suggestion for Treasury Regulations under Tax Reform Act of 1969," April 2, 1970, Folder 1184, Box 50, Fed-Cleveland. Sugarman wrote more than a dozen memos to Treasury on different aspects of the new law's application to public charities and philanthropic funds over the spring of 1970, all in Folder 1184, Box 50, Fed-Cleveland.

38. Letter from J. A. Tedesco, Chief, Rulings Section, Exempt Organizations Branch, IRS, to Jewish Community Federation of Cleveland, Oct. 28, 1970, reprinted in Norman Sugarman, "Handbook for Charitable Giving," published by the Jewish Community Federation of Cleveland, 1972, 50–51, Articles and Addresses, vol. 6, 1971–1974, Box 3, NS.

39. Letter from Norman Sugarman to Henry Zucker, Aug. 10, 1972; and Summary of Hearings on Certain Proposed Regulations Under the Tax Reform Act of 1969, Aug. 8, 1972, both in Folder 1060, Box 44, Fed-Cleveland. Sugarman's testimony helped inform §507 regulations, passed into law in December 1969. They can be found in full at https://www.irs.gov/irm/part7/irm_07-026-007.html#doe215. On the double tax benefit, see "Advantages of Establishing Your

Personal Philanthropic Fund Prior to the Liquidation or Sale of a Business or Real Estate or 'Going Public' or Other Disposition of Substantial Assets," attached to Memo from Lou Novins to Local Endowment Chairman, Endowment Fund Professionals and Federation Executives of Ongoing Endowment Programs, and Officers of the National Endowment Fund Development Committee, June 7, 1972, Folder 1141, Box 48, Fed-Cleveland. A contribution of cash offsets income by the amount of the contribution, while a contribution of appreciated assets receives a double benefit because it both provides an income tax deduction and avoids capital gains taxes on the appreciation. For an incisive overview of the capital gains tax and its structuring logic of racial and economic inequality, see Julia Ott, "Tax Preference As White Privilege in the United States, 1921–1965," *Capitalism: A Journal of History and Economics* 1, no. 1 (Fall 2019): 92–165.

40. Memo from Malcolm Stein (Office of Tax Legislative Counsel of the Treasury Department), "How the New Law Will Affect Foundation Operations—A View from within the US Treasury Department," April 17, 1970, Folder 1183, Box 50, Fed-Cleveland. Immediately after he delivered his test cases to the IRS—and even before he received formal word of the IRS's judgment—Sugarman shared his request with federation leaders in Baltimore, Boston, Chicago, Detroit, Los Angeles, Philadelphia, and Federation's national office. See Memo from Rudi Walter to Robert Hiller (Baltimore); Harold Morgan (Boston); Henry Bauling (Chicago); William Avrunin (Detroit); Julius Bisno (LA); Sigmund Cohen (Philadelphia); and Dan Rosenberg (CJFWF), May 12, 1970, Folder 1184, Box 50, Fed-Cleveland.

41. Transcript from Sept. 24, 1976, meeting, Folder 1144, Box 48, Fed-Cleveland, 12. Sugarman made the same suggestions about pursuing private family foundation assets to Jewish leaders in several cities. See "New Opportunities in Endowment Funds," Nov. 1970; "Outline of Remarks before the Jewish Federation of St. Louis," Oct. 13, 1975, Articles and Addresses, vol. 7, 1975–77, Box 3, NS; and "Use of Charitable Gifts in Tax Planning," Address before a Tax Seminar Sponsored by Jewish Federation of Rhode Island, Providence, June 19, 1978, Articles and Addresses, vol. 8, 1978–1979, Box 3, NS. For an example of a discussion of investment committees, policies, and objectives, see Minutes of Administrative Committee, Jewish Federation Pooled Income Fund, Sept. 12, 1974, Folder 1142, Box 48, Fed-Cleveland; and the Nov. 27, 1974 Ballot, Folder 1142, Box 48, Fed-Cleveland. For his remarks in St. Louis, see "Outline of Remarks before the Jewish Federation of St. Louis," Oct. 13, 1975, Articles and Addresses, vol. 7, 1975–77, Box 3, NS. Also see Board of Trustees, Feb. 7, 1972, UJA-FedNY, for a description of the New York Federation's finance committee, which oversaw investments. In 1976, a separate investment committee was established and assigned the specific task of supervising investment portfolios. See Board of Trustees, Nov. 8, 1976, UJA-FedNY. In 1980, a portion of the investment committee's responsibility was transferred to a professional investment service, and the finance and investment committee became responsible for overseeing this professional management. See Board of Trustees, Sept. 22, 1980, UJA-FedNY. On Sugarman's efforts to popularize philanthropic funds to non-Jewish charitable organizations, see Norman Sugarman, "New Requirements and Problems in Maintaining Tax Exempt Status," 11th Annual Meeting of the National Council on Community Foundations, Inc., May 1960, Articles and Addresses," Articles and Addresses, Vol. 3, 1955–1960, Box 2; Sugarman, "State Regulation of Tax-Exempt Foundations: Panel Discussion," American Bar Association Midyear Meeting, New Orleans, LA, April 1967 (reported in the Bulletin of the Section of Taxation, ABA, no. 3), Articles and Addresses, Vol. 5, 1966–1970, Box 2; Sugarman, "Foundations in the Eyes of the Federal Government,"

16th Annual Conference of the Council on Foundations, Pittsburgh, PA, May 1965, Articles and Addresses, Vol. 4, 1961–1965, Box 2; Sugarman, "The Effect of the Tax Reform Act of 1969 on Charitable Trusts: Problems and Possible Alternatives," a memorandum prepared for distribution by the New York Community Trust, March 29, 1971, Articles and Addresses, Vol. 6, 1971–1974, Box 3; Sugarman, "Community Foundations: New Ways to Raise and Invest Funds," Council on Foundations Annual Conference, San Antonio, TX, May 8, 1974, Articles and Addresses, Vol. 6, 1971–1974, Box 3; and Sugarman, "Proposed Tax Legislation on Charitable Deductions," United Way of Cleveland, Aug. 29, 1979, Articles and Addresses, Vol. 8, 1978–1979, Box 3, all in NS Papers. Also, Cleveland's Federation obtained copies of letters between John Carroll University and its attorney about this issue. See Letter from John Houck (at Jones, Day, Cockley, and Reavis) to Bill Fissinger (John Carroll University), Feb. 12, 1974, Folder 1142, Box 48, Fed-Cleveland.

42. For a concise history of community foundations, see Roger Colinvaux, "Defending Place-Based Philanthropy by Defining the Community Foundation," *Brigham Young University Law Review* 2018, no. 1 (Fall 2018): 2–3.

43. Norman Sugarman, "Community Foundations," *Filer Commission*, 1689, at https://archives.iupui.edu/handle/2450/892. Sugarman quote cited in Colinvaux, "Defending Place-Based Philanthropy by Defining the Community Foundation," 15. For a description of the establishment of the Filer Commission, the private commission established in 1973, see the preface to *Giving in America: Toward a Stronger Voluntary Sector, Report of the Commission on Private Philanthropy and Public Needs* (1975), 12, at https://archives.iupui.edu/bitstream/handle/2450/889/giving.pdf?sequence=1&isAllowed=y. On the growth of community foundations, see Brilliant, *Private Charity and Public Inquiry*, 106; Eleanor Sacks, "The Growing Importance of Community Foundations," Lilly Family School of Philanthropy, 2014, at https://philanthropy.iupui.edu/files/file/the_growing_importance_of_community_foundations-final_reduce_file_size_2.pdf; and Eleanor Sacks, "The Growth of Community Foundations Around the World: An Examination of the Vitality of the Community Foundation Movement," Council on Foundations, 2000, at http://wings-community-foundation-report.com/gsr_2010/assets/images/pdf/2000_COF_Growth_of_Community_Foundations_Around_the_World.pdf.

44. Board of Trustees, Dec. 14, 1970, UJA-FedNY.

45. Board of Trustees, March 8, 1971, UJA-FedNY.

46. Board of Trustees, March 8, 1971, UJA-FedNY.

47. Rosenblatt, "The Life and Death of a Dream Revisited."

48. Rosenblatt, "The Life and Death of a Dream Revisited," 39.

49. Board of Trustees, Nov. 13, 1972, UJA-FedNY. For Jicks's reaction, see Rosenblatt, "The Life and Death of a Dream Revisited," 46.

50. Isidore Sobeloff, "The Disturbing '70s: Challenges and Solutions," *Journal of Jewish Communal Service* (Spring 1972): 251. For a similar analysis, see Bertram Gold, "The Urban Crisis and Its Effect Upon Jewish Communal Services," *Journal of Jewish Communal Service* (Fall 1968): 34.

51. On the allocations to health and human services, see Charles Liebman, "Leadership and Decision-making in a Jewish Federation: The New York Federation of Jewish Philanthropies," *American Jewish Year Book* 1979, 27. For a description of the student takeover of New York's offices, see Board of Trustees, April 13, 1970, UJA-FedNY. For an analysis of the debates that New York City's federation leaders had in the 1960s and 1970s about extending funding for agencies

that primarily served non-Jews, including arguments about whether non-Jewish people could serve on agency boards, see Matthew Berkman, "Transforming Philanthropy: Finance and Institutional Evolution at the Jewish Federation of New York, 1917–86," *Jewish Social Studies* 22, no. 2 (Winter 2017): 174–177.

52. Sidney Vincent, "The Emerging Agenda of Jewish Communal Life—The Role of Jewish Communal Service," *Journal of Jewish Communal Service* 49, no. 1 (Fall 1972): 17, 18. On the Jewish Association of College Youth, see Berkman, "Transforming Philanthropy," 180–181.

53. On the student occupation of the New York federation's offices, see Board of Trustees, April 13, 1970, and on federation responses, see Board of Trustees, June 22, 1970 and Oct. 19, 1970, UJA-FedNY. A similar indication of younger people demanding more attention within the system of American Jewish philanthropy can be found in the establishment of the Big Apple Tzedekah Cooperative, which was founded in 1975 by eleven young Jews who wanted to pool their funds into a giving circle model so they could fund initiatives that they did not believe were receiving adequate attention from more established Jewish funding sources. For a record of this, see "Basic Operating Procedures of the Big Apple Tzedakah Cooperative," n.d., written on letterhead for *Response: A Contemporary Jewish Review*, Folder 1, Big Apple Tzedakah Cooperative Records, MS-606, The Jacob Rader Marcus Center of the American Jewish Archives, Hebrew Union College-Jewish Institute of Religion, Cincinnati, OH. For a discussion of similar Jewish giving collectives in other cities, see Steven M. Cohen, "The Case for Conflict in Communal Life," *Response* (Summer 1976): 5–12.

54. For plans to orient the 1976 General Assembly around the theme of continuity, see Donald Hurwitz, "Shaping the Quality of Jewish Life: The Central Role of Federations," *Journal of Jewish Communal Service* 49, no. 4 (Summer 1973): 286–289. I was able to track the rise of the term "continuity" within Jewish communal circles through the spike in its use in the *Journal of Jewish Communal Service*. Also see Lila Corwin Berman, Kate Rosenblatt, and Ronit Stahl, "Continuity Crisis: The History and Sexual Politics of an American Jewish Communal Project," *American Jewish History* (2020).

Chapter 7: The Market

1. Outline of Remarks before the Jewish Federation of St. Louis," Oct. 13, 1975, Articles and Addresses, vol. 7, 1975–77, Box 3, NS.

2. Stanley Surrey, "Tax Incentives as a Device for Implementing Government Policy: A Comparison with Direct Government Expenditures," *Harvard Law Review* 83, no. 4 (Feb. 1970): 706, 721, 723. Also see W. Elliot Brownlee, *Federal Taxation in America: A Short History*, 2nd ed. (New York: Cambridge University Press, 2004).

3. "Use of Charitable Gifts in Tax Planning," Address before a Tax Seminar Sponsored by Jewish Federation of Rhode Island, Providence, June 19, 1978, Articles and Addresses, vol. 8, 1978–1979, Box 3, NS. He gave similar speeches in several cities throughout the 1970s. See, for example, Norman Sugarman, "New Opportunities in Endowment Funds," Address before the 39th Annual General Assembly of the Council of Jewish Federation and Welfare Funds, Kansas City, MO, Nov. 1970, Articles and Addresses, vol. 5, 1966–1970, Box 2, NS; and "New Opportunities in Endowment Funds," Nov. 1970; and "Outline of Remarks before the Jewish Federation of St. Louis," Oct. 13, 1975, Articles and Addresses, vol. 7, 1975–77, Box 3, NS.

4. On this shift in philosophies of governing and economics from New Dealism and Fordism toward privatization and neoliberalism, see Wendy Brown, *Undoing the Demos: Neoliberalism's Stealth Revolution* (Cambridge, MA: Zone Books, 2015); Jefferson Cowie, *The Great Exception: The New Deal and the Limits of American Politics* (Princeton, NJ: Princeton University Press, 2016); Nancy MacLean, *Democracy in Chains: The Deep History of the Radical Right's Stealth Plan for America* (New York: Viking, 2017); Kim Phillips-Fein, *Invisible Hands: The Making of the Conservative Movement from the New Deal to Reagan* (New York: W.W. Norton, 2009); and Bryant Simon, *The Hamlet Fire: A Tragic Story of Cheap Food, Cheap Government, and Cheap Lives* (New York: New Press, 2017).

5. On tax policy in the 1980s, see Brownlee, *Federal Taxation in America*, ch. 5. On the rights revolution, see Robert Self, *All in the Family: The Realignment of American Democracy Since the 1960s* (New York: Hill & Wang, 2012).

6. Letter from Henry Zucker to Norman Sugarman, June 28, 1977, Folder 1033, Box 43, Fed-Cleveland. Similarly, Gerald Bubis, a professor of Jewish communal service, speculated in 1978 that total assets of Jewish federations and foundations could reach $1 billion in just four or five years. See Bubis, "Confronting Some Issues in Jewish Continuity: The Response of the Profession," *Journal of Jewish Communal Service* 55, no. 1 (Sept. 1978) 10–22, here 13.

7. Henry Zucker presentation on "The Trust Fund Idea and Service to Independent Foundations," in Proceedings, Institute on Endowment Funds, Jan. 24–25, 1967, Folder 1159, Box 49, Fed-Cleveland. On their work at the Cleveland Foundation, see Memo for review with William Treuhaft, March 11, 1963; Memo from Rudi Walter to Henry Zucker, April 3, 1963; Letter from William Treuhaft to John Sherwin, July 9, 1963; Letter from Rudi Walter to Philmore Haber, July 22, 1963; Letter from John Sherwin to William Treuhaft, Sept. 24, 1963; and Letter from Henry Zucker to Kimball Johnson, May 16, 1969, all Folder 131, Box 43, Fed-Cleveland.

8. "Handbook for Charitable Giving," published by the Jewish Community Federation of Cleveland, 1972, 50–51, Articles and Addresses, vol. 6, 1971–1974, Box 3, NS.

9. In 1971, New York had $11.5 million in endowment funds and $15.3 million in emergency funds; both of these funds were invested and intended to provide long-term capital. In 1979, New York reported $29.6 million in endowment funds, which included legacies and pooled income funds, and $20.3 million in emergency funds. See Board of Trustees, March 8, 1971; and Board of Trustees, Sept. 29, 1979, UJA-FedNY.

10. Board of Trustees, Sept. 29, 1979; and Board of Trustees, Sept. 22, 1980, UJA-FedNY.

11. Letter from Henry Zucker to Norman Sugarman, Dec. 20, 1978, Folder 1033, Box 43, Fed-Cleveland.

12. Board of Trustees, Sept. 14, 1981, UJA-FedNY.

13. Board of Trustees, Sept. 14, 1981, UJA-FedNY.

14. Board of Trustees, Sept. 14, 1981, UJA-FedNY. On Solender, see Eric Pace, "Sanford Solender, a Leader of Jewish Charities, Is Dead at 89," *New York Times*, Sept. 8, 2003, at https://www.nytimes.com/2003/09/08/nyregion/sanford-solender-a-leader-of-jewish-charities-is-dead-at-89.html.

15. On the holdings at New York's Jewish Communal Fund, see "CJF Endowment Development Program for 1979," Dec. 28, 1978 (prepared by Louis Novins), Folder 1033, Box 43, Fed-Cleveland. For financial details about Cleveland's endowment, see Tentative Agenda, Philanthropic Fund Advisory Committee, Sept. 15, 1978, Folder 1080, Box 45, Fed-Cleveland.

16. "Guidelines for Operation: Philanthropic Advisory Committee," May 10, 1977, Folder 1080, Box 45, Fed-Cleveland.

17. See "Guidelines for Operation: Philanthropic Advisory Committee," May 10, 1977; and on the minimum, see Form Letter from Joseph Persky (chair, Endowment Fund Committee) to "Friend," Aug. 31, 1978, Folder 1080, Box 45, Fed-Cleveland. On the Chautauqua request, see Minutes, Philanthropic Fund Advisory Committee, Endowment Fund Committee, Jewish Community Federation, June 19, 1981; and on the American Council for Judaism request, see Report to the Endowment Fund Committee from the Philanthropic Advisory Committee, Nov. 30, 1981, both in Folder 1083, Box 45, Fed-Cleveland. On the Chautauqua Institution, see Andrew Rieser, *The Chautauqua Moment: Protestants, Progressives, and the Culture of Modern Liberalism* (New York: Columbia University Press, 2003); and Jeffrey Simpson, *Chautauqua: An American Utopia* (New York: Harry N. Abrams, 1999). On the American Council for Judaism, see Thomas Kolsky, *Jews Against Zionism: The American Council for Judaism, 1942–1948* (Philadelphia: Temple University Press, 1990); Geoffrey Levin, "Another Nation: Israel, American Jews, and Palestinian Rights, 1948–1977" (PhD diss., New York University, 2019), ch. 4; and Monty Noam Penkower, "The Genesis of the American Council for Judaism: A Quest for Identity in World War II," *American Jewish History* 86, no. 2 (June 1998): 167–194.

18. This is a liberal estimate. It includes one month (Dec. 1978) during which disbursements exceeded the average disbursements from the six prior months by over $200,000. For data, see minutes and correspondence from the Endowment Fund Committee, Dec. 11, 1978; Nov. 29, 1978; Oct. 25, 1978; Sept. 25, 1978; Aug. 29, 1978; July 26, 1978, Folder 1033, Box 43, Fed-Cleveland.

19. Tentative Agenda, Philanthropic Fund Advisory Committee, Sept. 15, 1978, Folder 1080, Box 45, Fed-Cleveland.

20. "CJF Endowment Development Program for 1979," Dec. 28, 1978 (prepared by Louis Novins), Folder 1033, Box 43, Fed-Cleveland.

21. Jonathan Woocher, "The Politics of Scarcity: Jewish Communal Service in an Era of Resource Pressure," *Journal of Jewish Communal Service* 58, no. 3 (Spring 1982): 189; and Lucy S. Dawidowicz, "A Century of Jewish History, 1881–1981: The View from America," *American Jewish Year Book*, vol. 82 (Philadelphia: Jewish Publication Society, 1982), 95.

22. On the trend of economic privatization and its effects on the politics of the American state in the late twentieth century, see Lily Geismer, *Don't Blame Us: Suburban Liberals and the Transformation of the Democratic Party* (Princeton, NJ: Princeton University Press, 2015); Matthew Lassiter, "Political History beyond the Red-Blue Divide," *Journal of American History* 98, no. 3 (Dec. 2011): 760–764; Sarah Milov, *The Cigarette: A Political History* (Cambridge, MA: Harvard University Press, 2019); Self, *All in the Family*, part 4; and Simon, *The Hamlet Fire*. On the expansion of nonprofits in these same years, see Emily Barman, "Classificatory Struggles in the Nonprofit Sector: The Formation of the National Taxonomy of Exempt Entities, 1969–1987," *Social Science History* 37, no. 1 (Spring 2013): 103–141; Peter Dobkin Hall, *Inventing the Nonprofit Sector and Other Essays on Philanthropy, Voluntarism, and Nonprofit Organization* (Baltimore, MD: Johns Hopkins University Press, 1992); Rob Reich, Lacey Dorn, and Stefanie Sutton, "Anything Goes: Approval of Nonprofit Status by the IRS," Center on Philanthropy and Civil Society, Draft Report, Oct. 25, 2009; and Jonathan Levy, "Altruism and the Origins of Nonprofit

Philanthropy," in Rob Reich, Chiara Cordelli, and Lucy Bernholz, eds., *Philanthropy in Democratic Societies* (Chicago: University of Chicago Press, 2016).

23. Daniel Rodgers, *Age of Fracture* (Cambridge, MA: Belknap Press of Harvard University Press, 2011), 29–31.

24. On the reluctance of conservative American Jews to commit to the Republican party because of its coalition with the Christian right, see Herbert Weisberg, *The Politics of American Jews* (Ann Arbor: University of Michigan Press, 2019), 85–88.

25. On Cummings's cochairship, see Joseph Polakoff, "Reagan to Meet with Prominent Jewish Republicans to Discuss Nation's Domestic, Foreign Affairs," JTA Daily News Bulletin, March 9, 1981, Folder 3, Box 220, MF Papers. On Cummings, see Alfred Clark, "T. E. Cummings, 74; Envoy to Austria," *New York Times*, April 1, 1982, at https://www.nytimes.com/1982/04/01/obituaries/te-cummings74-envoy-to-austria.html.

26. Memo from Gordon Zacks to Ed Meese, re: "Liaison between American Jewish Community and the Reagan Administration," Jan. 9, 1981, Folder 3, Box 220, MF Papers.

27. Memo from Zacks to Meese, re: "Liaison between American Jewish Community and the Reagan Administration.".

28. Polakoff, "Reagan to Meet with Prominent Jewish Republicans to Discuss Nation's Domestic, Foreign Affairs."

29. Participants for Meeting with the President and Jewish Supporters, March 9, 1981, includes names, birthdates, and redacted social security numbers, Folder 3, Box 220, MF Papers.

30. For a copy of the statement, see untitled document, March 9, 1981, Folder 3, Box 220, MF Papers. Also see Wolf Blitzer, "Discord Splits Delegation to Reagan on F-15s; Fisher Softens Protest to Reagan on Saudi Deal; Draws Criticism," *Jewish Week*, March 19–25, 1982, copy in Folder 1, Box 43, PS Papers.

31. Organization Structure for the Jewish Republicans, March 19, 1981, Folder 3, Box 220, MF Papers. On Fisher's strategy, see, for example, Memo from Jack Stein to Ed Meese, March 20, 1981, re Cummings/Fisher Group, Folder 3, Box 220, MF Papers.

32. Organization Structure for the Jewish Republicans, March 19, 1981, Folder 3, Box 220, MF Papers.

33. On the Heritage Group Council, see Letter from David Weinstein, director, Outreach Program, Republican National Committee, to Max Fisher, March 18, 1981, which includes a copy of a letter from Anna Chennault, of the National Republican Heritage Groups (Nationalities) Council, to Richard Richards, Chairman, Republican National Committee, March 9, 1981, Folder 3, Box 220, MF Papers. Also see Letter from David Weinstein, director, Outreach Program, Republican National Committee, to Max Fisher, April 23, 1981, and Letter from Fernando Oaxaca, chair of Republican National Hispanic Assembly, to Fred Balitzer and copied to Richard Richards (chairs of the Republican National Committee), April 22, 1981, both in Folder 220, Box 3, MF Papers. On Weinstein's move to the United Jewish Appeal, see Letter from David Weinstein to Leonard Greenberg, May 12, 1981, Folder 4, Box 220, MF Papers.

34. Minutes of May 6 Meetings, transmitted to Max Fisher from Gordon Zacks, in a note referring to "our May 6 meeting," May 17, 1981, Folder 4, Box 220, MF Papers; and Organization Structure for the Jewish Republicans, March 19, 1981, Folder 3, Box 220, MF Papers.

35. Text of the 1971 NCRAC guidelines can be found in Wolf Blitzer, "Mobilizing the Jewish Vote," *Jerusalem Post*, Oct. 12, 1976, Folder 1, Box 43, PS Papers. On the broad institutional

support for the lobbying effort, see Minutes of May 6 Meetings, transmitted to Max Fisher from Gordon Zacks, in a note referring to "our May 6 meeting," May 17, 1981, Folder 4, Box 220, MF Papers. On AIPAC, see J. J. Goldberg, *Jewish Power: Inside the American Jewish Establishment* (New York: Basic Books, 1996), ch. 8; and John J. Mearsheimer and Stephen M. Walt, *The Israel Lobby and U.S. Foreign Policy* (New York: Farrar, Straus and Giroux, 2008). On NCRAC, see Matthew Berkman, "Coercive Consensus: Jewish Federations, Ethnic Representation, and the Roots of American Pro-Israel Politics" (PhD diss., University of Pennsylvania, 2018), ch. 5.

36. Letter from Douglas Glant, President, Pacific Group, to Max Fisher, May 20, 1981, Folder 4, Box 220, MF Papers; and Letter from Douglas Glant addressed to Al Spiegel, but in his salutation, Glant drew a slash through Al and wrote Max, May 24, 1982, Folder 6, Box 220, MF Papers. On his appointment to the Export Council, see Letter from Douglas Glant to Max Fisher, Oct. 12, 1981, Folder 5, Box 220, MF Papers.

37. Statement from Max Fisher, undated Folder 4, Box 220; Letter from President Ronald Reagan to Fisher, June 29, 1981, Folder 4, Box 220; and "Republican Jewish Coalition Urges Passage of Reagan Plan," *Texas Jewish Post*, June 25, 1981, Folder 5, Box 220, all in MF Papers. For press coverage of its establishment, see "Coalition for Reagan-Bush Leaders Agree to Continue as Organization of Jewish Republicans," *JTA Daily News Bulletin*, May 22, 1981, Folder 4, Box 220; Jean Herschaft, "Coalition Becomes a Permanent Body," *Jewish Post and Opinion*, July 3, 1981, Folder 5, Box 220; and "The Jewish Coalition," *Jewish Post and Opinion*, July 10, 1981, Folder 5, Box 220, all in MF Papers.

38. Memo from Richard Krieger to Chairman Richard Richards, RNC, May 24, 1982, Folder 6, Box 220, MF Papers; on Krieger, see https://www.jta.org/1987/02/13/archive/krieger-resigns-as-executive-director-of-the-u-s-holocaust-memorial-council.

39. Memo from Frank Fahrenkopf, RNC Chair, to National Republican Jewish Coalition, July 12, 1983, re Political Plan for Jewish Voters, Folder 7, Box 660, MF Papers.

40. On American Jews' support for the Democratic party, see Kenneth Wald, *The Foundations of American Jewish Liberalism* (New York: Cambridge University Press, 2019); and Weisberg, *The Politics of American Jews*.

41. "The Political Plan for Jewish Voters," National Republican Jewish Coalition, Dick Fox (chair), Max Fisher (honorary chair), George Klein and Gordon Zacks (co-chairs), printed on Political Management Resources stationery, Dec. 9, 1983, Folder 8, Box 220, MF Papers. The following May, the Republican National Committee reported it had spent $23,000 on consulting fees to Political Management Resources. See Letter from Frank Fahrenkopf to Max Fisher, May 16, 1984, Folder 2, Box 221, MF Papers.

42. Letter from A. Mark Neuman, Executive Director, to "Coalition Member," Oct. 17, 1984, Folder 3, Box 221, MF Papers. On the announcement of the bipartisan Jewish campaign to elect Reagan, see Press Release from National Jewish Coalition, Aug. 20, 1984, Folder 2, Box 221, MF Papers. See also press coverage about Jewish presence at the Republican convention: "Jews Enjoy Being Courted by Republicans," *Cincinnati Enquirer*, Aug. 22, 1984; David Friedman, "At the Republican Party Convention: Jewish Republicans, Lonely No More," *JTA: Daily News*, Aug. 22, 1984; and John J. Goldman and Betty Cuniberti, "Republicans Step Up Courting of Jewish Voters," *Los Angeles Times*, Aug. 22, 1984, all in Folder 2, Box 221, MF Papers.

43. The advertisement is signed by Meshulam Riklis and notes that he personally paid for it. Riklis was born in Turkey, raised in Tel Aviv, and immigrated to the United States in 1947,

where he became a successful investor in several companies. See advertisement, *New York Times*, Oct. 16, 1984, Folder 3, Box 221, MF Papers. On Riklis, see Michael Hiltzik, "A Borrowed Empire: Meshulam Riklis, Known to Most of the World as Mr. Pia Zadora, Is a Model for Today's Corporate Raiders, a Controversial Tycoon Who Built a Financial Kingdom on Debt," *Los Angeles Times*, Aug. 17, 1986, at http://articles.latimes.com/1986-08-17/magazine/tm-16503_1_pia-zadora.

44. Untitled, Aug. 4–5, 1982, Folder 6, Box 220, MF Papers. On Jewish political donations, see A.F.K. Organski, *The $36 Billion Bargain: Strategy and Politics in U.S. Assistance to Israel* (New York: Columbia University Press, 1990), tables on pp. 66 and 72, though notably Organski downplays the actual influence that American Jews, as a political bloc, had on the United States' policy in Israel. For an interpretation (and the subject of some notable controversy) that confers far more power to American Jewish political forces, see Mearsheimer and Walt, *The Israel Lobby and U.S. Foreign Policy*.

45. For his obituary, see "Norman Sugarman," *Washington Post*, Feb. 19, 1986, at https://www .washingtonpost.com/archive/local/1986/02/19/obituaries/5e93dc9c-3689-4511-ba6c -04b1d97a536c/?utm_term=.759311a3231e. On the assets donated to Fidelity's charitable fund, see Karsten Strauss, "The Charities that Raised the Most Money Last Year," *Forbes*, Nov. 1, 2017, at https://www.forbes.com/sites/karstenstrauss/2017/11/01/the-charities-that-raised-the -most-money-last-year/#45dbd81f6c00. On the Jewish Communal Fund's valuation of its assets, see its 2017 annual report, at https://jcfny.org/app/uploads/2017/11/JCF-2017-Giving -Report.pdf. On federation endowments, see 2013 Annual Survey of Planned Giving and Endowment Programs, Jewish Federations of North America, copy in author's possession. On the rise of charitable divisions connected to commercial investment firms, see Alan Cantor, "Donor-Advised Funds Let Wall Street Steer Charitable Donations," *Chronicle of Philanthropy* (Oct. 28, 2014), at https://philanthropy.com/article/Donor-Advised-Funds-Let-Wall /152337; Lewis Cullman and Ray Madoff, "The Undermining of American Charity," *New York Review of Books* 63, no. 12 (July 14, 2016), at http://www.nybooks.com/articles/2016/07/14 /the-undermining-of-american-charity/; and Monica Langley, "Fidelity Gift Fund Soars, But the IRS Is Skeptical," *Wall Street Journal*, Feb. 12, 1998, at http://www.wsj.com/articles /SB887235489239453000.

46. For calculations of assets held in donor-advised funds, see the National Philanthropic Trust's 2018 DAF Report, at https://www.nptrust.org/reports/daf-report/.

Chapter 8: The Complex

1. See Binyamin Appelbaum, David S. Hilzenrath, and Amit Paley, "'All Just One Big Lie,'" *Washington Post*, Dec. 13, 2018, at http://www.washingtonpost.com/wp-dyn/content/article /2008/12/12/AR2008121203970.html; Alan Feuer and Christine Haughney, "Standing Accused: A Pillar of Finance and Charity," *New York Times*, Dec, 12, 2008, at http://www.nytimes.com/2008 /12/13/nyregion/13madoff.html; Diana Henriques, *The Wizard of Lies: Bernie Madoff and the Death of Trust* (New York: St. Martin's Griffin, 2011); and Mark Seal, "Madoff's World," *Vanity Fair*, April 2009, at http://www.vanityfair.com/news/2009/04/bernard-madoff-friends-family-profile.

2. For a list of Jewish organizations immediately affected, see "YU Speaks," *EJewish Philanthropy*, Dec. 17, 2008, at https://ejewishphilanthropy.com/yu-speaks/. Also see Jacob Berkman, "Madoff Scandal Rocks Jewish Philanthropic World," *Jewish Telegraphic Association*, Dec. 15,

2008, at http://www.jta.org/2008/12/15/life-religion/madoff-scandal-rocks-jewish
-philanthropic-world; Ben Sales, "10 Years Ago, the Bernie Madoff Scandal Rocked the American Jewish World," *Jewish Telegraphic Agency*, Dec. 20, 2108, at https://www.jta.org/2018/12/20
/united-states/10-years-ago-the-bernie-madoff-scandal-rocked-the-american-jewish-world
-heres-how-those-victims-have-fared; Richard Silverstein, "Bernard Madoff, Bad for the Jews,"
Guardian, Dec. 23, 2008, at https://www.theguardian.com/commentisfree/cifamerica/2008
/dec/23/bernard-madoff-jewish-charities; and Anthony Weiss, "Madoff Scandal Rips Apart
Close World of Jewish Philanthropy," *Forward*, Dec. 18, 2008, http://forward.com/news/14757
/madoff-scandal-rips-apart-close-world-of-jewish-ph-03007/.?

3. On the language of freedom as a central trope of the Reagan years, see Daniel Rodgers,
Age of Fracture (Cambridge, MA: Belknap Press of Harvard University Press, 2011), ch. 1.

4. On the broader trends of capital growth through inequality, see Thomas Piketty, *The
Economics of Inequality* (Cambridge, MA: Belknap Press of Harvard University Press, 2015); and
Thomas Piketty, *Capital in the Twenty-First Century* (Cambridge, MA: Belknap Press of Harvard
University Press, 2014).

5. I am adapting the term "hollow prize" from urban history. See Michael Katz, *Why Don't
American Cities Burn* (Philadelphia: University of Pennsylvania Press, 2012), 85, citing H. Paul
Friesema, "Black Control of Central Cities: The Hollow Prize," *Journal of the American Institute
of Planners* 35, no. 2 (March 1969): 75.

6. The first characterization of Madoff's crime as an affinity scam that I have found appeared
in E. Scott Reckard, "Madoff Losses Go Deep in L.A.," *Los Angeles Times*, Dec. 16, 2008, at
https://www.latimes.com/archives/la-xpm-2008-dec-16-fi-madoff16-story.html. Also see Harold Pollack, "Why Were So Many Madoff Victims Jewish?" *Atlantic*, Feb. 8, 2016, at https://www
.theatlantic.com/business/archive/2016/02/madoff-jewish-affinity-fraud/460446/; Silverstein, "Bernard Madoff, Bad for the Jews"; and Jonathan Tobin, "The Madoff Scandal and the
Future of American Jewry," *Commentary*, Feb. 1, 2009, at https://www.commentarymagazine
.com/articles/the-madoff-scandal-and-the-future-of-american-jewry/. On affinity fraud, see
Keith Blois and Annmarie Ryan, "Affinity Fraud and Trust within Financial Markets," *Journal of
Financial Crime* 20, 2 (April 2013): 186–202.

7. See Reckard, "Madoff Losses Go Deep in L.A."

8. See Robin Pogrebin, "In Madoff Scandal, Jews Feel an Acute Betrayal," *New York Times*,
Dec. 24, 2008, at http://www.nytimes.com/2008/12/24/world/americas/24iht-24jews
.18903457.html?pagewanted=all.

9. On the December 23 meeting organized by the Jewish Funders Network, see Robin Shul-
man, "Jewish Charities Scramble to Cover Losses to Trader," *Washington Post*, Dec. 24, 2008, at
http://www.washingtonpost.com/wp-dyn/content/article/2008/12/23/AR2008122302651
.html; and "Plan in the Works to Help Nonprofits Hurt by Madoff," *Jewish Telegraphic Agency*,
Dec. 24, 2008, at https://www.jta.org/2008/12/24/archive/plan-in-the-works-to-help
-nonprofits-hurt-by-madoff-2. On speculations about changes in practice, see Weiss, "Madoff
Scandal Rips Apart Close World of Jewish Philanthropy"; and Tobin, "The Madoff Scandal and
the Future of American Jewry."

10. Steven M. Cohen, "Trends in Jewish Philanthropy," *American Jewish Year Book*, vol. 80
(Philadelphia: Jewish Publication Society, 1979), 43, 50. In the summer of 2018, Cohen was subject
to numerous allegations of sexual misconduct. See Hannah Dreyfus, "Harassment Allegations

Mount Against Leading Jewish Sociologist," *New York Jewish Week*, July 19, 2018, at https://jewishweek.timesofisrael.com/harassment-allegations-mount-against-leading-jewish-sociologist/.

11. Mordechai Rimor and Gary Tobin, "The Relationship Between Jewish Identity and Philanthropy," in Paul Ritterbrand and Barry Kosmin, eds., *Contemporary Jewish Philanthropy in America* (Savage, MD: Rowman and Littlefield, 1991), 53; and Barry Kosmin, "New Directions in Contemporary Jewish Philanthropy: The Challenges of the 1990s," *New Directions for Philanthropic Fundraising* 8 (Summer 1995): 50.

12. Cohen, "Trends in Jewish Philanthropy," 31. On the relationship between identity projects and Jewish philanthropy, see Joshua Friedman and Moshe Kornfeld, "Identity Projects: Philanthropy, Neoliberalism, and Jewish Cultural Production," *American Jewish History* 102, no. 4 (Oct. 2018): 537–561.

13. For this comparison, see Jeffrey Solomon, "Jewish Foundations: An Introduction," *Journal of Jewish Communal Service* 81, nos. 1–2 (Fall-Winter 2005): 101; and Jack Wertheimer, "Current Trends in American Jewish Philanthropy," *American Jewish Year Book*, vol. 97 (Philadelphia: Jewish Publication Society, 1997), 73.

14. By-Laws, The Arie and Ida Crown Memorial, adopted June 13, 1994, dated Aug. 16, 1994, Crown Papers.

15. By-Laws, 1994, Crown Papers.

16. "Henry Crown, Industrialist, Dies," *New York Times*, Aug. 16, 1990, at https://www.nytimes.com/1990/08/16/obituaries/henry-crown-industrialist-dies-billionaire-94-rose-from-poverty-by-joan-cook.html; and "Irving Crown; Helped Found Material Service," *Chicago Tribune*, March 2, 1987, at https://www.chicagotribune.com/news/ct-xpm-1987-03-02-8701170090-story.html.

17. By-Laws, Crown Papers.

18. For an overview of the survey, see Sidney Goldstein, "Profile of American Jewry: Insights from the 1990 National Jewish Population Survey," *American Jewish Year Book*, vol. 92 (Philadelphia: Jewish Publication Society, 1992), 77–173. For historical context about social-scientific measurements of American Jewish intermarriage, see Lila Corwin Berman, "Sociology, Jews, and Intermarriage in Twentieth-Century America," *Jewish Social Studies* 14, no. 2 (Winter 2008): 32–60. On the rising language of Jewish survival, see Michael Staub, *Torn at the Roots: The Crisis of Jewish Liberalism in Postwar America* (New York: Columbia University Press, 2002), chs. 3 and 7. On the deployment of Jewish continuity language, see Lila Corwin Berman, Kate Rosenblatt, and Ronit Stahl, "Continuity Crisis: The History and Sexual Politics of an American Jewish Communal Project," *American Jewish History* (2020); and John Ruskay and Alisa Rubin Kurshan, "American Jewry's Focus on Continuity—at Ten Years," *Journal of Jewish Communal Service* 76, nos. 1–2 (Fall 1999): 81–88. For information about how the finances of the Data Bank were structured, including the creation of a support foundation (in Berman's name) held at the Council of Federation as an endowment to support it, see Folder 1988, Data Bank Formation Doc. Original Letters of Agreement, Box 5, Berman Collection—unprocessed, Bentley Historical Library, University of Michigan.

19. By-Laws, The Arie and Ida Crown Memorial, Sept. 11, 2009, Crown Papers. Members of the family, representing three different generations, served on a committee to authorize grants to Jewish organizations. Author's conversation with Lesley Said Matsa, program officer at the Crown Fund in charge of Jewish giving, June 30, 2017.

20. By-Laws, 2009, Crown Papers. For the mission statement of the Crown Family Foundation, see its Guidestar profile at https://www.guidestar.org/profile/36-3330462. On supporting organizations, sometimes called supporting foundations, see Victoria Bjorklund, "Choosing among the Private Foundation, Supporting Organization, and Donor-Advised Fund," published by Simpson, Thatcher & Bartlett, LLP, May 29, 2003, at http://www.stblaw.com/docs/default-source/cold-fusion-existing-content/publications/pub239.pdf?sfvrsn=2.

21. On the growth of the Chicago federation's endowment, see Rudi Walter and Henry Zucker, "Study of Endowment Fund Programs of Thirteen Large City Jewish Federations," Prepared for the Endowment Fund Committee of the Jewish Community Federation of Cleveland, Nov. 1959, Folder 1124, Box 52; and Endowment Fund Development in Federations–1975," prepared by the Council of Jewish Federations and Welfare, June 1976, Folder 1033, Box 43, Fed-Cleveland. The total endowment figure was given in author's conversation with Steven Nasatir, the President of the Jewish United Fund/Federation of Metropolitan Chicago, Dec. 9, 2014; and author's conversation with Rachel Sternberg, then Senior Vice President of the Annual Campaign Jewish United Fund/Jewish Federation of Metropolitan Chicago, and Rose Jagust, then Associate Vice President of Donor Advised Programs, Nov. 12, 2014. See Crown Family Foundation tax filings, 2014, 990, which lists its year-end assets at $280 million. On the Crown family's donor-advised fund, see https://www.chicagobusiness.com/article/20130227/BLOGS03/130229773/crowns-give-family-trust-to-jewish-federation.

22. Donald Kent and Jack Wertheimer, "The Implications of New Funding Streams for the Federation System," *Journal of Jewish Communal Service* 76, nos. 1–2 (Fall-Winter 1999): 69–77.

23. Project on Jewish Family Foundations and Donors Mission Statement, Draft, May 8, 1991, margin note to change the name to "JFN" Mission Statement, copy in author's possession, furnished by the Jewish Funders Network, New York, NY, hereafter JFN.

24. Challenges and Opportunities for Jewish Funders in the 90's, Conference Schedule, Jan. 7–9, 1991, JFN; and Julia Goldman, "Focus on Issues: Collaboration Is 'Name of Game' in World of Jewish Philanthropy," *Jewish Telegraphic Agency*, April 30, 1999, at https://www.jta.org/1999/04/30/archive/focus-on-issues-collaboration-is-name-of-game-in-world-of-jewish-philanthropy-2.

25. Elissa Gootman, "Family Funders Meet at Florida 'Transfer of Wealth,'" *Forward*, March 6, 1998.

26. Gootman, "Family Funders Meet at Florida 'Transfer of Wealth.'"

27. Lori Silberman Brauner, "Finding a Place for Foundations in the Jewish Communal World," *MetroWest Jewish News*, Nov. 12, 1998, 37.

28. Michael Porter and Mark Kramer, "Philanthropy's New Agenda: Creating Value," *Harvard Business Review* 77, no. 6 (Nov.–Dec. 1999): 121–130. The article provided the seed for the two to collaborate on two new ventures: a philanthropic consulting practice (called FSG) and the Center for Effective Philanthropy. See https://www.fsg.org/blog/fsg-story.

29. Porter and Kramer, "Philanthropy's New Agenda," 126.

30. "Jewish Philanthropists Debate an Ethic of Plenty—In a Time of Uncertainty," *PR Newswire*, March 5, 2002, 1. On the end of Mendelson's tenure, see "As Nature of Jewish Funding Changes, Groups Assess Ethics of Philanthropy," JTA, April 4, 2001, at https://www.jta.org/2001/04/04/archive/as-nature-of-jewish-funding-changes-groups-discuss-ethics-of-philanthropy. On Charendoff, see author's conversation with him, June 2, 2014.

31. Board of Directors Meeting, Nov. 4, 2001, JFN. Author's conversation with Mark Charendoff, June 2, 2014.

32. On the Jewish Funders Network recordkeeping and recording, see, for example, Barbara Pash, "Foundations of Giving," *Baltimore Jewish Times*, Nov. 19, 1999, 50, where the executive director notes that more than 4,000 of the total 42,000 private foundations in the United States donate to Jewish causes.

33. Jeffrey Solomon, "Jewish Foundations: An Introduction," *Journal of Jewish Communal Service* 81, nos. 1–2 (Fall-Winter 2005): 101–105. Also, author's conversations with Jeffrey Solomon, July 10, 2014.

34. Bussel Philanthropy Associates, "Understanding collaboration between Federations and Foundations in community separately-incorporated Jewish Community Foundations," conducted for the Planned Giving & Endowments and Research & Analysis Departments, United Jewish Communities, Sept. 2007. On the Tarrytown Group, see Jack Wertheimer, "Giving Jewish: How Big Funders Have Transformed American Jewish Philanthropy," A Report of the Avi Chai Foundation, March 2018, 32–33. Also, author's conversations with Felicia Herman, July 17, 2014; and Jeffrey Solomon, July 10, 2014. On the trend of federation professionals leaving federations for private foundation staff positions, see Sara Berman, "Federations Are Hemorrhaging Donors, Staff: Executive Directors Swapping Seats as Some Head for Foundation World," *Forward*, Nov. 19, 1999.

35. Organizations that similarly sought to coordinate Jewish donors and steward their philanthropy toward Jewish causes include Slingshot (founded in 2005) and Natan (founded in 2002). These were both outgrowths of initiatives funded, in part, by Andrea and Charles Bronfman Philanthropies and its 21/64 division, with the goal of cultivating next-generation Jewish funders who many observers believed would not be attracted to federation-style philanthropy. Author's conversations with Sharna Goldseker, June 26, 2014, and Felicia Herman, July 17, 2014. On the other side of the equation, a number of ventures emerged that sought to coordinate Jewish nonprofits, train their leaders, and shape their practices to make them sustainable and attractive to funders—both private foundations and federations. Early examples include Joshua Venture Group (founded in 1998), Bikkurim (founded in 2000), PresenTense (established as a magazine in 2005 and then an "accelerator program" in 2007), and UpStart Bay Area (founded in 2008). In 2017, the four organizations merged into a new organization, called UpStart. Author's conversation with Martin Kaminer, Jan. 7, 2015; "Four Organizations Merge to Lead Next Stage of Jewish Innovation," *EJewish Philanthropy*, Nov. 10, 2016, at https://ejewishphilanthropy.com /four-organizations-merge-to-lead-next-stage-of-jewish-innovation/; and Upstart website, at https://upstartlab.org/about/history/. For an excellent contextualization of the efforts to buttress the Jewish philanthropic structure through the language of innovation and next-generation leaders, see Shaul Kelner, "In Its Own Image: Independent Philanthropy and the Cultivation of Young Jewish Leadership," in Jack Wertheimer, ed., *The New Jewish Leaders: Reshaping the American Jewish Landscape* (Hanover, NH: University Press of New England, 2011).

36. Shaul Kelner, *Tours that Bind: Diaspora, Pilgrimage, and Israeli Birthright Tourism* (New York: New York University Press, 2011), ch. 2.

37. Kelner, *Tours that Bind*, 41, 42.

38. Michael Steinhardt, *No Bull: My Life In and Out of Markets* (New York: Wiley, 2001), 274–275. For a similar rendering, see Leonard Saxe and Barry Chazan, *Ten Days of Birthright Israel* (Lebanon, NH: Brandeis University Press, published by University Press of New England,

2008), 5–6. On Steinhardt's net worth in 1994, see Michael Noer, "Michael Steinhardt, Wall Street's Greatest Trader, Is Back—and He's Reinventing Investing Again," *Forbes*, Jan. 22, 2014, at https://www.forbes.com/sites/michaelnoer/2014/01/22/michael-steinhardt-wall-streets -greatest-trader-is-back-and-hes-reinventing-investing-again/#21e85d555f75. Steinhardt established the Judy and Michael Steinhardt Foundation in 1987 and then, in 1994, the Steinhardt Foundation for Jewish Life (initially called Jewish Life Network/Steinhardt Foundation).

39. Leonard Saxe and Barry Chazan, *Ten Days of Birthright Israel*, ch. 1. Saxe directed the Steinhardt Social Research Institute at Brandeis University and served as the principal investigator on multiple studies measuring the effectiveness and outcome of Birthright.

40. For the Steinhardt Institute's mission, see https://www.brandeis.edu/ssri/. For a list of studies, see http://bir.brandeis.edu/handle/10192/22941/browse?value=Saxe%2C+Leonard &type=author&rpp=100&order=DESC&sort_by=2, which includes all of Leonard Saxe's publications. On Steinhardt's gift to Brandeis, see Richard Asinof, "Steinhardt to Fund Demographic Research," *Jewish Telegraphic Agency*, April 13, 2005, at https://www.jta.org/2005/04/13 /lifestyle/steinhardt-to-fund-demographic-research. On the broader trend of Jewish demography funded by philanthropic entities, see Michal Kravel-Tovi, "Introduction: Counting in Jewish," and "Wet Numbers: The Language of Continuity Crisis and the Work of Care among the Organized American Jewish Community," in Michal Kravel-Tovi and Deborah Dash Moore, eds., *Taking Stock: Cultures of Enumeration in Contemporary Jewish Life* (Bloomington: Indiana University Press, 2016).

41. Leonard Saxe, Michelle Shain, Graham Wright, Shahar Hecht, and Theodore Sasson, "Beyond 10 Days: Parents, Gender, Marriage, and the Long-Term Impact of Birthright Israel," Cohen Center for Modern Jewish Studies, Dec. 2017, at https://www.brandeis.edu/cmjs/pdfs /jewish%20futures/Beyond10Days.pdf.

42. For a sample of the rising critical literature about American philanthropy, see Anand Giridharadas, *Winners Take All: The Elite Charade of Changing the World* (New York: Knopf, 2018); Erica Kohl-Arenas, *The Self-Help Myth: How Philanthropy Fails to Alleviate Poverty* (Berkeley: University of California Press, 2015); Gara LaMarche, "Is Philanthropy Bad for Democracy?" *Atlantic*, Oct. 30, 2014, at https://www.theatlantic.com/politics/archive/2014/10/is -philanthropy-good-for-democracy/381996/; Jane Mayer, *Dark Money: The Hidden History of the Billionaires Behind the Rise of the Radical Right* (New York: Doubleday, 2016); Linsey McGoey, *No Such Thing as a Free Gift: The Gates Foundation and the Price of Philanthropy* (New York: Verso, 2015); and Rob Reich, *Just Giving: Why Philanthropy Is Failing Democracy and How It Can Do Better* (Princeton, NJ: Princeton University Press, 2018).

43. See Haviv Rettig Gur, "Billionaire Adelson Donates $25M to Birthright," *Jerusalem Post*, Feb. 7, 2007, at https://www.jpost.com/International/Billionaire-Adelson-donates-25m-to -birthright. For a review of Adelson's donations from 2007 to 2011, see Paul Abowd, "Super PAC Patron Sheldon Adelson Pours Riches into Pro-Israel Groups," posted at the Center for Public Integrity, Feb. 6, 2013 and updated May 13, 2014, at https://publicintegrity.org/federal-politics /super-pac-patron-sheldon-adelson-pours-riches-into-pro-israel-groups/. After this period, he continued to donate to Birthright, with a $45 million gift in 2015 and $70 million in 2018, marking 70 years since Israel's establishment and representing the largest gift Birthright had ever received. See "Birthright Gains $45 Million in New Gifts from Adelson, Azrieli," *Jewish Telegraphic Agency*, Feb. 9, 2015, at https://www.jta.org/2015/02/09/global/birthright-gains-45

-million-in-new-gifts-from-adelson-azrieli; and Jeremy Sharon, "Sheldon Adelson Donates 70 Million Dollars to Birthright," *Jerusalem Post*, April 24, 2018, at https://www.jpost.com /Diaspora/Business-magnate-Sheldon-Adelson-donates-70-million-dollar-to-Birthright -552607. It may be more accurate to put Adelson's share in Birthright's total capital raised at 47%, since according to Wertheimer, Birthright had raised $800 million from 1999 to the date of his report, which likely did not include Adelson's latest $70 million gift (increasing his total giving to Birthright to $410 million, and Birthright's total capital raised to $870 million). See Jack Wertheimer, "Giving Jewish: How Big Funders Have Transformed American Jewish Philanthropy," A Report of the AVI CHAI Foundation, March 2018,: 7. On Adelson's net worth, see the *Forbes* list, at https://www.forbes.com/lists/2007/10/07billionaires_Sheldon-Adelson_ER9O.html.

44. Theodore Sasson, Michelle Shain, Graham Wright, and Leonard Saxe, "Does Taglit-Birthright Israel Foster Long-Distance Nationalism?" *Nationalism and Ethnic Politics* 20, 4 (2014): 438–454.

45. Steven Bertoni, "Billionaire Sheldon Adelson Says He Might Give $100M to Newt Gingrich or Other Republican," *Forbes*, Feb. 21, 2012, at https://www.forbes.com/sites/stevenbertoni /2012/02/21/billionaire-sheldon-adelson-says-he-might-give-100m-to-newt-gingrich-or-other -republican/#4fdd77c54400. On campaign finance reform, see Mayer, *Dark Money*, chs. 9 and 10.

46. Ron Kampeas, "Sheldon Adelson, Political and Jewish Giving Are All of a Piece," *Jewish News Weekly of Northern California*, Aug. 10, 2012.

47. On Open Hillel, which began in 2013, see Michael Kaplan, "Open Hillel Plans First National Conference," *Forward*, May 15, 2014, and the organization's website at www.openhillel .org. For full disclosure, the author serves on the Academic Council Board of Open Hillel. On the hashtag campaign, see https://jewsnotfundedbysheldonadelson.tumblr.com/. On IfNotNow, see Abraham Riesman, "The Jewish Revolt," *New York*, June, 2018, at http://nymag.com /intelligencer/2018/07/ifnotnow-birthright-ramah-bds-israel.html. For a broader overview of the changing nature of American Jews' relationship to Israel, especially as refracted through their philanthropic behavior, see Dov Waxman, *Trouble in the Tribe: The American Jewish Conflict over Israel* (Princeton, NJ: Princeton University Press, 2016).

48. For a historical discussion of this point, see Berman, Rosenblatt, and Stahl, "Continuity Crisis: The History and Sexual Politics of an American Jewish Communal Project." For a social-scientific analysis focused on gender inequality in Jewish studies that also observes the sexual politics of continuity discourse, see Jennifer Thompson, "The Birdcage: Gender Inequity in Academic Jewish Studies," *Contemporary Jewry* 39, no. 3–4 (Dec. 2019): 427–446.

49. Dreyfus, "Harassment Allegations Mount Against Leading Jewish Sociologist"; Sharon Otterman and Hannah Dreyfus, "Michael Steinhardt, a Leader in Jewish Philanthropy, Is Accused of a Pattern of Sexual Harassment," *New York Times*, March 21, 2019, at https://www .nytimes.com/2019/03/21/nyregion/michael-steinhardt-sexual-harassment.htmll; and Sheila Katz, "Michael Steinhardt Sexually Harassed Me," *Jewish Telegraphic Agency*, March 26, 2019, at https://www.jta.org/2019/03/26/opinion/michael-steinhardt-sexually-harassed-me-i-spent -the-next-4-years-trying-to-hold-him-accountable. For Steinhardt's foundation's response, see https://steinhardtfoundation.org/home/an-important-message-from-the-steinhardt-family -and-foundations/?fbclid=IwAR3CSh7ivP5S3BCXKrto9xMC7HTgCCMPn54HWzQO6mU D5G4JLDXXSsPGxMc. On the investigative reporting that led to an explosion of #MeToo activism, see Ronan Farrow, *Catch and Kill: Lies, Spies and a Conspiracy to Protect Predators* (New

York: Little, Brown and Company, 2019); and Jodi Kantor and Megan Twohey, *She Said: Breaking the Sexual Harassment Story That Helped Ignite a Movement* (New York: Penguin Press, 2019)

50. For immediate critical responses that sought to tie Cohen's scholarship to a broader set of sexual politics, see Lila Corwin Berman, Kate Rosenblatt, and Ronit Stahl, "How Jewish Academia Created a #MeToo Disaster," *Forward*, July 19, 2018, at https://forward.com/opinion/406240/how-jewish-academia-created-a-metoo-disaster/; and Rokhl Kafrissen, "How a #MeToo Scandal Proved What We Already Know: 'Jewish Continuity' Is Sexist," *Forward*, July 20, 2018, at https://forward.com/opinion/406271/how-a-metoo-scandal-proved-what-we-already-know-jewish-continuity-is-sexist/. For a response that rejects this line of reasoning, see Jane Eisner, "How Do We Separate Bad Behavior from Good Work?" *Forward*, July 31, 2018, at https://forward.com/opinion/406949/in-this-metoo-era-how-do-we-separate-bad-behavior-from-good-work/. On responses to Steinhardt, see Lila Corwin Berman, "Michael Steinhardt and the Takeover of Jewish Philanthropy by Mega-Donors," *Washington Post*, March 22, 2019, at https://www.washingtonpost.com/outlook/2019/03/22/michael-steinhardt-takeover-jewish-philanthropy-by-mega-donors/?utm_term=.e2531201ed97; and "Jewish Funders Speak Out on Michael Steinhardt," *EJewish Philanthropy*, March 22, 2019, at https://ejewishphilanthropy.com/jewish-funders-speak-out-on-michael-steinhardt/.

51. On Wexner's ties to Epstein, see Steve Eder and Emily Steel, "Leslie Wexner Accuses Jeffrey Epstein of Misappropriating 'Vast Sums of Money,'" *New York Times*, Aug. 7, 2019, at https://www.nytimes.com/2019/08/07/business/wexner-epstein.html. Also, see Lila Corwin Berman, "Jeffrey Epstein Has Tainted Jewish Philanthropy. Now What?" *Forward*, Aug. 1, 2019, at https://forward.com/opinion/428734/jeffrey-epstein-has-tainted-jewish-philanthropy-now-what/. On the Sackler family and its philanthropy, see Anand Giridharadas, "When Your Money Is So Tainted Museums Don't Want It," *New York Times*, May 16, 2019, at https://www.nytimes.com/2019/05/16/opinion/sunday/met-sackler.html; and Alex Marshall, "Museums Cut Ties with Sacklers as Outrage Over Opioid Crisis Grows," *New York Times*, March 25, 2019, at https://www.nytimes.com/2019/03/25/arts/design/sackler-museums-donations-oxycontin.html.

Conclusion: Reform

1. Laura Wernick, "Leveraging Privilege: Organizing Young People with Wealth to Support Social Justice," *Social Justice Review* 86, no. 2 (June 2012): 323–345. Also see Helaine Olen, "Can Rich Millennials Be Convinced to Give Their Money Away?" *Atlantic*, Nov. 20, 2017, at https://www.theatlantic.com/business/archive/2017/11/resource-generation-philanthropy/546350/. For a brief mention of the organization and an indication that it has some broad recognition, see David Callahan, *The Givers: Wealth, Power, and Philanthropy in a New Gilded Age* (New York: Knopf, 2017), 213, 307.

2. Wernick, "Leveraging Privilege," 334. On the origins of the Jewish praxis group, see "Meet Iris Brilliant!" August 12, 2014, https://resourcegeneration.org/?s=%22Jewish+praxis%22, and author's conversation with Karen Pittelman, June 12, 2017 (part of a group conversation). I am unaware of any demographic surveys of Resource Generation; however, the executive director who stepped down in early 2017 told me that Jews are a "disproportionate" segment of the total membership. Author's conversation with Jessie Spector, Aug. 4, 2014. Furthermore, in

interviews with participants, I was told by each that the organization has an overwhelming number of Jewish members alongside what many characterized as other "outsiders." In one interview, for example, the two women with whom I spoke described Jews, queers (including transpeople), and women as constituting the core of the group and even discussed efforts to recruit non-Jews and men to join. Author's conversation with Jessica Rosenberg and Rachel Adler, June 13, 2017.

3. Margot Seigle, "Walking the Wealthy & Jewish Tightrope," April 28, 2016, at https://thejewandthe5carats.wordpress.com/. Author's conversations with Margot Seigle, Nov. 4, 2014 and Oct. 8, 2015.

4. Seigle, "Walking the Wealthy & Jewish Tightrope."

5. Seigle, "Walking the Wealthy & Jewish Tightrope." Author's conversations with Rachel Adler, June 13, 2017; Gabe Kravitz, June 12, 2017 and July 14, 2017; Sara Narva, June 28, 2017; Karen Pittelman, June 12, 2017; Kate Poole, June 26, 2017; Jessica Rosenberg, June 13, 2017; Naomi Sobel, June 12, 2017; Jessie Spector, Aug. 4, 2014; Samantha Waxman, June 12, 2017 and June 29, 2017. In more general terms, this follows the pattern of individual transformation leading to social transformation described in Wernick, "Leveraging Privilege."

6. See https://resourcegeneration.org/what-we-do/social-justice-philanthropy-and-giving/.

7. See https://resourcegeneration.org/raise-our-taxes-rg-s-tax-justice-platform/.

8. For the press release, see https://resourcegeneration.org/rich-millennials-join-trump-tax-march-demand-end-to-corrupt-tax-system-that-favors-rich/. On Resource Generation responses to tax legislation, see https://resourcegeneration.org/webinars/taxscambill-webinar/; https://resourcegeneration.org/2017/12/08/how-ive-benefited-from-tax-evasion-wealth-hoarding-at-26/; and https://resourcegeneration.org/2017/11/30/why-young-people-with-class-privilege-wont-stand-for-the-trumptaxscam/.

9. See "JLens Hosts First Impact Investing Summit for Jewish Communal Leadership," *EJewish Philanthropy*, Dec. 15, 2017, https://ejewishphilanthropy.com/jlens-hosts-first-impact-investing-summit-for-jewish-communal-leadership/.

10. The entire conference was recorded. For a recording of the panel from which these quotations are taken, see https://www.youtube.com/watch?v=gQCDff-hGLw&feature=youtu.be. On Lustig, see http://www.jfnainvestmentinstitute.org/speakers/michael-lustig. A copy of the program can be found at http://docs.wixstatic.com/ugd/3aa597_f2371bafc17e46a38d85c4292 80cc714.pdf.

11. See JLens's Jewish Advocacy Strategy, at http://www.jlensnetwork.org/jewishadvocacy strategy. Also, author's conversation with Julie Hammerman, April 15, 2015.

12. For a recording of the panel, see https://www.youtube.com/watch?v=CbSJvDP1 QXo&feature=youtu.be. Similar ideas can be found in JLens's Jewish Advocacy Strategy at https://www.jlensnetwork.org/jewishadvocacystrategy.

13. On the Airbnb controversy, see JLens's statement, "Airbnb Abandons Corporate Social Responsibility Values by Acquiescing to BDS Campaign," at http://www.jlensnetwork.org /single-post/2018/11/27/Airbnb-Abandons-Values-of-Corporate-Social-Responsibility-by -Acquiescing-to-BDS-Campaign. For background on Airbnb's decision, see Isabel Kershner, "Airbnb Bans Listings in Israeli Settlements on West Bank," *New York Times*, Nov. 19, 2018, at https://www.nytimes.com/2018/11/19/world/middleeast/airbnb-west-bank.html. Five months later, Airbnb reversed its decision as part of settlements of four lawsuits brought by the

United States and Israel, but said it would donate all profits from these listings to humanitarian nonprofit organizations unrelated to the conflict in Israel/Palestine. See Julia Jacobs, "Airbnb Reverses Policy Banning Listings in Israeli Settlements in West Bank," April 9, 2019, *New York Times*, at https://www.nytimes.com/2019/04/09/world/middleeast/airbnb-israel-west-bank .html, and the Airbnb statement at https://press.airbnb.com/update-listings-disputed-regions/.

14. See JLens's statement, "Gun Violence and Investing," at http://www.jlensnetwork.org /single-post/2018/05/19/Gun-Violence-and-Investing.

15. See JLens's 2017 Impact Report at http://www.jlensnetwork.org/2017advocacy.

16. "Furloughed Federal Worker Loan Fund Investment," draft of letter written by Sue Reinhold, January 2019, copy in author's possession.

17. "Furloughed Federal Worker Loan Fund Investment." Reinhold never sent this email because as she was finalizing her plan, the government shutdown ended.

18. "Furloughed Federal Worker Loan Fund Investment." On Hebrew Free Loan Society, see Shelly Tenenbaum, *A Credit to Their Community: Jewish Loan Societies in the United States, 1880–1945* (Detroit, MI: Wayne State University Press, 1993).

19. Sue Reinhold, "Investing with Jewish Values," Sept. 6, 2018, italics in original, copy in author's possession. Reinhold posted a similar version of these remarks as a blog on the Jewish Community Federation and Endowment Fund of San Francisco, the Peninsula, Marin and Sonoma Counties website on Nov. 5, 2018 at https://jewishfed.org/news/blog/what%E2%80%99s -jewish-about-impact-investing. For full disclosure, in her remarks, she made direct reference to my article (Lila Corwin Berman, "How Americans Give: The Financialization of American Jewish Philanthropy," *American Historical Review* 122, no. 5 [Dec. 2017]: 1459–1489). On grant-making from endowment funds, see Sue Reinhold email to author, Sept. 14, 2018.

20. See Reinhold, "Investing with Jewish Values." Also see Sue Reinhold's prepared remarks for "Panel on Impact Investing," Jewish Funders Network International Conference, March 19, 2019, copy in author's possession.

21. Reinhold, "Investing with Jewish Values."

INDEX

Note: Page numbers in italic type indicate illustrations.

Adelson, Sheldon, 181–84, 251n43
Adelson Family Foundation, 181
African Americans, 45, 46
AIPAC. *See* American Israel Public Affairs Committee (AIPAC)
Airbnb, 192, 254n13
Alliance Israélite Universelle, 26
American Bar Association, 82
American Birth Control League, 91
American Council for Judaism, 148
American Israel Public Affairs Committee (AIPAC), 156, 157
American Jewish Committee, 105
American Jewish Congress, 166
American Jewish Joint Distribution Committee (JDC), 26, 93
American Jewish philanthropic complex, 164–86; Birthright as example of, 178–84; complexity of, 3; Crown Foundation as example of, 169–73; defined, 2–3; durability and strength of, 167, 178, 184–86; emergence of, 116, 141, 161; historical construction of, 2–3, 11, 161, 197; Jewish Funders Network as example of, 173–77; Madoff case and, 164–67; overview of, 11; reform challenges to, 186–96; statecraft imbricated with, 2–3, 7, 11, 163, 197
American Jewish philanthropy: American state's role vis-à-vis, 5–7, 11, 112, 197; compatible with Reagan political philosophy, 150–51, 163; defining, 1–2; early years of, 4; foundations as expression of, 64;

future-oriented focus as shift in vision of, 78, 115, 118–20; gender politics in, 185; identity linked to, 115–22, 136–38, 167–72, 178–84, 191–92; impact of, 1; individualist conception of, 27; and Israel, 11, 93–98; late-twentieth/early-twenty-first-century reconception of, 173–78, 250n35; Madoff's fraud and, 164–67; monetary value of, 2, 161–63; political engagement of, 88, 90–91, 95–96, 100, 111–12, 122–29, 141, 149, 184; private finance as model for, 141; property associated with, 51, 54–69, 124, 128; psychological component of, 3–4; public-private relationship in, 4–5, 7, 11, 129–30, 133; role of, in governance, 2, 3, 4, 7; scholarship on, 6, 212n8; traditional view of, 6; unity/consensus imputed to, 89, 90–91; values-based investing by, 192–93; during World War II, 55–57; youth demands of, 114–17, 135–37, 241n53
American Jewish Year Book, 150, 154, 167
American philanthropy: capitalism-democracy balance achieved by, 31–32; defense of, 31–32, 70–71, 81–82; defining organizations in, 80–81; in Great Depression, 48–49; origins of, 29; partnerships in, 124; reform efforts aimed at, 20, 67, 69, 80–83, 86, 89, 122–29; social justice–oriented, 189–90; statecraft imbricated with, 34; suspicions and investigations of, 31, 41, 62–63, 70–71, 80–81, 87, 123. *See also* American Jewish philanthropy

257

A NOTE ON THE TYPE

This book has been composed in Arno, an Old-style serif typeface in the classic Venetian tradition, designed by Robert Slimbach at Adobe.